SHARING GOD'S GOOD COMPANY

Sharing God's Good Company

A THEOLOGY OF THE COMMUNION OF SAINTS

David Matzko McCarthy

WILLIAM B. EERDMANS PUBLISHING COMPANY

GRAND RAPIDS, MICHIGAN / CAMBRIDGE, U.K.

Published 2012 by

Wm. B. Eerdmans Publishing Co.

2140 Oak Industrial Drive N.E., Grand Rapids, Michigan 49505 /

P.O. Box 163, Cambridge CB3 9PU U.K.

Printed in the United States of America

18 17 16 15 14 13 12   7 6 5 4 3 2 1

Library of Congress Cataloging-in-Publication Data

McCarthy, David Matzko.

Sharing God's good company: a theology of the communion of saints /

David Matzko McCarthy.

p.   cm.

ISBN 978-0-8028-6709-4 (pbk.: alk. paper)

1. Christian saints — Biography — History and criticism.   I. Title.

BR1710.M36   2012

235'.2 — dc23

2011049265

www.eerdmans.com

To St. Anthony of Padua
and the people of St. Anthony Shrine Parish,
Emmitsburg, Maryland

One of my first Sundays at the parish, I found a pamphlet titled *Our Parish, Our Patron, Saint Anthony* (Ligouri Publications, 1998). The pamphlet ends with the following prayers (pp. 22-23). If we can live by these prayers just a little, we will have done great things.

OUR COMMON PRAYER

Almighty God, you have given Saint Anthony to us as our patron. Inspire us with his zeal for preaching the gospel. With his help may we become faithful followers of Jesus. Grant this through Christ our Lord. Amen.

FOR PRIVATE PRAYER

Saint Anthony, you are always willing to help those in need. I come before you with my petitions. . . . You were gracious to the poor who approached you in your day, and you worked miracles in response to their needs. Please obtain the favors I ask of you this day. I promise to live the teachings of the gospel of Jesus more faithfully and devote myself to helping those in greatest need. Amen.

Contents

ACKNOWLEDGMENTS		viii
INTRODUCTION		1
1.	Social Desire	9
2.	Saints	29
3.	Realism	43
4.	Participation	60
5.	Images	79
6.	Miracles	97
7.	Pilgrimage	115
8.	History	134
9.	Hagiography	153
CONCLUSION		169
INDEX		171

Acknowledgments

—⚍—

Thank you, St. Anthony Shrine and Our Lady of Mount Carmel Parishes. We are hardly extraordinary. Every year, it seems, we get by with a little less. Yet we have each other, and this sharing seems to become greater every year. We have managed to become part of every part of each other's lives. Everywhere the McCarthys go, you are there. At work, school, neighborhood, grocery store, playground, fund-raiser, building project, basketball court, and ball field, you are with us. When we join in procession to Communion, we have some saints with us. But, for the most part, we bring a modest faith. To this degree, I think, we do well in representing the world at the Lord's Table. Our hope is that when we are blessed and sent forth, we play our part in opening the world to God.

I would like also to thank Mary Kate Birge, David Cloutier, Bill Collinge, Jim Donohue, and Rodica Stoicoiu of the Theology Department at Mount St. Mary's University, English professor Carol Hinds, Bridget McCarthy, Gloria Balsley, and MacKenzie Sullivan for reading chapters of the book, for talking through various points and problems, and for helping me attend to the details of life especially when distracted by big thoughts. I thank our children, Abigail, Quinlan, John, Daniel, and Timothy, for keeping big questions of life in circulation and particularly for their love of books. Because of them, our lives at home flow on a river of stories. For them, we hope we can live by the stories of the saints.

Introduction

—⟋⟍⟋—

A basic presumption of this study is that saints and the communion of saints are problems. Many studies and biographies of the saints put their lives in an unproblematic frame. That is not to say that saints' lives are described as problem-free. To the contrary, lives of the saints are marked by obstacles to faith, missteps in following their calls, and opposition from community, state, and church. Saintly lives are full of troubles, misunderstandings, and outright hostility. Witness often brings suffering and death. The stories of the saints are about problems, but underlying questions about hagiography and the saints are often passed over without a second thought. Consider, for example, the story of St. Polycarp in Robert Ellsberg's outstanding collection, *All Saints: Daily Reflections on Saints, Prophets, and Witnesses for Our Time.*[1]

Ellsberg tells us that Polycarp (70-155) is "one of the most revered of the apostolic fathers," who is remembered for his wisdom and composure in the midst of persecution. His long, faithful life ends with love and trust in God. The written record of his death, *Martyrdom of Polycarp*, is "the oldest account of Christian martyrdom outside the New Testament." Ellsberg tells us that the narrator of the ancient account "emphasizes the fact that Polycarp's death was 'a martyrdom conformable to the gospel.'" He explains the point further. "[T]he death of the holy bishop was a mystical reenactment of the passion of Christ, who lived and died to save the world." Ellsberg highlights Polycarp's prayer in the face of a horrible

1. Robert Ellsberg, *All Saints: Daily Reflections on Saints, Prophets, and Witnesses for Our Time* (New York: Crossroad, 1997).

1

death. The martyr prays in thanksgiving for salvation in Christ, for the good company of the martyrs, and for our participation in Christ's dying and being raised to new life.[2]

Ellsberg concludes his entry on Polycarp by recounting miraculous signs described in the ancient narrative. Amid the flames of execution, the martyr is untouched. The flames part around him and form something like a walled chamber ("like a ship's sail filled by the wind"). Amid the flames, Polycarp is not consumed but baked like bread or "as gold and silver [are] refined in a furnace." "Seeing that he remained alive amid the flames, the executioner stabbed him in the heart, which issued in such a quantity of blood 'that the fire was quenched and the whole crowd marveled.'"[3] With this picture of the marveling crowd, Ellsberg's description of Polycarp's life and death comes to an abrupt conclusion. He offers no reflection or commentary. He does not attend to Polycarp's symbolic victory over the powers of the world and over death itself. He leaves out the metaphysical implications of the supernatural event: the flames do not kill Polycarp, but only purify him for higher life. The ancient account likens him to gold in a furnace, which is an allusion, surely, to Wisdom 3:6:

> As gold in the furnace, he proved them,
> and as sacrificial offerings he took them to himself.

As Polycarp dies, the blood issuing directly from his heart extinguishes the flames of death completely. Ellsberg does not note these liturgical and biblical allusions (e.g., John 19:34). He does not mention the cosmic implications carried by Polycarp's miraculous manner of death. He does not indicate that the martyr triumphs over death and the worldly powers that deal in death. In the ancient account, Polycarp's death signifies life.

In his abrupt conclusion, Ellsberg does not develop these figurative meanings of the martyr's story. He also abbreviates the story itself. The actual account does not end with the saint's death. There is a final episode that Ellsberg does not include. In the ancient account, Polycarp's Christian brothers and sisters attempt to secure his body, so that they may "have fel-

---

2. Ellsberg, *All Saints*, 89. Ellsberg cites the translation of the *Martyrdom of Polycarp* in Cyril C. Richardson, *Early Christian Fathers* (New York: Macmillan, 1970), 149-58.

3. Ellsberg, *All Saints*, 89-90.

lowship with his holy flesh."[4] To thwart their desires, a centurion, on the urging of Jewish interlopers, makes sure that Polycarp's body is set upon the fire and cremated. Nonetheless, the community of Christians is able to collect the saint's remaining bones and deposit them "in a suitable place." They hold the martyr's remains to be "more valuable than precious stones and finer than refined gold." This final episode is self-referential for the storyteller and audience. It reads like a defense of the cult of the saints. The narrator is sure to distinguish worship of Christ from love for the martyrs as "disciples and imitators of the Lord." The resting place of Polycarp's bones becomes a gathering place where, "with joy and gladness, the Lord will permit us to celebrate the birthday of his martyrdom in commemoration of those who have already fought in the contest, and for the training and preparation for those who will do so in the future."[5]

In highlighting the symbolism of Polycarp's death and by including the story's practices of veneration and their justification, I have introduced problems that are not explicit in Ellsberg's straightforward account. He simply reports the miraculous movement of flames and how they are extinguished. He does not comment on the rhetorical and figurative elements of the miracles as signs. He avoids issues of veneration. Instead, he simplifies our orientation to the life of Polycarp by introducing a spiritual lesson in the form of an epigraph. The heading for Ellsberg's entry on Polycarp reads "He who has given me strength to face the flames will also enable me to stay unflinching at the stake." In Ellsberg's frame, the martyrdom of Polycarp offers a dramatic illustration of our hope that God will provide, especially when we have faith that God is all that we need. The lesson of the epigraph puts the death of Polycarp in a straightforward and manageable framework. This workable approach is what a book like Ellsberg's *All Saints* should provide for our daily reflections. It is not the approach of this book on saints, realism, and history.

Chapters that follow will deal with difficult and troublesome questions presented by the lives of the saints. For example, Ellsberg's excerpt on Polycarp's martyrdom does not include the desire of his community to gather in the presence of his bones and have fellowship with his holy flesh. Ellsberg narrows our concerns to Polycarp's exemplary trust in God. His

---

4. See J. B. Lightfoot and J. R. Harmer, eds., *The Apostolic Fathers: Greek Texts and English Translations of Their Writings* (Grand Rapids: Baker, 1992), 240-41.

5. *Martyrdom of Polycarp*, in *The Apostolic Fathers*, 241.

account does not require us to ask questions about what is going on in the veneration of the martyrs. If all that Polycarp offers is a lesson of faith, would he have been remembered at all? Would he be a saint or simply a good example? What is the difference between an exemplar and a saint? These questions have pressed upon me for a number of years. What makes the saints so attractive to us? Why do they continue to be part of our lives? Why do I keep Ellsberg's daily reflections on "witnesses for our time" within arm's reach, right above my desk? Why are most of Ellsberg's witnesses for our time, like Polycarp, from an entirely different time and place?

In chapter 1, I argue that figures like Polycarp are remembered precisely because their relationship to us broadens our connections in time and place. In the chapter, I call our longing for nearness to the saints a "social desire." It is a desire for communion with others who populate the pathways and form social relations that embody the union of heaven and earth. Our deep social desires are longings to be connected to life as a whole, to the meaning of things, to God, and to neighbor in God's good company. When I introduced the phrase "social desire" to my wife, Bridget, she expected that the "social" would suggest a desire for fame, fashionable clothes, and exclusive neighborhoods. The saints typically turn away from these kinds of worldly desires. This turning away is an important theme of the book. But the main theme is that the communion of saints brings an alternative social desire to the surface. While fame and fortune can be called material desires, the lives of the saints reveal a deeper metaphysical desire — a desire to be connected to God in our time and to human community across time and place.

Chapter 2, titled "Saints," develops an initial understanding of the saints as people with whom we share common life. With the saints, we share a community that embodies the kinship of God. It is kinship that extends social relationships through time and place to all times and places; it is social life filled out in metaphysical relations. Like Polycarp and the ancient account of his martyrdom, countless saints do not fit into a purely modern, this-worldly frame of reference. The saints are eccentric; they are off center in our world. Their ill fit with our time might explain why their presence is as wide as ever. Certainly, devotion to the saints is far less integrated into common life. But if we go merely by the numbers, they are remembered and addressed in prayer as much now as at any other time in history. My view is that the saints are as present to our time as ever because the communion of saints offers distinctive and at the same time expansive avenues of social/metaphysical relations. In our world of material desires, the saints open up metaphysical pathways.

In short, chapters 1 and 2 attend to the questions, Why saints? What role do they play in our time? In chapters 3 ("Realism"), 4 ("Participation"), and 5 ("Images"), I approach problems concerning the reality embodied and represented by the lives of the saints. For example, in the *Martyrdom of Polycarp*, the saint's death is described with obvious figurative elements. The account abounds in symbols and metaphors as well as scriptural and liturgical allusions. It is no coincidence that Polycarp's blood extinguishes the fire of death. With the figurative language, questions arise. Is the account invented through wishful thinking of the faithful? Or is it real? Or is it both? You will see that, in chapters 1 and 2 ("Social Desire" and "Saints," respectively), I am struggling with the problem of saints as texts — as written and told, read and heard. You will also see that, in chapter 2, I suggest that the saints as icons and statues — as inhabiting a spatial and visual field — might be a more promising avenue for thinking about the role and place of the saints in our lives. I begin with the textual problem because, as one who deals in words and texts, I see textual problems of symbol and metaphor as a way to approach issues of visual representation.

Chapters 3 and 4 ask these questions: Can the lives of the saints as they are received in texts (in hagiography) count as realism? And if so, how does this figurative or hagiographic realism work? How do the lives of the saints situate us with relationships where we might have a glimpse of how things really are? In chapter 3, I try to understand the key elements of figurative realism. Chapter 4 develops the central element of this kind of realism — that it invites our participation in what is real and true. Chapter 5 deals with issues of symbol and metaphor, and the representations of saints in icons, images, and statues. Putting the issues and chapters in this order ("Realism," "Participation," and "Images") allows me to begin with questions of realism and representation and return to the reality of kinship and social relations outlined in chapters 1 and 2. Visual representation in statues and stained glass points us to another time and place and, at the same time, occupies space in the here and now. Visual depictions of saints are usually full of anachronisms. Ancient people are clothed in modern dress. Anachronisms are required because the realism is a representation of real communion across time. The saints embody a real kinship of God.

Chapters 6, 7, and 8 deal will the reality of God's nearness to us. Chapter 6, on miracles, attends to scientific questions. In the main, it presents a case for miracles in terms of a conversation and debate among scientists. Some scientists close off the possibility of miracles while others see the openness of the world. The scientific debate also raises theological questions. If the scientist wonders if the world can be changed by God, the theologian asks whether or not God can be changed by us — by our prayers and petitions. As the question is popularly raised, it appears that God's will and presence are static things that have to be pushed by us one way or another. In reality, God is "changeless" as ever-present actuality. God is pure action and love. In this regard, miracles require, not a change in God, but a change in the world, a change that makes God's pure action more immediate to us. In our prayers, we are asking God to clear the way, to "make straight his paths" (Mark 1:3). A prayer for a miracle is a prayer for a change in the world. The miracles in the lives of the saints, by and large, follow this pattern. They are psychosomatic. The saints have been changed, and they become the holy embodied. They are living things of the world where the holy comes through.

Chapter 7 is about pilgrimage. Pilgrimages are basic practices of devotion to the saints, to places where we discover more about them (and ourselves) through sight and touch. Chapter 8 is on history and how the lives of the saints connect us to a sense of the whole. In other words, the chapter on miracles is about the holy in the world, the chapter on pilgrimage is about holy places, and the chapter on history is about holy time. A fundamental problem in understanding the connections of place and time is our modern conception of progress. The meaning of place and time has been flattened to a horizontal plane, so that progress is made only by stages — by leaving something behind and marching on to the next, better thing. Is this not the logic of the market, whether in China or the United States? The great modern social philosophies — capitalism and Marxism in their various incarnations — require this-worldly stories of history. They require corresponding conceptions of evil, human nature, and the fulfillment of human life. They require that human beings and human history be divided, that various human histories are defeated and overcome.

The pilgrim's progress is different. It puts the horizontal plane of time in reference to the vertical relations (figuratively speaking) of heaven and earth. Without this metaphysical relation in time and place, human progress is fragmented. Without metaphysical relations in time, much of human history is alienated or lost to us. Chapter 8 (on history) will develop the historical significance of being "in Christ." It will indicate that being in Christ connects times and places through communion (i.e., the communion of saints) and, at the same time, preserves the uniqueness of persons and events in their own time. The metaphysical landscape of holiness — of holy people and events in time — gives to them greater, rather than less, historical significance. Often it is said that the lives of the saints are full of myth and legend and, therefore, are not adequately historical. Although this may be true in particular cases, the lives of the saints provide a restoration of history as a whole. With this claim about history, I have returned to my concluding point in chapter 1: social desire. The saints populate a nearly deserted space between our social relations and the meaning of life. The lives of the saints embody the relationships that draw out this deep and powerful social desire.

The final chapter, chapter 9, is on hagiography and social desire. Sainthood and naming saints are unavoidably metaphysical and relational. When saints are remembered, venerated, and depicted in painting, stone, or stained glass, they form a metaphysical landscape of relationships. People from various times and places form a backdrop of common life. The saints invite us into a communion of patrons and benefactors, which Peter Brown, in *The Cult of the Saints,* calls "democratization from on top."[6] Chapter 9 begins with the social nature of salvation and the intimacy between love of God and neighbor. It concludes with an outline of the relations of God's Trinity and the role of the saints in a Trinitarian economy of salvation. The book as a whole deals with modern questions and problems pertaining to the lives of the saints. Given the metaphysical nature of these questions and problems, it is apt that chapter 9 deals, in the main, with ancient and medieval hagiography. Medieval hagiography, in particular, often displays a broad dissemination of grace and a democratization of holy life. When all is said and done, my goal has been to see in the problems of sainthood and hagiography basic questions of theology and the Christian life. The lives of the saints, all in all, are about God's grace and holiness in the world.

This is a book on the saints, but it does not offer straightforward biographies and inspirational stories. Instead, it puts weighty modern ques-

6. Peter Brown, *The Cult of the Saints: Its Rise and Function in Latin Christianity* (Chicago: University of Chicago Press, 1981), 48.

tions on the backs of the saints. The book is an exercise in thinking through theological and philosophical questions. It is different from books that treat similar questions because here the context for these questions is the reality of the communion of saints. In a world that weighs me down, the saints live out Christ's promise, "For my yoke is easy, and my burden light" (Matt. 11:30). A significant part of the modern yoke is the question of whether or not my life, which means something to me, has any connection to the course of things and the meaning of life. The question of "connections" is relational, and the weight of the question is metaphysical. That is, do I have connections to life beyond the things physically near to me and beyond simple material relations? The saints offer a pathway to pursue this question. They offer "embodiment" and practical/material relationships with metaphysical implications.

This metaphysical embodiment is the heart of the problem. Much of my work up to this point (e.g., *The Good Life*) has been an attempt to work out practical problems in living a more fully human life. What kind of material environment or human habitat is needed to live out a rich common life? Here, in *Sharing God's Good Company*, I am working on the same basic question. If we are to flourish, what do we need for a home? My work up to this point has been concerned with familial, neighborhood, and community relationships that form an environment for our lives. Here, the question of home goes deeper. Does our life together here and now have any connection to the course of things and to life as a whole? The question speaks of a profoundly human, social desire. This desire is the topic of chapter 1.

ONE

Social Desire

—ɯ—

The saints desire to be near God, and many of us desire to be near the saints. In either case, it is a social desire, a longing to be in good company with God. The saints are attractive because (among other things) they situate our lives on a landscape of metaphysical yet social relations. In this chapter and throughout the book, I will repeatedly use the word "metaphysical," and by it I mean an understanding of reality and one's place in it that goes beyond physical connections and beyond knowledge that limits itself to material relations. One way of putting it is this. Social relationships can be understood in terms of physical proximity — genetically as a family or race and spatially as neighborhood or state. The saints, in contrast, are set within social relationships that are figurative and metaphysical. They embody our kinship of adoption and shared relationship to God. The communion of saints is a network of relationships on an expansive landscape of times and places throughout the ages and across the world. The lives of the saints embody a desire for kinship that connects us to the meaning and source of life. They are media of participation in the full and future presence of the kingdom of God.

This chapter (along with chapter 2) reviews conceptual and intellectual problems in understanding the saints. The following chapters (chapters 3 through 8) reverse the process. They ask how openness to the communion of saints can reorient our way of thinking about the world. For example, how do we think about the holy in history, in events (e.g., miracles), and in a place (e.g., pilgrimage sites)? If the conceptual problems can be described well, then we might be able to see more clearly what the saints are doing in our world. If we can get a better perspective on what the saints are about, perhaps we can see more clearly and more theologically who we are, where God is, and how things really are. People, as much as ever, tell the stories of saints and are devoted to them. But people, as much as ever, find the saints survivors of a bygone age of leprechauns and fairies. This chapter reviews problems in accounting for saints, and it asks what these problems and our persistent attraction to saints tell us about our world.

The communion of saints populates the cosmos with personal relations. In accounting for the saints here, I could step back and offer a purely academic review of theories, but it seems appropriate to begin with my personal investment. I have been feeling an attraction to the saints for a long time. About twenty years ago, I managed to include a few saints and the meaning of sainthood in two chapters of my dissertation. At one family get-together in 1992, during my years of research and dissertation writing, my two older sisters happened to ask me about my topic. I offered a complex and convoluted explanation, which was for them a great source of delight. "David, so many years of school, and you can't even explain what you are doing. Need a few more years?" After that day, they took every opportunity to ask me about my progress. Since then, when asked about my dissertation, I have been honest. I say it is about "books I have read." The answer does not satisfy friendly inquirers; they think I am being evasive. They persist by asking for a title, and I say the real title is "Things I Wanted to Know." From here, the conversation is always the same. I have to convince them that I am not just putting them off — that it really was a loosely connected set of chapters unified by what, at the time, I wanted to know. By giving specifics, I am able to show that I have not been disingenuous; I am so convincing that it is rare for someone to ask again for the actual, printed title. A large portion of my explanation is that I desired and still desire to know the saints.

In my dissertation (ca. 1992), I made enough progress with saints and hagiography to keeping wanting more. As a matter of full disclosure, the title of my dissertation was "Hazarding Theology: Theological Descriptions and Particular Lives."[1] I just cringed as I typed the words. I can hear my sisters feigning sophistication as they dwell on the word "hazarding." The dissertation was good enough to earn a degree, but entirely unsatisfy-

---

1. David Matzko, "Hazarding Theology: Theological Descriptions and Particular Lives" (Ph.D. diss., Duke University, 1992).

ing as a "work." A few years later (around 1995), I expanded my dealings with the saints and produced another entire manuscript (280 pages). After one rejection from a publisher, I threw it in a filing cabinet. The editor told me what I already knew. It may have been worth writing (for me) but was not worth reading. The title was "Fortunate Saints," in reference to the reversal of fortunes in the Beatitudes (Matt. 5:1-12). In the introduction, I put the main point in italics: *Stories of particular women and men function for us as fortunate saints when the telling of their lives creates access to a landscape for our faithfulness.* The italics compensate for the lack of clarity, as though talking slower and louder would make a difference. For a thesis, it does not illuminate much about the saints. It seems that I have constructed a thesis sentence in which the saints are passive: it is their stories and our telling of their lives that do something. Looking back at "Hazarding Theology" and "Fortunate Saints," I can see both my dissatisfaction and why my straight-talking sisters would poke fun at their academic little brother. Although I was trying to account for the saints, I seemed to have been pushing them aside and talking over them.

In my study of the saints up to that point, I had delineated a set of problems.[2] The main problem was a disjunction between definitions of sainthood and the actual saints.[3] In my thesis on fortunate saints, I used "fortunate" as a modifier because I was committed to giving a definition and yet aware that any definition would not hold for a multitude of saints. My concern was to delineate a political space and a social function for the saints. The question of social function is the right question, but I reduced this role to the social world of the storyteller and "interpreter." Without going into the content of the manuscript further, allow me to use the phrase "fortunate saints" in this chapter to refer to a failed attempt to un-

2. I work through these problems in the following articles: David Matzko McCarthy, "The Gospels Embodied: Lives of Saints and Martyrs," in *The Cambridge Companion to the Gospels,* ed. Stephen C. Barton (Cambridge: Cambridge University Press, 2006), 224-44; "Moral Theology with the Saints," with James Keating, *Modern Theology* 19, no. 2 (April 2003): 203-19; "The Performance of the Good: Ritual Action and the Moral Life," *Pro Ecclesia* 7, no. 2 (Spring 1998): 199-215; "Christ's Body in Its Fullness: Resurrection and the Lives of the Saints," in *Resurrection Reconsidered,* ed. Gavin D'Costa (Oxford: Oneworld Publications, 1996), 102-17; "Postmodernism, Saints, and Scoundrels," *Modern Theology* 9, no. 1 (January 1993): 19-36.

3. In *Making Saints,* Kenneth Woodward suggests that this gap is often a problem in the church's canonization process. *Making Saints: How the Catholic Church Determines Who Becomes a Saint, Who Doesn't, and Why* (New York: Simon and Schuster, 1990).

derstand the saints. It is a failed postmodern attempt. Although attempting to understand the saints, I focused on the relationship between interpreter and texts (not people).

In "Fortunate Saints" I undercut and talked over the agency of the
saints while trying to solve a different problem. I was troubled by what
seemed to be an adversarial relationship between saints and those who are
devoted to them. I remember reading Hippolyte Delehaye's *Legends of the
Saints* (first published in 1905).[4] I was more than a bit dismayed that re-
trieving the saints was in large part a project of rooting out and overcoming popular distortions — the simplifications, abstractions, and hidden
social interests of popular legends. Could the saints withstand the scrutiny
of history? I had the inclination to defend popular devotion and stories,
which I realized were not superimposed on the saints (as saints) but were
an important part of their real history and identity. In the process, stories
and storytellers became the agents of my study of saints. As Kenneth
Woodward puts it in *Making Saints,* "saints are their stories."[5] This fusion
of saint and story relieved the tension between saints and their cults, but
the agency of so-called fortunate saints receded into the background. Storytellers were in control; saints were not persons as much as texts.

I was attempting to be "postmodern." I note this point now because
this chapter is, in large part, about modern and postmodern struggles
with realism. Given the unsatisfactory results of these struggles, chapters
3 and 4 take up the issue of realism from the point of view of the communion of saints. In this chapter, I am using "modernism" and "postmodernism" in the following ways. Modernism distrusts realism and our ability to
refer to reality as it really is out there beyond us. It is, in a sense, Newtonian: it concerns itself with texts as worlds in themselves with their own,
autonomous laws of operation. The mechanisms of language govern the
reality of the text. Postmodernism distrusts these seamless textual worlds
and shows how interpreters intrude upon them. Like quantum physics,
postmodernism imagines many textual worlds. Every text has multiple
universes. The subjective intrusion of the interpreter on the text does not
retrieve but creates a world, and there are countless possible worlds. My
"Fortunate Saints," in short, was postmodern. It was an attempt to ac-

---

4. Hippolyte Delehaye, *The Legends of the Saints,* trans. Donald Attwater (New York:
Fordham University Press, 1962).

5. Woodward, *Making Saints,* 18.

count for the social world of the saints through the interaction of story and interpreter. The actual saints receded into the background, and the storytellers became the agents.

Despite its problems, there is a valid point in this thesis on storytelling. I just expanded the point too far. I allowed two saintly figures to define sainthood — martyred Salvadoran archbishop Oscar Romero (d. 1980) and Dorothy Day (d. 1980) of the *Catholic Worker*. My interest in Romero and Day was religious and personal; it was not at first academic. But once I read everything I could find by and about them, I made a discovery about how to interpret the saints. Each becomes a focal point of common life and a way of living faithfully: Day in the *Catholic Worker* (beginning in New York in the 1930s) and Romero in El Salvador in the late 1970s. They become focal points largely because they tell the stories of others. Romero is archbishop amid the violence, poverty, and injustices of El Salvador in the 1970s, and as the common epithet explains, he becomes "the voice for the voiceless."[6] Not only does he represent the poor and tell their story in general, but many of his homilies and addresses name and tell the stories of particular people.[7] Likewise, Dorothy Day's books and her writing in the *Catholic Worker* newspaper are almost always autobiographical, and the autobiography is almost always about other people.[8] My interest in Romero and Day had something to do with their faith and their politics, and I found that they inspired devotion (now as servants of God) largely because they were devoted to the lives of others. They could see the way of God in the poor, not the poor as a category or concept, but particular people with distinctive gifts and callings. Romero and Day are media for people to tell about their own lives and to express their own hopes and faith.

With Romero and Day in view, the social role of the saints came into focus for me in relationship to Edith Wyschogrod's *Saints and Postmodernism* (1990).[9] It is a heady book, and it represents a stage in my intellectual

6. In Romero's pastoral letter on the mission of the church, he calls the church to be the voice of the voiceless. Archbishop Oscar Romero, *Voice of the Voiceless: The Four Pastoral Letters and Other Statements*, trans. Michael J. Walsh (Maryknoll, N.Y.: Orbis, 1985), 138.

7. Monseñor Óscar Romero, *Homilías*, Tomo II ciclo A, 27 de noviembre de 1977–28 de mayo de 1978 (San Salvador: UCA, 2005).

8. Consider part III of Day's *The Long Loneliness* (New York: Harper and Row, 1952) and her *Loaves and Fishes* (Maryknoll, N.Y.: Orbis, 1997).

9. Edith Wyschogrod, *Saints and Postmodernism: Revisioning Moral Philosophy* (Chicago: University of Chicago Press, 1990).

life when I was captivated by a hyper-theoretical postmodernism, especially with its criticisms of modern moral theory. I was young; theories about theories were interesting for what they could do in the academic world of theories. I was young and had the time to wade through Wyschogrod's discussions of Heidegger, Levinas, Derrida, Foucault, and Deleuze. I was disoriented by *Saints and Postmodernism*. Disorientation is the intended effect, I suspect. I found an orientation (a point of reference) to the book when I reached Wyschogrod's discussion of Nelson Mandela, in a section called "Political Saints."[10] With Mandela in view, I was able to see that what Wyschogrod had been developing (for 150 pages or so) as saintly self-sacrifice and radical altruism was simply the negative image of modern self-possession.[11] Saints were supposed to be selfless, and this standard of radical altruism had long been a modern way of setting piety and religious aspiration outside of practical life. In the modern frame, to be a person who lacks rational self-interest is to be an entity outside the social contract. Saints, in this frame of radical altruism, are by definition otherworldly. For moderns the radically selfless saint inhabits another world. With postmodern flair, Wyschogrod simply inverts the modern self (who defines itself) and creates a saint who is inexplicably "other" in the world.

As far as I could tell, Wyschogrod's inverted modern saint did not explain the life and aspirations of Nelson Mandela.[12] Mandela was imprisoned at the time of Wyschogrod's writing and released (after twenty-seven years) just months before I was reading the book. Mandela was noble and self-possessed, not self-emptied (as Wyschogrod argued). He was full of hopes and ambitions of a whole people for a free South Africa. He seemed to me to be self-abundant. Wyschogrod thinks of him as selfless. She highlights Mandela's refusal to be released from prison in 1985 because "the people are not free."[13] Mandela and other political prisoners were offered release from prison if they promised to not continue their former political activities. Note Wyschogrod's explanation. "[T]he self must inspect its conduct retrospectively, approve or disapprove of itself,

10. Wyschogrod, *Saints and Postmodernism*, 150-55.

11. Wyschogrod, *Saints and Postmodernism*, 34-39.

12. David Matthew Matzko, "Postmodernism, Saints, and Scoundrels," 19-36.

13. Winnie Mandela, *Part of My Soul Went with Him*, adapted by Mary Benson and edited by Anne Benjamin (New York: Norton, 1985), 147, cited by Wyschogrod, *Saints and Postmodernism*, 152.

and thus always admire or despise itself. What is deemed admirable, however, is the choice of political freedom, but the moment this freedom becomes an object of admiration it ceases to be free. The freedom that has become admirable undergoes yet another reversal: it cannot be the object of admiration because it is freedom for the Other who resists discursive articulation."[14] Contrast Mandela's own explanation, in a statement, from prison in 1985, given through his daughter. "Too many have died since I went to prison. Too many have suffered for the love of freedom. I am in prison as a representative of the people and of your organization, the African National Congress, which was banned. What freedom am I being offered while the organization of the people remains banned [?]"[15] After his criticism of this false freedom, Mandela begins a litany of oppression. What freedom is offered when our people cannot live, work, gather, maintain a home, and move about freely? He concludes, "The people are not free. . . . Your freedom and mine cannot be separated."[16] In effect, the freedom that I am being offered is a sham. I will simply be trading one kind of imprisonment for another.

Wyschogrod does follow Mandela's own line of interpretation. She gives a tortuous explanation about Mandela's self-inspection. Mandela, in contrast, offers no introspection at all. He says, in effect, "It is not about me, but about us, and whether or not I am in prison, we will not be free." He does not imagine himself to be separated from his people or somehow "other." On the contrary, he is inescapably "same." If he were released, he would not be free, as they were also not free in South Africa. He is connected to the people, and with them, he has an abundant and dignified self. The wonder of Mandela's life is that the identity of the people of South Africa spills over into him, and as a result, he stands for them. Hardly selfless, he is full of his people's good.

I had learned this point about the abundant self from Oscar Romero and Dorothy Day. Reading *Saints and Postmodernism*, by way of contrast, made the point plain. The identity of the saints is far more complex and attractive than Wyschogrod's radically altruistic saints, who live noble but miserable, selfless lives. Her postmodern saint shares the sorrow and suffering of others, but none of us would want to share this kind of saint's

14. Wyschogrod, *Saints and Postmodernism*, 155.
15. Mandela, *Part of My Soul*, 147.
16. Mandela, *Part of My Soul*, 148.

joyless and vacant identity. Wyschogrod's saints are lonely modern heroes. She holds that the postmodern saint is outside the customary self and beyond representation. While the modernist views saints as other-worldly, Wyschogrod's postmodern saint, as noted above, is "other" in the world. The selflessness of her saints is self-imposed. Their radical altruism seems to be, ironically, just another form of modern self-making: the making of the empty self. Because their altruism is complete, they give only and need nothing from us. They are autonomous and self-sufficient. In contrast, Romero and Day represent porous selves; they need as much as they give. They put their lives into others, and they are filled as others put their lives into them.[17] Their so-called self-emptying is like a vacuum, empty for the slightest instant before being filled by an active, multifaceted, unpredictable, and densely populated network of people. This is Mother Teresa's dark night when alone in prayer and her contrasting joy with the poor in the abundant love of God.[18] It is Romero's hope to live, after death, with Christ, in the Salvadoran people. It is Dorothy Day's appeal for voluntary poverty and affinity with Dostoevsky's "harsh and dreadful love" — to be at once in community with the poor and filled with the love of God.

These saints live out Jesus' recommendation for self-preservation: "For whoever wishes to save his life will lose it, but whoever loses his life for my sake and that of the gospel will save it" (Mark 8:35). The context for this declaration is Jesus' teachings on the cost of discipleship and on taking up the cross and suffering persecution. In Mark 8:31-38 and Matthew 16:21-28, Jesus tells the disciples that he will die in Jerusalem, and Peter objects. Jesus, in rebuttal, explains that the cross is the way of the kingdom. The cross and resurrection will usher in the bounty of God's reign, a bounty to be enjoyed by those who lose themselves to it. This way of losing and finding oneself is not a contradiction. It is sharing in the death and resurrection of Christ; it is St. Paul's assertion that in Christ we die to the old self and are raised in "newness of life" (Rom. 6:4). We live in Christ, but it is Christ who lives in us (Gal. 2:19-20). When Archbishop Romero anticipated his violent death, he proposed that "If am killed, I shall arise again

17. I am thinking, here, of the idea of the "porous self" that is developed by Charles Taylor in contrast to the "buffered self." See Taylor, *A Secular Age* (Cambridge, Mass.: Belknap Press, 2007), 27.

18. Mother Teresa, *Mother Teresa: Come Be My Light,* ed. Brian Kolodiejchuk (New York: Doubleday, 2007).

in the Salvadoran people."[19] On the surface, the statement suggests that Romero was full of himself. However, it is not about him as an individual; he was not claiming to be a second Christ. On the contrary, his identity is shared with a people in Christ. He shares the abundance of eucharistic communion. His point is that the church is the body of Christ. He shares life in the body of Christ and, therefore, will live abundantly after death.

By narrowing in on this "abundant self," the thesis of my discarded "Fortunate Saints" was an attempt to be faithful to this communion between saints and those who draw near to them. It was an attempt to understand how the saints continue to live. They are fulfilled in God's communion but their lives are not complete. They continue to change and to grow in relationship to us. We participate in the lives of the saints by telling their stories in relationship to our own lives. The saint is permeable, not only to God, but also to us. This point is undeniable; but in my earlier account of "Fortunate Saints," I allowed postmodern theory to get the best of me. The underlying idea was that the saints continue to live in relationship to us. But I conceived of the continuing lives of saints, not as people, but as open-ended texts (as elements of a theory). In this frame, the interaction was primarily not between the saints and us, but between one set of storytellers and another. The saint lived insofar as we remembered and passed on her story. But ironically, she did not share in the story. She was dead. The saint was living only as a multilayered text.

I did not have a clear sense of this "reduction to the text" until later, when working through Elizabeth Johnson's *Friends of God and Prophets.*[20] The book was issued with some anticipation.[21] In a *Commonweal* review (1998), Robert Imbelli observes that Johnson's "faith-filled and critical reappropriation" of the communion of saints is "imperative in a culture often marked more by fragmentation and disconnection than communion."[22] He adds that "following a talented theologian in the skillful exercise of her craft generates genuine excitement."[23] After outlining the book's virtues, Imbelli turns his attention to its doctrine of God. He ex-

---

19. James Brockman, *Romero: A Life* (Maryknoll, N.Y.: Orbis, 1989), 248.

20. Elizabeth Johnson, *Friends of God and Prophets* (New York: Continuum, 1998).

21. I was familiar with Johnson's approach to the saints, "Saints and Mary," in *Systematic Theology: Roman Catholic Perspectives,* vol. 2, ed. Francis Schüssler Fiorenza and John P. Galvin (Minneapolis: Augsburg Fortress, 1991), 143-78.

22. Robert P. Imbelli, "A Catholic Work," *Commonweal* 125, no. 18 (October 23, 1998): 24.

23. Imbelli, "A Catholic Work," 24.

plains that "the doctrine of God reflected in the book's radiant celebration of the Communion of Saints strikes me as a peculiarly undifferentiated one." Diminished, he claims, are the relations of the three persons of the Trinity, of Father, Son, and Holy Spirit, and the result is that *Friends of God and Prophets* "risks countenancing a less than trinitarian, ultimately impersonal, vision and prayer."[24] When I picked up the book, I did so, like Imbelli, with excitement. As I began to read, I did not notice his issue with the doctrine of God. I did, however, feel the impersonal character of the book's reappropriation of the saints.

My immediate reaction was visceral. Page 1: Johnson refers to the communion of saints as a symbol. Page 2: she censures "the social system of patronage" that permeates the history and much of contemporary devotion to the saints. I felt this rejection of patronage — of relationships of devotion and benefaction — in my gut. I felt a loss. The feeling made me turn back a page and reread what kind of symbol was in view.

> This doctrinal symbol [of the communion of saints] does not in the first instance refer to paradigmatic figures, those outstanding individuals traditionally called "saints," but rather names the whole community of people graced by the Spirit of God. Neither does it point exclusively to those who have died; rather, the community of living persons is its primary referent. Furthermore, while obviously interested in human beings, the symbol does not allude to them exclusively but embraces the whole natural world in a "communion of the holy." . . . Ultimately it points to the Creator Spirit who vivifies creation, weaves interconnections, and makes holy the world.[25]

From this quotation, one can see the insight, which I applied to my own failed account of "Fortunate Saints," that they have become tropes rather than people, figures of speech that we use to refer to ourselves as well as inanimate things, symbols of meaning rather than living agents in our lives.

Johnson's outright dismissal of patronage brought this point into view. Certainly, I do not want to defend what Johnson calls a patriarchal "pyramid of power." But the power and assistance of the saints serve to

---

24. Imbelli, "A Catholic Work," 26.
25. Johnson, *Friends of God*, 1-2.

overturn that pyramid far more and far more often than they might support it. Johnson cites Peter Brown on this point. He shows that, in late antiquity, the saint as patron "ensures that in their world, there should be places where men could stand in the searching and merciful presence of a fellow human being."[26] Rather than tending to a few at the top, the patron saint gives access to those at the bottom. "The saint became the good patron whose intercessions were successful, whose power was exercised benevolently, and in whose name the church's wealth was at the disposal of the whole community."[27] This kind of reversal is described, in modern life, by Robert Orsi in his *Thank You, St. Jude*. Orsi studies devotion to St. Jude in mid-twentieth-century Chicago. He finds that relationships with Jude are empowering. "To pray to Jude . . . whose particular role in the American Catholic pantheon was to make the impossible possible, the hopeless hopeful — was to enter upon the path of reversal. As one woman exclaimed after her faithful Jude had come to her assistance in a difficult situation, 'the trick has been turned again.'"[28] Orsi, like Brown, shows that the saint is benefactor, friend, and the focal point of expanding relationships of friendship and benefaction.[29]

The saints are friends and sponsors. They connect us to redemptive associations. This point could have been retained by Johnson, even while she rejects patriarchal pyramids of power. Instead, she establishes an either/or: either we are companions of the saints who are symbols of meaning, or we are only supplicants of the saints as our patrons.[30] Johnson notes that these paradigms are mixed throughout Christian history: she refers to the "ambiguity" of models in Augustine, and identifies Latin America as a place where saints are venerated as both companions and patrons.[31] "[T]hese popular saints are helpers of the people in their daily

26. Peter Brown, *Cult of the Saints* (Chicago: University of Chicago Press, 1981), 127, cited in Johnson, *Friends of God*, 91.

27. Johnson, *Friends of God*, 90-91.

28. Robert A. Orsi, *Thank You, St. Jude* (New Haven: Yale University Press, 1996), 100.

29. Orsi, *Thank You, St. Jude*, 129-30; Brown, *Cult of the Saints*, xxx; Claudia Rapp, "'For Next to God, You Are My Salvation': Reflections on the Rise of the Holy Man in Late Antiquity," in *The Cult of Saints in Late Antiquity and the Middle Ages: Essays on the Contribution of Peter Brown*, ed. James Howard-Johnston and Paul Antony Hayward (New York: Oxford University Press, 2000), 63-82; John Bossy, *Christianity in the West, 1400-1700* (New York: Oxford University Press, 1985), 3-33.

30. Johnson, *Friends of God*, 91.

31. Johnson, *Friends of God*, 81.

struggle for life. By providing them with understanding and power to deal effectively with harsh situations, these saints open an avenue of relationship to God who can then be thought to be actively present in their lives. . . . [M]illions of people have set about creating meaningful lives for themselves and their families in the company of the saints."[32] Given this relationship as helpers and companions, why does Johnson divide the role of the saints in two contrasting models? I can identify, not specific reasons, but some presuppositions of Johnson's study. These assumptions have pulled this way and that within my own desire to be near the saints.

The main point is that Johnson writes as a theological reformer. Her task is to harvest the bounty of the tradition, weed out the tares, gain an orientation to the present, and propose a pathway to move forward. Johnson puts social and political concerns in the forefront. *Friends of God and Prophets* is "a feminist theological reading of the communion of saints." Johnson consistently attends to questions of injustice and human suffering, especially of the poor and disenfranchised. This perspective, generally speaking, has a default position of democratic politics and social contract theory. Democratic society is an implied social contract between autonomous individuals who enter social life in order to fairly balance individual interests.[33] In the Christian theologian's work, this democratic politics also includes the common good and an ultimate common end and unity of humanity in God.

In relationship to this reformist theological project, most of the saints appear to be barriers to be overcome. A close look at the most famous lives of the saints reveals harsh asceticism, eccentric behavior, obedience to ecclesiological authority, intolerance of rival points of view, and a triumphalism of Christianity over paganism. Traditional piety and devotion to these saints can seem counterproductive, nostalgic at best, and at its worst, a desire to return to superstition and outdated forms of piety. What do we do with the self-imposed suffering of St. Rose, St. Francis, and countless other saints? What good is self-inflicted humiliation when we are trying to relieve the suffering of the world? Even more to the point, should we allow the inequities of the world — systems of nepotism and preferential treatment, patronage, and supplication — to be mapped onto

32. Johnson, *Friends of God,* 13.

33. For an analysis of this default position, see Robert Kraynak, *Christian Faith and Modern Democracy* (Notre Dame, Ind.: University of Notre Dame Press, 2001).

the company of heaven? Ought not heaven to provide the paradigm of equality under God? If we will achieve the kingdom, should not we see ourselves as equal to the saints?

Johnson explains, with some regret, that the age of special, personal relationships to saints has passed. "The modern and postmodern spirit offers a poor fit for traditional appreciation of the saints. . . . Tales of their holy lives and images of their devout selves make them seem too perfect, too miraculous, too otherworldly, too eccentric to have anything useful to say."[34] She asks us to face the fact that the metaphysical world that provided a busy avenue between this world and the next has collapsed. Traditional practices in relationship to the saints are fragmented survivors, like medieval ruins. Something of the old age is still standing, but the remaining structure is uninhabitable. Johnson's project is to push the communion of saints forward in our time. A traditional dependence upon the saints will have to be left behind for the sake of a saint who is an example and inspiration: passionate, not too perfect, self-sufficient yet interdependent, deeply personal and socially active, and faithful to a compassionate and companionate God.[35]

Johnson's project — as passionate, intelligent, and evocative as it is — produced in me a sense of loss, which required a close evaluation of my own thinking about the saints. We shared the same basic point: we have a relationship, not to the saints, but to their stories. My own thesis (in relationship to Wyschogrod and Mandela) was that we are the subjects of their stories, and their identity is filled and enriched with our lives.[36] Along these lines, Johnson holds that saints live in our memory. "Memory has an intrinsically narrative structure. . . . By telling and listening to stories, persons locate themselves in a cultural, historical, or religious tradition and allow its insights and challenge to shape their identity as human subjects."[37] In Johnson's framework, saints are not approached as individuals to whom we have a living relationship, but are named as part of a litany of saints. "In modern and postmodern culture, such prayer through acts of remembrance and hope awakens consciousness and revitalizes the spirit."[38] The

---

34. Johnson, *Friends of God*, 17-18.

35. Johnson, *Friends of God*, 231-32.

36. My thesis on the saints (from my "Postmodernism, Saints, and Scoundrels") is cited in Johnson, *Friends of God*, 238-39.

37. Johnson, *Friends of God*, 170.

38. Johnson, *Friends of God*, 245.

saints provide "lessons of encouragement" and "inspiration to hope."[39] In short, these friends of God are texts and not living friends.

Johnson's *Friends of God and Prophets* put me at an impasse. What I had been thinking about as communion with the saints was really a kind of narrative control, weeding out the bad by ignoring their stories, looking for lessons of encouragement for my social sensibilities, and in general, putting modern subjectivity in modern/postmodern terms. The modern point is that "saints are their stories," and the postmodern twist is that the real agents of the stories are, not the saints, but the storytellers and interpreters. I wasn't getting nearer to the actual saints. The lives of the saints are attractive partly because they are wild; that is, they are not easily domesticated in my nice middle-class world. This is the irony of postmodernism in general. It looks, on the surface, to be "transgressive," but really just conforms to a bourgeois privatization of meaning. The impasse was, for me, that in trying to understand the saints in moral, social, and textual terms, I was also trying to tame them.

This problem stayed on the back burner for a number of years. It came to the fore, in August of 2007, when I began to undertake this project. For a week at the end of the summer, I read, paced, read again, paced again, and reached an embarrassing level of proficiency in Microsoft's Spider Solitaire. I read and studied without clear direction. Toward the end of the week, I sat down with *Sex Lives of the Saints: An Erotics of Ancient Hagiography*, by Virginia Burrus.[40] I was baffled and intrigued. I laughed out loud a few times at Burrus's talent for misreading texts, and I have no doubt that Burrus would be delighted by my reaction. With the delight, I began to see the saints from a different point of view.

To measure my reaction to *Sex Lives of the Saints*, I consulted a *Theological Studies* review of the book. The review (like others that I found later)[41] expressed both admiration for *Sex Lives of the Saints* and incomprehension. Michael McCarthy concludes his review in this way:

---

39. Johnson, *Friends of God*, 79-85.

40. Virginia Burrus, *Sex Lives of the Saints: An Erotics of Ancient Hagiography* (Philadelphia: University of Pennsylvania Press, 2004).

41. Andrew S. Jacobs, review of *The Sex Lives of the Saints: An Erotics of Ancient Hagiography*, by Virginia Burrus, *Church History* 73, no. 4 (December 2004): 838-41. "Burrus brings together history, theology, critical theory, philosophy, and autobiography in a dazzling series of readings of early Christian hagiographies that will, by turns, delight, confound, illuminate, and challenge diverse historians, theologians, and theorists" (838).

The book is difficult to read, both because it is so drenched in mind-bending theory and because erotics itself treats a subject that resists containment. B.'s discussion will surely frustrate those who wish to pin down the Lives of Saints, their writers, and herself. Yet that is presumably her point. What may be particularly interesting to readers of this journal is what the ancient Christian "counter-erotics" tells us about God, who defies discursive delimitation yet remains the measure "of such a sublime erotic ambition" (15). B. suggests that to reckon with such a God is to reconsider the history of sexuality.[42]

In one sense, the thesis of *Sex Lives* is indisputable. The lives of the saints do reveal a "counter-erotics."[43] The saints (by and large) are not "selfless" in our modern sense of disinterested love. They do not love as we have come to see the paradigmatic Good Samaritan: he helps a stranger along the road, departs as a stranger, and receives nothing in return for his kindness. The saints' indomitable desire for God, to be full of God, animates their asceticism, their poverty, and their attraction to the poor, lame, and blind. The general point is clear: the saints love with passion rather than disinterest, with *eros* rather than *agape*. Burrus's general point is clear, but the details of her *Sex Lives* are unfaithful to the saints as people. The "saints" are merely texts yet again; in this case texts for deconstruction and postmodern play. As stated by Michael McCarthy in *Theological Studies*, the details about the saints (Jerome, Martin of Tours, and so on) are awash in postmodern/post-Freudian/Foucaultian/sexual transgressions, sublimations, ambiguity, and deviance. In a delightful but self-referential way, *Sex Lives of the Saints* is unapologetically about Burrus's own skills of interpretation.

After reading *Sex Lives of the Saints*, I was fixated on a single question, "Why write a book like this on the saints?" This question applies to any book (on any topic), and I recognized that reading *Sex Lives* was an occasion for reflection, and very little hinged on my answer in relation to Burrus's work in particular. In Burrus's case, however, I did invent an answer: Burrus has come to love the saints; she wants to live with them, but she does not want to make a commitment. Her postmodern irony allows her to study the saints *as if* their lives were real and true, without any com-

---

42. Michael McCarthy, review of *The Sex Lives of the Saints: An Erotics of Ancient Hagiography*, by Virginia Burrus, *Theological Studies* 66, no. 2 (June 2005): 491.

43. Burrus, *Sex Lives*, 147-59.

mitment to what is real and true. In effect, in trying to understand *Sex Lives of the Saints,* I simply turned its postmodern questions toward the author. The book is about Burrus's own desire for the saints, and perhaps, a desire to share their desire for God. Its postmodernism makes the relationships playful, temporary, and safe, but full of passion like a Hollywood version of a weekend affair.

By bringing desire to the surface, Burrus enjoys her relationships with the texts far more than Johnson does in *Friends of God and Prophets* or than I have in the past. Johnson's book is far more restrained because she is far more serious about the moral and religious reality represented by the lives of the saints. As noted above, she is a prominent theologian and a reformer; Burrus appears to be an intellectual who is concerned primarily with showing us what can be done with texts. Johnson and Burrus are much different, but there is a similarity between the serious modern and playful postmodern approaches. In a modern (Johnson) and postmodern (Burrus) frame of material relations, any commitment to real social relations will dissolve on a metaphysical level. The way that I put this point above is that the modern approach sees saints as otherworldly and the postmodern as "other" in the world. In each case, however, there is no bridge between the worlds — between the social world that we inhabit and a metaphysical communion of saints. In neither approach do we have living relationships to the saints. The modern approach encloses the saint within the text and our social/political world; the postmodern approach fragments the text and encloses the saint within endless interpretations.

The "bridge" between the worlds is the basic problem. Burrus's postmodern play appears to be an attempt to free us from modern constraints, but the frantic play of interpretation suggests a metaphysical anxiety of the modern buffered (metaphysically closed) self.[44] We are drawn to the saints because of their otherworldly desires. But Burrus's postmodern theory and interpretive strategies provide only a great setting for an affair, exotic and temporary. She can throw herself into the saints with the safety of postmodern irony. Her passion has no social or metaphysical implications.

After seeing this interpretive play at work in Burrus, it struck me that I love the saints and want to live with them too. Then it struck me how many new books on saints I see every year. How do people from worlds gone by

---

44. Taylor, *A Secular Age,* 300. Fredric Jameson, *Postmodernism, or the Culture of Late Capitalism* (Durham, N.C.: Duke University Press, 1992).

keep appearing among us in a world where they do not belong? Then, the question hit me hard, "Why am I adding my bit to a sea of books on the saints?" Burrus's book helped me see the answer: like her, I am being drawn to them and cannot help but write on the saints. Unlike Burrus, I am a homebody not tempted by the exotic. I am in a different intellectual setting than Burrus and her *Sex Lives of the Saints*. I am the nice guy, about whom even my wife has said, "He is the kind of guy you could marry but don't want to date." I cannot feign detachment in order to make an intellectually safe and ironic but passionate space. Likewise, I am drawn to the saints, without irony, because they find a way to what is real and true. The saints offer networks of social relations that bridge time and place; their associations trample the metaphysical limits of modern thought and imagination. This overflow of metaphysical relations makes the communion of saints difficult to display reasonably. But we write (as academics will do) on the saints because we want to be near them. We want to be part of their world.

But another question emerged. How do I justify my concern for the saints without creating an interpretive hedge around them, the kinds of interpretive and textual strategies deployed by Wyschogrod, Burrus, Johnson, and my "Fortunate Saints"? To approach an answer, I listed the various problems that the communion of saints presented to modern/postmodern thought. I listed the reasons why I would give up on a serious study of the saints. The main problem (noted above) is that they are not really present to us, except as texts, icons, and statues. Hagiography is not historical. The traditional hagiographer imposes his or her religious concerns on history; we cannot be sure of knowing the real saints of the ancient and medieval world. Likewise, the "communion" of saints appears to be an invention of our desire for social and metaphysical unity. As much as Johnson protests that the patronage system was imposed upon heaven, doesn't she impose modern democratic polity and personal autonomy upon the kingdom of God? Aren't I just doing the same? I took these problems and simply turned them around, perhaps affected by Burrus's eye for sublimation. I outlined this book, *Sharing God's Good Company*, in terms of how the kinship of the saints overflows modern conceptual limits of reality and history, and modern conceptions of social life.

The starting point is the saint's relation to social desire. Our social desire, put simply, is our desire for shared life. It is a desire for a meaningful life. It is a desire and hope that my everyday endeavors do not stop with me, that who I am as a son, brother, father, friend, theologian, neighbor, and coach does not end with how it makes me feel or how it is meaningful just to me or how I am simply useful to others. This question about the meaning of my life is not simply a question about social life, but a question about life, about the meaning of how things really are. The purposes in our personal lives "always originate from a metaphysic, a worldview that identifies our place in the cosmos. Moral space itself thus implies a metaphysical space in which our lives are also situated."[45]

In *Landscapes of the Soul*, sociologist Douglas Porpora identifies a malaise in contemporary life due, in part, to our inability to locate our place in the meaning of things. "We are who we are not just in social space, not just in moral space, but in metaphysical space as well. If to know who we are is always to know our position in space, then part of who we are is our position in the cosmos. As a culture, we may fail to think cosmologically; we may fail to imagine our entire cosmos. But we cannot fail to do so without endangering our own personal sense of identity. What is closest to us individually — our very souls — is connected to what is most distant and most grand — the meaning of life."[46] Charles Taylor, in *Sources of the Self*, holds that this crisis of meaning and identity is a consequence of a moral impulse that calls for a detachment and "disembedding" in modern life.[47] In the modern democratic rejection of higher callings and higher time, we have uprooted ourselves from a common horizon or standpoint from which we can see, however indistinctly, where the land meets the sky.[48] In contrast to this loss of bearings, the communion of saints spans out and populates a metaphysical horizon, and by occupying this horizon, it provides an orientation to an otherwise formless space.

45. Douglas Porpora, *Landscapes of the Soul: The Loss of Moral Meaning in American Life* (New York: Oxford University Press, 2001), 20.

46. Porpora, *Landscapes of the Soul*, 20-21.

47. The summer after I completed a first draft of the project, I found this social desire articulated in Charles Taylor's *A Secular Age*. Part of Taylor's brilliance is his ability to tell an intellectual history that resonates with how we experience the everyday and feel placed and displaced in the world. I feel both the domestication and the displacement every day, at home and yet alienated. How do we live as part of the family of God in a world where kinship, God, and the meaning of life divide rather than unite, where I recognize that my neighbor or colleague has a conception of the world that might contradict my own and yet we carry on together, happily, on the surface of things? As a friend of mine likes to say, "Just keeping it shallow." Contemporary life and modern reality sustain and spur on our social desire but cut it off, usually by privatizing its pathways, its routes of pilgrimage.

48. Charles Taylor, *Sources of the Self* (Cambridge: Harvard University Press, 1989), 27.

Although we cannot map out the borderlands in their entirety, we can have, through the saints, a relationship to their inhabitants. Not everyone feels a sense of disorientation. In *Landscapes of the Soul*, Porpora finds that "many of us individually not only are without answers, but we never even ask the questions. . . . [A]s individuals, many of us seem to live quite contentedly without at all considering life's ultimate questions."[49] Likewise, not everyone will feel a social desire to the point of disorientation. Nor will everyone be attracted to the communion of saints. But I wonder if the wide and varied appeal of the saints is evidence of a deeply felt need among many of us for friends, mentors, and sponsors who connect us to the cosmos as a whole — to what things really are as a whole. The saints provide associations, lines of communication, and close connections that join us to God. The desire for nearness to the saints — to the eccentric, noble, passionate, patient, strange, kind, joyous, and melancholy people of God — is at its core a social desire for a kinship that is settled in the cosmos and connects us to God.

This mediated character of communion with God can be seen as objectionable or inviting. Many of us have been raised with a metaphysics of the direct line between God and human. This book is for those looking for connecting relationships, those who do not want to stand alone with God in the cosmos. In *Friends of God and Prophets*, Johnson argues that saints ought to be attractive as lessons of encouragement, rather than for their aid and "their [so-called] ability to mediate the presence and power of the transcendent God."[50] She sees this role of mediation tied up, inextricably, with patriarchal power and privilege.[51] It is hard to know why she ties heavenly benefaction so tightly to the earthly exclusion of the powerless. In any case, her rejection of saintly sponsorship fits a modern religious spirit and our democratic sense that each of us has his or her own relationship to God. Often, however, this quest for personal intimacy turns out to be hollow, lonely, and abstract. It is, in the end, just our own spirituality.

Our modern problem is not that God has made himself a distant monarch, but that our lives, especially our social roles and personal space, have become distant from what we presume to be an ever-present and loving God. We have difficulty mapping out the meaning of things. Before

49. Porpora, *Landscapes of the Soul*, 132.
50. Johnson, *Friends of God*, 86.
51. Johnson, *Friends of God*, 16, 27, 235-36, 244-45.

God, we are all equal; nonetheless, many of us recognize that we are not all equally situated in relationship to God. Whether we have not situated ourselves or have not been situated equally, we look to a community to draw us near. We need family. We who are poor in spirit need friends and benefactors to populate the pathways, people to meet on pilgrimage, friends of friends who live in borderlands, someone who knows someone who is ready to take us in and show us the way in a strange land.

Two

Saints

—ᴍ—

Lawrence Cunningham begins his *Brief History of Saints* by showing the difficulties of defining sainthood. Simply sketching common characteristics of the saints hardly seems possible. They are kings, paupers, mystics through and through, entirely practical minded, brilliant, anti-intellectual, conventional, and unconventional. Cunningham notes that many saints are luminous and attractive to their contemporaries and to us. Hildegard of Bingen (d. 1179) and Catherine of Siena (d. 1380) come to mind. Cunningham also admits that "other saints strike us as odd, outrageous, or eccentric. The late medieval mystic Richard Rolle was so peculiar that his sister cried out: *Frater meus insanus est* (My brother is bonkers)."[1] Holy fools, like St. Benedict-Joseph Labre (d. 1783), evoked disdain and disgust in their times. In addition, the lives of some saints, like St. Christopher, are constituted entirely of legend and folklore. Cunningham concludes that "the category of saint is so generic that we can only call a person a saint because we recognize that this or that person belongs under that title, i.e. that this or that person bears a 'family resemblance' . . . to what we consider a saint to be."[2] Cunningham's use of family resemblance is the best we can do to circumscribe the saints, with one point of clarification. We are able to see family resemblances because the communion of saints resembles a family. Their connection is that they share the kinship of God.

---

1. Lawrence S. Cunningham, *A Brief History of Saints* (Oxford: Blackwell, 2005), 3.
2. Cunningham, *Brief History of Saints*, 127. Cunningham takes the phrase "family resemblance" from Ludwig Wittgenstein's *Philosophical Investigations*, trans. G. E. M. Anscombe (New York: Macmillan, 1973).

The centrality of communion is portrayed beautifully by Beverly Donofrio in her memoir *Looking for Mary; or, The Blessed Mother and Me*.[3] Donofrio is widely known for an earlier memoir, *Riding in Cars with Boys*, which was adapted and released as a film of the same name.[4] The success of this book and film surely laid the ground for new opportunities. Donofrio appears to have not taken them. Imagine if Drew Barrymore were cast as you on the big screen. Where would you go from there? The savvy author would rush another book out on the same trajectory. Donofrio, however, has not followed the success. She has kept to her commitments as a writer insofar as her work has followed the course of life. The spirit and energy of *Looking for Mary* lie not in religious commitments per se, but in a writer's relentless quest to be honest with life as it really is. This is the power of *Riding in Cars with Boys* as well. After the success of that earlier memoir, Donofrio had standing enough for *Looking for Mary* to be reviewed in the *New York Times Book Review* and the *Washington Post Book World*. Clearly disappointed, the *New York Times* called the book "strange," and the *Washington Post* lamented that the edgy, hip girl of *Riding in Cars with Boys* had become a bundle of religious sentimentality and clichés.[5] In effect, *Riding in Cars with Boys* was well received because Donofrio, with her mastery as a writer, made her life porous to us. *Looking for Mary* was not so well received in the same venues because in it and through it she became porous to God.

In the previous chapter, I discussed theories about the saints and hagiography in order to point to an underlying social desire. Donofrio allows me to highlight the need for social and metaphysical connections through her narrative. No doubt, she is able to go beyond the limits of theories because she is a magnificent writer. For me and in the context of this chapter, she provides a contemporary example and guide to the role of the saints in our lives. Actually, Donofrio would put it better: she is searching for a role in the life of Mary, and Mary has a role in the life of the world. Donofrio develops rich intertextuality between her story and the story of Mary. Mary's life is not conceived of as a "text" but as a real, extratextual referent.

3. Beverly Donofrio, *Looking for Mary; or, The Blessed Mother and Me* (New York: Viking Compass, 2000).

4. Beverly Donofrio, *Riding in Cars with Boys* (New York: Penguin Books, 1990). The film of the same title was directed by Penny Marshall (2001); screenplay by Morgan Ward.

5. David Kelly, "Looking for Mary," *New York Times Book Review*, August 13, 2000, 9; Laura Ciolkowski, "In Brief: Memoirs," *Washington Post Book World*, October 22, 2000, 10.

Looking for Mary works through the insights that "saints are their stories" and that we tell the stories of the saints through our relationships to them. However, one common effect of theories of sainthood is that they buffer us from the eccentricities of the saints. We find a place for them in our world. In contrast, Donofrio's narrative positions her own life in Mary's world — in the world as it is known through Mary.

Looking for Mary chronicles Beverly Donofrio's search for Mary as she struggles for a practical and spiritual orientation in her life as a whole. She is looking to connect herself to the meaning of life through a relationship (to Mary) that bridges social and metaphysical space. Her questions are about having a role and place. These questions pivot on her role as a mother, which she shares with and resists in Mary. In this quest and in motherhood, Beverly is both the driving force in the narrative and its main obstacle. She pursues relentlessly and passionately, but what she pursues is sometimes vague, sometimes full of contradictions, and often a false image of what she really, deeply desires. Her pursuit of love and wholeness for herself and her son is a flight from them as well. In this pursuit and resistance, she reflects a common experience. Looking back on my life, I see that more than once I sought refuge in an unsatisfactory or even destructive relationship because it was doomed to fail; I experienced a kind of intimacy, and I was safe from it as well. Don't many of us do the same with matters of faith: close enough to keep life with God in view but far enough away to keep our lives steady and safe?

In *Looking for Mary*, Donofrio recounts her unsatisfactory relationships, destructive tendencies, and low points with rigorous honesty. She is merciless in her self-scrutiny.[6] She is candid also about the faults of others, and sometimes impatient and uncharitable toward them. In her uncharitable moments, she invites us to scrutinize her too. This rigorous honesty is where *Looking for Mary* reveals and leaves behind the edgy, hip girl of *Riding in Cars*. As a memoir, *Looking for Mary* is retrospective and therapeutic, but its purpose is clearly not to encourage admiration for the author. After reading the book, I was unsure about my attitude toward her. Would her honesty be intimidating? Would she set me on edge? My reaction accords with her narrative. She is not concerned with her own image or the reader's relationship to her; rather, she is pointing us beyond herself. She

6. Donofrio, *Looking for Mary*, 72.

points us to two ennobling gifts, Jason and Mary, her son and her new patron and companion.

Beverly's slow reconciliation with her son and growing relationship
with Mary are conveyed through the tensions and unity of three plotlines.
The weaving together of these plotlines is my main interest in the book.
Donofrio weaves together (1) her pilgrimage to Medjugorje; (2) a fuller
story of her life, lost loves, and struggles of motherhood; and (3) the story
of Mary, from the annunciation to her activity in the world today.
Donofrio's first chapter begins with her trip to Bosnia so that we see her
life (which she simply sketches at this point) as groundwork for the pilgrimage. "Six years before I landed in Bosnia, the Virgin Mary was no
more than a dim memory, another fairy tale from my childhood as I sat in
the rocker day after day, heartbroken over a man, but really over my life,
which I thought of as pathetically impoverished. I was forty and alone and
had just moved to a tiny village by the sea called Orient, where I knew no-
body."[7] Beverly tells us about her heartache over a failed relationship, her
time in Orient, and her growing attraction to figurines, prayer cards, and
glossy prints of Mary. Combing yard sales, she fills her house with them.
To frame the chapter, she draws a comparison between her own cold
heart, "too defended, too brittle, too pockmarked by life," and the heart of
Mary on a print that hangs near her bathroom mirror.[8] With its typical
symbolism (flames, sword, tears, and roses), "that heart told a story like a
novel. It was just like life: complicated, changing, never the same."[9]
Beverly concludes the story of her time in Orient (not the chapter as a
whole) by shifting agency. Mary becomes the actor: "I'd made a shrine of
my house, and knowing a good opportunity when she sees one, the
Blessed Mother came in."[10] She ends the chapter with an account, from
the Gospel of Luke, of the angel Gabriel's announcement to Mary that she
will bear Jesus.

As Beverly's pilgrimage to Medjugorje begins, the account of her life
goes back to earlier, pivotal events, and the story of Mary moves forward.
Beverly is a reluctant pilgrim. She is part of a pilgrimage tour and package
of experiences. She endures her annoying and enthusiastic group with the

7. Donofrio, *Looking for Mary*, 3.
8. Donofrio, *Looking for Mary*, 3.
9. Donofrio, *Looking for Mary*, 14.
10. Donofrio, *Looking for Mary*, 15.

cool distance of a journalist. For most of the pilgrimage, she inhabits what Charles Taylor, in *A Secular Age*, calls a "middle realm." It is a "free and neutral space, between religious commitment and materialism."[11] In this middle space, we moderns are pulled two ways — by "the cross pressure felt by the modern buffered identity, on the one hand drawn toward unbelief, while on the other, feeling solicitations of the spiritual."[12] Beverly's pilgrimage and her spiritual longings work upon her and draw her to reflect upon her own life. She moves from spiritual and personal isolation to surrender — from the buffered to the porous self. Beverly's growing relationship with Mary — the "solicitations of the spiritual" and her openness to "forces beyond our senses" — is experienced as true but irrational.[13] By the end of the memoir, she will make sense of it. She will resolve the tensions of the buffered self by finding a place to live and worship in Mexico, a place that is porous — that integrates divine solicitations in day-to-day life.

Beverly begins her life story with her pregnancy as a high school student. She ends, many years later, with the funeral of her son's father and her short-time husband. In between, we learn of friends, lovers, abusers, giving parents, and an interesting but self-centered grandparent. Donofrio's *Looking for Mary* is a confession, both a catalogue of missteps and a retrospective identification of Mary's sometimes subtle and sometimes undeniable workings in her life. Each chapter (like chapter 1) concludes with the story of Mary, from the annunciation in chapter 1 to stories of Mary's self-determination in our lives in later chapters. Note the contrast with the textual approach outlined in the previous chapter. When approaching the saints as tropes and texts, we become the agents of their stories. In contrast, Donofrio's recollections of life develop a separate story line for Mary so that Mary becomes an agent of Beverly's pilgrimage and the story of Beverly's life.

Along this line of reversal, the contrasts and conjunctions of the three plotlines have a powerful effect. First, the pilgrimage is a mix of irritations, disagreements, intimate moments, wonder, prayer, fasting, and self-evaluation. Second, all these tensions flow steadily toward Beverly's memories, self-scrutiny, and attempts to understand her life as a whole. Finally,

11. Charles Taylor, *A Secular Age* (Cambridge, Mass.: Belknap Press, 2007), 360.
12. Taylor, *A Secular Age*, 360.
13. Donofrio, *Looking for Mary*, 242.

the third story line, the story of Mary, does not fit at the beginning of the book. The first two sequences (pilgrimage and life story) are written from a personal point of view, interpretive and introspective. The sequence on Mary, in contrast, has an objective and impersonal tone. Beverly is not in it; the point of view is detached, and it is written to inform, as a matter of fact. Here we have an indication (which I did not recognize at first) that Beverly is slowly finding a real place, that her life on its own is adrift and that the life of Mary is a firm place with a real orientation to life.

It had been building, but I felt the full force of the contrast between Beverly's memoir and the objective report of Mary's story when I reached the fourth chapter. Most of the chapter deals with the low points of Beverly's life: estrangement from her son Jason, an abusive relationship, depression, despair, and therapy. Just before the story of Mary begins, she notes that, by misdirection and isolation rather than openness, she begins to identify with Mary.

> [When my therapist commented that my shoes looked like a nun's] I confessed that I did fantasize about being a nun sometimes, but it was only a fantasy about wearing the same cool outfit every day, and being cloistered away from the world, safe, and man-independent. It was not about anything spiritual. I was not obedient, and did not like following rules, and certainly would never marry a here-in-spirit-only Son of God, born of a virgin, impregnated by a bird.
>
> It did not escape me that I'd become like Mary: a mother who didn't have sex. Born-Again Virgin was what I called myself for laughs.[14]

In the subsequent section on Mary, Donofrio turns to the apocryphal *Gospel of James* (ca. 150) to recount Mary's birth, dedication to the temple, betrothal, pregnancy, and perpetual virginity. A long last sentence of the chapter points out the contrast between the "walled garden" of Mary's virgin womb and its "fertile soil where something new and unexpected could grow; her abiding virginity was a sign that even the impossible is possible with God."[15] The walled garden is also Beverly. Apart from this literary cue that she will also be fertile soil (a porous self), the power of *Looking for Mary* is the slow unveiling of a profound truth: Beverly has lived the "in-

---

14. Donofrio, *Looking for Mary*, 73-74.
15. Donofrio, *Looking for Mary*, 77.

vented" life, and Mary's life is the real story, where we can find a place to live truthfully, the story of compassion, peace, and openness to God.

In chapter 11 (out of fourteen), Beverly's time in Medjugorje comes to a conclusion, and Mary makes her presence plain. The pilgrimage and the story of Beverly's life begin to merge in chapter 10 where the sacrament of reconciliation and the Eucharist frame a set of painful memories, accusations ("You're a selfish person," Jason had once said), and forgiveness for her ex-husband, Stephen. Beverly becomes vulnerable and open to Mary as Mary is open to God and the suffering of the world. Throughout the pilgrimage, signs had been received by several members of the group, some credible but most wishful thinking. The fellow pilgrims appear to be too open to anything that hints of the supernatural. Earlier (chapter 9), Beverly had enough of the pilgrimage: "I do not want to be a crazy, sign-seeing, rose-smelling, rigid, right-to-life Catholic. I do not want to participate in this pilgrimage anymore."[16] In chapter 11 she decides to leave her pride on a hilltop in Medjugorje. She will have Mary in her life whether or not she is seen as a crazy, sign-seeking simpleton. Later, she will speak of Mary's role in helping her form new lines of identity.[17] At this time of surrender and openness, Beverly receives concrete signs from Mary.

The signs are media of communication between Beverly and Mary. They take Beverly out of the "middle realm" of the modern buffered self and the enclosed space of materialism (described by Taylor above). The physical signs point to a real metaphysical relationship. This metaphysical kinship is where Beverly will resolve the tensions and disjunctions of her pilgrimage and her struggle to see with some clarity her life as a whole. One sign is natural/ordinary, and the other is supernatural and extraordinary. The extraordinary sign, precisely because it evokes wonder, is the unambiguous sign. Mary is sending a clear message. The natural sign is ambiguous, and the meaning of it requires interpretation. Beverly's interpretation — her participation in the meaning of the event — is her response to Mary. The signs, natural and supernatural, form a conversation and affirmation of shared life.

The supernatural sign is the vanishing of a ceramic tear that was an obvious feature of a statue (recently purchased) that Beverly had been carrying about the town in a shopping bag. Others witnessed the obvious

---

16. Donofrio, *Looking for Mary*, 160.
17. Donofrio, *Looking for Mary*, 193.

change, and the miracle is reported as a matter of fact. The point of its supernatural character is not that nature has been transcended, but that the
supernatural cannot be denied. The change is plain to any observer. It is a
pledge that is witnessed and confirmed by others. Mary is making a public
commitment to Beverly. Mary has given an unmistakable sign *to her.*

The "natural" sign is a common and certainly understandable event. A
hand breaks off the same statue of Mary. Unlike the vanishing tear, evidence of the fracture is obvious. Although this broken hand does not require supernatural explanation, it does evoke interpretation. It seems to
mean nothing at all. But Beverly is impelled to make something of it as her
gesture to Mary — as her active reception of Mary's pledge that is evinced
through the unmistakable sign of the vanishing tear. When Beverly arrived in Medjugorje, she brought with her a rash upon her hands, itchy
blisters that a physician had diagnosed as "a recurring nervous condition
for which there was no cure."[18] The rash functions as a psychosomatic
measure. By the end of the pilgrimage, her hands are "ragged and hideous,
but feel fine," and it looks like every inch of old blistered skin will peel
off.[19] Alongside this image of baptism and rebirth, Beverly interprets the
broken hand of the statue in terms of her new relationship to Mary. She
asks her spiritual adviser, Fr. Freed, "Do you think her hand broke off because she wants to give me a hand?" After a pause, she answers for him,
"You think it means I'm supposed to give *her* a hand?" He responds, "I
think it means both."[20] Here, the unmistakable sign (the tear) and the ambiguous sign (the hand) work together. The miracle — the real metaphysical connection — is filled out through interpretation, which is the ground
for having a place, a purpose, and a relationship that offer a way to participate in the divine source of all life.

In the chapters that follow, I will try to work out the kinds of connections found in *Looking for Mary,* not only Beverly's narrative realism and
reference to miraculous signs, but also her weaving together of pilgrimage, holy place, and holy time. Through holy Mary, she sees and inhabits
God's good world. Donofrio is not attempting a philosophical or theological inquiry. She opens her life to us. In relationship to the saints (for her,
specifically Mary), she gives a personal account that opens space for mak-

18. Donofrio, *Looking for Mary,* 18.
19. Donofrio, *Looking for Mary,* 192.
20. Donofrio, *Looking for Mary,* 189.

ing theological connections between the practices of devotion to the saints, hagiography, and broad philosophical questions about meaning, history, and community. She raises fundamental questions that are evoked by an encounter with the saints. The most obvious question is the possibility of making real metaphysical connections and opening up a place for working through our deeply felt social desires. With great literary skill and thoughtfulness, honesty, and vulnerability, Donofrio narrates the conversion of the buffered self to the porous self. I will set myself to understanding how to think about the world given that such experiences are possible, real, and true. *Looking for Mary* is about Beverly's struggle to get beyond the "middle realm" — to chart a spiritual topography and to make her way through a one-dimensional, material world to a world open to real, transcendent relationships.

The saints are defined by their kinship. They form a connecting web of relations that bridges the divide of the "middle realm" — the divide between our buffered world and divine meaning. This chapter began with the difficulty of defining saints, given their eccentricities and the fact that some saints, like Christopher, are constituted by legend and lore. Given this set of problems, Lawrence Cunningham notes that definitions of saints tend to be far narrower than the numerous characters that are actually called saints. He suggests that sainthood is not so much a precise set of qualities as persons whose lives bear a family resemblance. Donofrio's *Looking for Mary* pushes this definition by association further. Her memoir suggests that relationships (rather than individual qualities) are primary when encountering the saints. We gain our bearing on life through the relationships of the saints to God, the communion among the saints, and a saint's role and place in our lives. These relationships, rather than specific moral characteristics or habits of piety, form a kinship that is the basis for what we are able to recognize as holy in life.

Holiness is a relation to God, and the saints are the bounty of God's concrete and ever-extending associations. For this reason, ideas of sainthood, as Cunningham explains, will have to be embodied. Sainthood is not so much defined as named; the saint is not a category but a person-in-relationship to God and us. The varied, eccentric, noble, passionate, and poor saints embody God's kinship in the world. Sometimes we meet a person and immediately, because of mannerisms or facial structure, recognize that person as a brother or sister, son or daughter of someone we already know. Consider St. Polycarp, whose martyrdom was described in the introduction. Polycarp's faith in the face of death follows the pattern of St. Stephen (Acts 7:59-60), who follows the pattern of Christ. This connection of pattern and type is where Cunningham's use of family resemblance seems to apply best to the saints.

However, there are times when we see little resemblance among the saints. Think of St. Rose of Lima disfiguring her own face with lye.[21] We should have to be convinced against our objections that two people, say St. Rose and St. Catherine of Siena, are siblings or cousins of faith. "Okay, I see it now," we might say.[22] Yet, at other times we do not see it but trust that the two are related somehow. In this case, resemblance is something we learn to see, like faith seeking understanding. In each case, the family relationship is the ground for finding a commonality; or put better, the kinship is the commonality. The kinship of sainthood is first of all a set of relationships to God, and the kinship of God extends further than we can ever imagine. People find their way to sharing divine life in innumerable ways. In other words, the unmanageable diversity of the saints is a conceptual problem for us, but in practice it is a wonder of grace.

This appeal to kinship attends to the set of problems raised in the last chapter and its discussion of modern and postmodern theories (Elizabeth Johnson, Edith Wyschogrod, Virginia Burrus, and me). Saints are described in two basic ways in the modern/postmodern perspective: as moral or religious exemplars. The modern tendency is to explain and justify religion, in general, primarily in terms of morality.[23] According to this view, prayer, worship, and the veneration of saints make good if they produce a moral good. Usually, the modern saint is defined as a moral archetype and a social activist. For example, Johnson speaks of an egalitarian communion, Wyschogrod of radical altruism, and my "Fortunate Saints" of political engagements. There is enough truth in these moral definitions to keep enough saints in our lives. Certainly, a moral sense is important to the saints: if a person were known to be immoral, he or she could not be considered a saint. Virtue is necessary. The holiness of God will have to shine through.

21. See Sara Maitland, "Passionate Prayer," in *Sex and God*, ed. Linda Hurcombe (New York: Routledge and Kegan Paul, 1987), 125-40.

22. See Sr. Mary Alphonsus, O.S.S.R., *St. Rose of Lima* (Rockford, Ill.: Tan Books, 1982).

23. Immanuel Kant, *Religion within the Limits of Reason Alone*, trans. Theodore M. Greene and Hoyt H. Hudson (New York: Harper and Row, 1960); Jeffrey Stout, *Democracy and Tradition* (Princeton: Princeton University Press, 2004).

Nevertheless, as a justification for the saints, the moral approach encounters the problem of accounting for those who are actually called saints. Most contemplatives and mystics spend their lives in prayer without what we usually think of as extraordinary moral works. They are, by definition (as mystics), not social activists. I have told my son Daniel that his namesake, St. Daniel the Stylite, spent thirty-two years living on a pillar and dispensing spiritual advice. This bit of information is delightful for the young Daniel, but probably not of much practical use. Some saints, as Cunningham notes, are eccentric to the point of distraction. I wonder if the contemporary popularity of St. Francis of Assisi has to do with the fact that most of us know very little about him. When I told a friend about my work on this book, he made sure to lend me his copy of *The Little Flowers of St. Francis of Assisi*.[24] Then he gave me a commission: "Francis coerces Brother Bernard into stomping on his (Francis's) neck and insulting him brutally. See what you can do with that. The extreme fasting is disturbing as well. No spiritual director would allow it." The trial and error of holiness can be distressing. The lives of the saints may have been righteous, but we would hardly recommend them as examples for our children.

If saints are supposed to be moral exemplars per se, then saints are likely to distract us from what is important. We will have to overlook the passions that lead them to religious extremism and immovable witness to the faith. Among other saints, we will have to overlook the otherworldly piety that leads to inaction in this world. If a moral standard precedes and measures the saints, most martyrs and mystics will have to be weeded out. Dying for political or humanitarian reasons is good, but is there a doctrine or religious sentiment to die for? Spirituality is good, but can we countenance harsh asceticism and self-scrutiny for the sake of personal union with God? What kind of God is this that asks for suffering? If the saints are mere exemplars, then a moral system will have to circumscribe them, regulate them, and dismiss the extremism and quietism.

If this weeding out were the case, then saints would be moral exemplars only in a weak sense. They would simply provide ornamentation for our moral claims, and the ornamentation would be considered, more often than not, a distraction that gets in the way of serious moral endeavors. The eccentric and excessive saints will have to be disregarded. Devotion

24. Ugolino di Monte Santa Maria, *The Little Flowers of St. Francis of Assisi*, trans. W. Heywood (New York: Vintage Books, 1998).

and prayer for the dead will have to be ignored. Devotion to the saints would be tolerable, as in the case of Archbishop Oscar Romero, when it translates to a hope for social and political reform. In the modern framework, the typical view is that our fundamental allegiances should not be to people but to abstract moral ideals: justice, fairness, equality, and freedom.[25] Likewise, in Wyschogrod's postmodern context, the saints are disinterested and dedicated entirely to an anonymous "other." Wyschogrod's postmodernism is framed by her shift from an abstract principle (modernism) to an abstract other-regard (the postmodern "other"). For the modern and postmodern view, relationships with saints (like other personal relationships) will form biases and preferential associations that will get in the way.

When morality fails, there is another common option in defining the saints. Rather than seeing them as moral guides, we can define the saints in terms of their religious consciousness. The appeal to religious feeling seems to put religious practices as well as the saints in their proper context. We are able to admit that many saints are less apt moral exemplars than ordinary people we know. St. Thérèse of Lisieux (d. 1897), for example, would agree. Her "little way" makes a claim to sainthood by doing nothing extraordinary in this life. Her bold claims are found in her religious vision of the relationship between heaven and earth. In this regard, saints from Thérèse to Francis of Assisi can be defined by their religious sensitivity and understanding. St. Thérèse gives hope and encouragement for ordinary people who attend to the little matters of day-to-day life, to people who will not be recognized by their communities as saints. St. Francis calls us to attend to what we say through our actions.[26] Even if their own piety is extreme and not worthy of imitation, their uncompromising faith motivates us to put God first and to live faithfully.

Lawrence Cunningham takes this approach in a book written twenty-five years before his appeal to "family resemblance" in his *Brief History of Saints*. In *The Meaning of Saints* (1980), he defines saints in terms of their religious consciousness. He holds that "a saint is a person so grasped by a religious vision that it becomes central to his or her life in a way that radically

25. Joseph Reimer et al., *Promoting Moral Growth: From Piaget to Kohlberg* (Prospect Heights, Ill.: Waveland Press, 1983).

26. Note the "Prayer of St. Francis" or his oft-misquoted line, "Preach the gospel and when necessary use words." See *Francis and Clare: The Complete Works*, trans. Regis J. Armstrong, O.F.M. Cap., and Ignatius C. Brady, O.F.M. (Mahwah, N.J.: Paulist, 1982), 123.

changes the person and leads others to glimpse the value of that vision."[27] St. Thérèse might seem to fit here. Her case for sainthood will be treated in detail in chapter 3. A definition of sainthood based on her religious consciousness and vision misses the obvious and practical point. St. Thérèse does not make a claim to a specific vision as such; she urges activity in the world after her death, giving of aid and care. Countless people have come to love her and depend upon her. They are grasped, not by the way she pictures the world, but by her. She is present to them. They are introduced to her through family and friends, and friends of friends. Person by person, the devotion extends. For instance, St. Thérèse entered my life, not through her religious vision (her *Story of a Soul*), but through her relationship to my sister. One finds Thérèse in every room of her home. A sense of the presence of St. Thérèse is the basis from which to begin to grasp her understanding of "the little way." Her vision is that she will have a relationship to us, and the friendship then cultivates the shared vision.

In sum, theories of the saints as moral or religious exemplars avoid mention of the direct dealings of saints with us — our interchanges of devotion and benefaction, advocacy and care. The theories are not wrong as much as they are incomplete. The moral archetype gives us a map for taking action, and the "person grasped by religious vision" gives us an inspirational perspective. But in neither of these definitions do the saints give us themselves. This point was the basic claim of chapter 1 and its discussion of theories of sainthood. When we imagine self-giving, for example, we should not picture abstractions like Wyschogrod's radical altruism, which is the creation of the empty self.[28] The self-giving of the saints, like other living relationships, is an interaction of giving and receiving, care and affection, attentiveness, forgetfulness, renewal, and common life over time.

Interaction with the saints might be intense and extraordinary, but it tends not to be. In *Looking for Mary*, Donofrio seeks to move from the extraordinary experiences of her pilgrimage in Medjugorje to a place where a relationship with Mary is built into the practices of ordinary life (in San Miguel). Likewise, St. Thérèse of Lisieux is pictured in every room of my sister's house. My relationship to Thérèse is similar to my relationship to

---

27. Lawrence Cunningham, *The Meaning of Saints* (New York: Harper and Row, 1980), 65.

28. Edith Wyschogrod, *Saints and Postmodernism: Revisioning Moral Philosophy* (Chicago: University of Chicago Press, 1990), 155.

my sister. Sherrie will clear up my vision, especially when clouded by academic lingo. She can be critical; she worries a lot. She never misses the
birthdays of my five children, but frequently forgets mine. When I was
young, educated, and jobless, I lived with her and entertained her children.
On rare occasions over the years, my sister and I have had special moments together, and they make me uncomfortable every time. Our intimacy comes through keeping up with each other, care and favors for sure,
but ultimately because we are brother and sister. The bond precedes us,
and in a sense, we simply yield to it. At our best moments, we build on it.
Likewise, the saints are our kin; the communion of saints is a kinship, and
by giving us themselves — by being present to the world — we become
part of their sets of relations. It is a matter of faith to see that we are called
to the banquet, along with the saints. There are some that we avoid sitting
next to, others that we have not had a chance to meet, and others we race
to sit near. But by drawing near to one, we have a place with all the others
at the table. This is the communion of saints, varied and particular yet far-
reaching and far more than we can manage. But intimacy with one opens
up communion with all.

"Kinship" is a generic term that takes on the character of particular relationships. The term does not require a theory of organization (as *polis* or
"church" may); it allows for different kinds of saints and for a common
identity as a people. It is loose-fitting in general, and requires attention to
the particular to make the participation of family possible. I don't yield to
family in the abstract, but to learning to be a brother to a specific person,
my sister Sherrie. We do not grasp the whole meaning of "family" and certainly do not represent all families, but we have relationships to the near
and distant in our families, even to the forgotten of generations past, that
give us a place in the whole. Likewise, the communion of saints is kinship
that extends beyond the reach of its members. It is a community, not primarily of one saint in relation to another, but of each and all in relation to
God. The origin and center is God, so that a unifying characteristic or paradigm of the saint is not necessary. What is needed is a family resemblance
based in the fact that the saints are gathered people. This point about kinship will be important throughout the book; the saints populate edges of
the modern, secular world and establish various alliances on the borders
of modern realism, history, and social life. They breach the seams of the
buffered self.

THREE

Realism

———∿∿∿———

In his *Realist Vision*, Peter Brooks studies novels of the nineteenth-century realist tradition, but he locates his study within a context that transcends specific literary and philosophical styles. We have, he proposes, "a thirst for reality . . . [w]hich is curious, since we have too much reality, more reality than we can bear."[1] The problem with our lived reality is that we are busy working with it day to day, in a sequential order, one moment to the next. Like parts moving along an assembly line, the moments pass by. We are always in the middle of things with instrumental connections to the before and after but no link to the whole. Without a place in a whole, the realist vision sets out to offer segments of life in bold relief. In this approach, realism rejects an appeal to an extraordinary or a higher picture of life. It offers ordinary moments of time highlighted in bold through a stylized narrative.[2] An underlying point to Brooks's study of nineteenth-century realism is that it tends to resist symbol, metaphor, allegory, and higher meaning, but fails in its resistance. Realism at its best highlights the particular as a way to envision the whole, but envisioning the whole requires meaning that transcends a specific time and place.

The representation of life in modern realism and a parallel form of hagiographic realism are the subjects of this chapter. Hagiography varies throughout history according to conventions of time and place. Ancient or medieval hagiography is like ancient or medieval history and biogra-

---

1. Peter Brooks, *Realist Vision* (New Haven: Yale University Press, 2005), 1.
2. Donald Pizer, *Realism and Naturalism in Nineteenth Century American Literature* (Carbondale: Southern Illinois University Press, 1966), 3-10.

phy. In this chapter our concern is the conventions of nineteenth-century realism and a parallel form of hagiography. Both put us amid the tensions of the "middle realm" outlined by Charles Taylor, between the commitments of materialism and an indeterminate metaphysical pull.[3] Realism intends to refer to life as it really is.[4] In this frame, hagiographic realism takes a modern, representational approach to ordinary life, but unlike modern realism, it connects the ordinary to the whole of life through metaphysical relations. Ordinary life, in other words, includes relationships that have their source in God. Modern realism contracts meaning, time, and space in order to put events in relief. Hagiography, in contrast, is

3. Charles Taylor, *A Secular Age* (Cambridge, Mass.: Belknap Press, 2007), 360.

4. Realism, therefore, provides an important comparison with contemporary hagiography. As noted above, realism and hagiography share parallel concerns — a concern for the meaning of things. They are alike, but realism is also the clearest challenge to hagiography. In contrast to nineteenth-century realism, modernism and postmodernism allow spaces for the textuality of the lives of the saints. Each begins with a conviction about the world that is counter to realism: life itself is fragmented and cannot be represented in the passage of time. In contrast to the transcendental stability of the religious world, realism represents historical change and the progressive development of human culture. It provides a story that replaces traditional forms of salvation history. Realism, however, is unmasked by modernism as unity and coherence imposed on things rather than as representative of them. The realist skepticism of transcendence is turned upon its own account of the material world. Modernism, in its challenge to realism, does not represent the everyday coherence of things. Think of surrealism and the metaphysical elements of Salvador Dali's *Last Supper* or *Crucifixion*. The individual thing is depicted on a landscape that lacks rational organization. The individual thing (or text) does not refer, but has a reality in itself. It is. Further still, postmodernism rejects a stability of being and strives toward the creation of worlds as simulacra of being. Modernism and postmodernism, ironically, provide homes for the lives of the saints because they can be worlds unto themselves without reference to the here and now.

It would appear that hagiography would be destabilized when representation is lost. But it is modern realism (whether in literature, science, or history) that undermines hagiography at its core. It sees the mediation of a world of transcendent relations as patently false. Modernism, in its challenge to realist representation, allows the lives of the saints to be textual worlds without need of referents, without need for the coherence between material and transcendent worlds. The modern lives of the saints become significant for us because of their formal or structural qualities. They are disruptive and dangerous memories. Postmodernism, insofar as it collapses the textual world into the play of interpretation, goes further still and allows the saints to be any kind of memory we want them to be. If the modern saint is disruptive, the postmodern saint provides wish fulfillment. The postmodern possibility that the saints live through us (through our interpretations) is not far from a premodern possibility that we live through the saints.

expansive. Reality is not circumscribed in order to be seen; rather, the particular becomes more than it is as it participates in higher life. In this sense, hagiographic realism has a sacramental character where participation in the wholeness of reality is transferred to specific things and events in time, transferred not primarily as thing or text but through living relationships. Wholeness is instantiated as communion.

Chapter 1 discussed the problems of modern and postmodern approaches to the saints, and chapter 2 outlined a realist challenge through Donofrio's story of Mary as a living agent in her life. This chapter and chapter 4 put the lives of the saints in relationship to literary realism. One of the characteristics of realism (and its shift to naturalism) in modern literature is a refusal to allow received conventions, philosophies, and doctrines to gloss over the realities of ordinary life. Realism offers a stylized conception of the ordinary that fits with a mid- and late-nineteenth-century structure and conception of social life.[5] The passing of the old social order, the rise of a socially mobile middle class, and a wave of scientific positivism culminate to a point where a gap is seen to exist between fact and received interpretations, between real life and doctrines and frameworks of the old order. Like the scientist in the laboratory, the literary realist "produces his case histories as part of the prevailing inventory of experience. Each starts with the particular man, hoping perhaps to reach generality, but initially disenchanted with all previous generalities."[6]

In his *Realist Vision*, Brooks maintains that realism is animated by a "thirst for a reality that we can see, hold up to inspection, understand."[7] Reality has to be manageable. At the beginning of his study, he points to this impulse in contemporary reality TV. The lives of ordinary and otherwise uninteresting people are contrived and edited to create an exhibit, which allows us to observe human interaction.[8] Some reality programs, like *Dating in the Dark*, are set up as experiments with real-life consequences. The program's promoters explain: "Looks are taken out of the equation as guys and girls get to know each other in total darkness. . . . Is love truly blind or will these daters be scared away by the light of day?"[9] Later in his study of realism, Brooks suggests a similarity between reality

5. George J. Becker, *Realism in Modern Literature* (New York: Frederick Ungar, 1980), 4-5.
6. Becker, *Realism in Modern Literature*, 17.
7. Brooks, *Realist Vision*, 1.
8. Brooks, *Realist Vision*, 217.
9. "Dating in the Dark," http://abc.go.com/shows/dating-in-the-dark/about-the-show.

TV and the works of nineteenth-century naturalist Émile Zola. Zola claims "that he composes novels on the model of the scientific experiment, taking a certain temperament, a certain bundle of psychological traits, then putting it into a certain socioeconomic situation — and standing back to observe and record the inevitable results."[10] How much different is this experiment than putting a collection of ordinary people in a microcosm of our world, a *Survivor* island, where a person's character is tested against the standards of guile and utilitarian self-interest?

Like reality TV, Zola's descriptive efforts to "make the visible comprehensible" have a tendency to "veer into myth and allegory."[11] In Zola's *Germinal,* for example, the sabotage and collapse of a coal mine, in the last part of the book, speak of upheaval across Europe. The scene is allegorical as Zola describes the destruction of the mine in order to signify broad historical transitions. As the anarchist saboteur leaves the scene of the heaving mine, we are told, "He will be there, without doubt, when the middle class in agony shall hear the pavement of the streets bursting up beneath their feet."[12] With this pull of figurative meaning — a pull of transhistorical and metaphysical connections — the key to realism is not a rejection of transcendent meaning, but its commitment to find it in the ordinary. Realism turns to the seemingly insignificant rather than the exceptional; it turns to ordinary people, the passing of time, and the multitude of ordinary things in the world.

The modern realist attempt to represent life requires a disinterested, objective tone. The opposition between this realism and realist hagiography is that hagiography seeks to represent the unity of life through personal engagement and participation. Nineteenth-century realism reflects a disengaged position of a freestanding humanism (the laboratory image

10. Brooks, *Realist Vision,* 216.

11. Brooks, *Realist Vision,* 120.

12. Émile Zola, *Germinal,* trans. Havelock Ellis (New York: Knopf, 1925). The following are the last few sentences of part VII, chapter 3 on the collapse of the mine. "Then on the shaken pit-bank Souvarine [the anarchist and the saboteur of the mine] rose up. He had recognized Maheude and Zacharie sobbing before this downfall, the weight of which was so heavy on the heads of the wretches who were in agony beneath. And he threw down his last cigarette; he went away, without looking back, into the now dark night. Afar his shadow diminished and mingled with the darkness. He was going over there, to the unknown. He was going tranquilly to extermination, wherever there might be dynamite to blow up towns and men. He will be there, without doubt, when the middle class in agony shall hear the pavement of the streets bursting up beneath their feet" (428).

noted above). It situates the observer on the outside at the same time that there is a high regard for ordinary life.[13] Even with the pessimistic and determinist turn of naturalism, the unsophisticated commoner, who is not destined to be set apart, achieves a measure of self-determination and dignity — set in relief by the narrative without deviating from the ordinary course of things.[14]

In Theodore Dreiser's *Sister Carrie*, for example, the world is structured by cold and impersonal exchanges of the city, the fate of social and economic class, and how one's life is determined by one's place in the economy and the acquisition of things. Carrie's desire for more of life is mediated by her desire for and possession of things.[15] In his *Realist Vision*, Brooks argues that modern realism is, in essence, about things.[16] There is a cataloguing of things accumulated. Things are the medium of who we are and what the world is like, and there is an expectation that "an accumulation of details [will] evoke a whole."[17] To this end, nineteenth-century realism employs metonymy (representing the whole through continuity in space and time) to bring real life into relief: "the selected parts that we must construct sequentially into a whole."[18] It condenses and intensifies attention to things and to the temporal connections of reality to produce an allegory for modern life.[19]

In his study of modern realism in literature, George J. Becker also attributes the realist impulse to features of modern disengagement: the industrial economy, the ensuing social change, and the increasing dominance of scientific explanation. Mixed with this new way of seeing the world is a complementary optimism about progress. The new philosophy of life, although scientific, will have to overlook the disinterested goals of Darwinian evolution.[20] It is not pure science; it is the practical economic

13. Charles Taylor, *Sources of the Self* (Cambridge: Harvard University Press, 1990), 211-33.

14. Pizer, *Realism and Naturalism*, 12-13.

15. Theodore Dreiser, *Sister Carrie* (Cleveland: World Publishing, 1927). See Pizer, *Realism and Naturalism*, 19-24.

16. Brooks, *Realist Vision*, 16.

17. Brooks, *Realist Vision*, 128.

18. Brooks, *Realist Vision*, 16.

19. Hayden White, *Figural Realism: Studies in the Mimesis Effect* (Baltimore: Johns Hopkins University Press, 1999), 1-26.

20. Becker, *Realism in Modern Literature*, 27. Popular Darwinism becomes "a vulgarization of the doctrine of evolution . . . [such that] evolution means development, a forward movement, an ascent toward something better."

and social effects of science that give life to realism. Industry brings abundance to ordinary life. An optimism (which appears even within the determinism of naturalism) allows realism to give forward-looking meaning. There is confidence that things are moving upward. Becker takes the effect of science to be less about the specifics of scientific findings and more about a new faith in rational authority over the old Christian orthodoxy. The mood of the times is taken with freedom from the old ways, both religious and social, for the sake of progress and a happy future. Modern advancement brings social anonymity and atomization; yet, the rapid acquisition of wealth presents the possibility of "effervescent social mobility."[21]

The saint of this realistic age is Thérèse of Lisieux (1873-97). She reflects a democratization of ambition and the new world of the ordinary. She is the unsophisticated member of the rising middle class who replaces the traditional hero. The youngest child of a pious family in a French village, she enters a Carmelite convent at age fifteen. She lives in the cloister until she dies of tuberculosis nine years later. After her death in 1897, devotion to her grows quickly and widely, and the process of her canonization begins in 1914. She is canonized in 1925. She comes to be known for her "little way" — for making small insignificant sacrifices, trusting in God's grace, looking to make a real and powerful effect upon the world through the power of prayer — in other words, for living a way of holiness that is available to the ordinary person.

In fact, if we had visited her convent, we would have given her little notice, and that is essential to her place in the communion of saints. She is the antihero. She undertakes no extraordinary battles, but she certainly does struggle day to day. She is the antisaint; she performs no heroic deeds and does not attain mystical heights. But she undergoes the pains of common life and the kinds of losses (of family members, for example) that we all feel.[22] She founds nothing, no institutions or religious orders, and hints at frustrated ambitions of becoming a missionary and priest.[23] She is the saint of the common people, and her journey to holiness is through the details of everyday life.

St. Thérèse was declared a doctor of the church (in 1997), but she was

21. Becker, Realism in Modern Literature, 11-13.

22. St. Thérèse of Lisieux, Story of a Soul, trans. John Clarke, O.C.D. (Washington, D.C.: Institute of Carmelite Studies, 1976), 156-57.

23. St. Thérèse, Story of a Soul, 192, 217-18.

an antischolar. In her autobiography, she describes her impatience with books, particularly by those authors most familiar to her within her own Carmelite community, such as St. John of the Cross. "If I open a book composed by a spiritual author (even the most beautiful, the most touching book), I feel my heart contract immediately and I read without understanding, so to speak. Or if I do understand, my mind comes to a standstill without the capacity of meditating."[24] Instead, Thérèse turns to the Gospels; she cites Luke 17:21, "The Kingdom of God is within you." She notes that "Jesus has not need of books or teachers. . . . Never have I heard Him speak, but I feel that He is within me at each moment."[25] When giving Thérèse the title of doctor, John Paul II pointed to her emphasis on mercy and love in contrast to cold justice and rigorist tendencies in the church. He put Thérèse's theology in brief: "Through spiritual childhood one experiences that everything comes from God, returns to him and abides in him, for the salvation of all, in a mystery of merciful love."[26]

As a saint of the age, Thérèse shifts the analogy of the spiritual life from a painstaking craft of holiness to the wonder and ease of the machine. She suggests an image of the saint, not as one who stands apart, but as one who is produced, possibly mass-produced, by God's mercy and grace. Thérèse explains, first, that she feels a deep and abiding desire to be a saint but sees an insurmountable difference between herself and the saints. It is "the same difference that exists between a mountain whose summit is lost in the clouds and the obscure grain of sand trampled underfoot by the passers-by." Here she announces "a means of going to heaven by a little way, a way that is very straight, very short, and totally new."[27] "We are now living in an age of inventions, and we no longer have to take the trouble of climbing the stairs, for, in the homes of the rich, an elevator has replaced these very successfully. . . . I searched, then, in the Scriptures for some sign of this elevator, the object of my desires, and I read these words coming from the mouth of Eternal Wisdom: 'Whoever is a *LITTLE ONE*, let him come to me [Prov 9:4].'"[28] In her book on Thérèse, Dorothy Day (in 1960) contrasts the little way with the power of the modern state and its military force. Thérèse's little way is the way of the people because

---

24. St. Thérèse, *Story of a Soul*, 179.
25. St. Thérèse, *Story of a Soul*, 179.
26. John Paul II, *Divini Amoris Scientia* (October 19, 1997).
27. St. Thérèse, *Story of a Soul*, 207.
28. St. Thérèse, *Story of a Soul*, 207-8.

it draws on a life of prayer, simple goodness, and faith. This little way, according to Day, is counter to the powers of the age and liable (in the view of these powers) to be seen as unrealistic. But Day asks, "Is the atom a small thing? And yet what havoc it has wrought. [The little way] is an explosive force that can transform our lives and the life of the world, once put into effect."[29] Thérèse's way of love, for Day, is the counterforce and countermode of the people.

St. Thérèse of Lisieux is the saint of her age, not only because she makes spiritual progress through banal details of life, but also because the ordinary is mapped onto transcendent terrain. Life after death is real. Here she is the antirealist in the modern, secular sense. Some would call her sentimental, and a romantic. Dorothy Day thinks she is a saint of the unsophisticated yet no-less-real people. She says Thérèse is like the indigenous ciders of Normandy as opposed to the fine wines of France. St. Thérèse's pragmatic contemporary, William James, would put her on the side of sentimental and useless piety. To be fair to his evenhanded approach, James would probably view Thérèse with a great deal of ambiguity and pity. On one hand, she embodies saintly characteristics that James puts under the positive headings of asceticism, strength of soul, purity, and charity.[30] Further, he would find common sense in the "little way" insofar as it is an alternative to excessive asceticism and scruples about purity. In James's conceptual frame, the little way's focus on mercy would be notable for supporting a criticism of a Catholic understanding of merit. He would find Thérèse's Thoreau-like reverence for the smallest details of life noble, and would commend her boundless sympathy and humility that transcends invidious comparison.[31]

On the other hand, James would certainly hold that Thérèse suffered from a narrow intellectual outlook (shared by her sister Carmelite St. Teresa of Ávila). This outlook, according to James, transforms the virtues of sensible devotion into fanaticism. With her gentle heart, Thérèse's fanaticism would be seen as benign. But she was a fanatic in the sense that she allowed herself and the entirety of her daily life to be absorbed by her relation to God, who appears to want exclusive claim on her. She takes

29. Dorothy Day, *Thérèse* (Springfield, Ill.: Templegate, 1979), 174-75.

30. William James, *The Varieties of Religious Experience* (New York: Longmans, Green, and Co., 1902), 273-74.

31. James, *Varieties of Religious Experience*, 275-84.

loyalty to God to a "convulsive extreme" in "an imaginative absorption in the love of God."[32] In James's framework, Thérèse's *Story of a Soul* falls into a "voluble egoism" and "stereo-typed humility and return upon herself" as one unworthy, yet a special recipient of grace.[33] In James's pragmatic perspective, all that St. Thérèse has to say about her relationship to God is shallow, perhaps not because of what she says, but because she does not actually do anything useful. In the Jamesian outlook, the *Story of a Soul* amounts to self-referential words. She imposes her personality upon God but makes no mark upon the world. She has fanciful ambitions with little to show for her life.

St. Thérèse would agree that she has little to show, and it is in relation to James's pragmatism where hagiographic realism comes to the fore. Thérèse expected to be useful after death. Near death, she told her superior, "I feel that my mission is about to begin, my mission of making others love God as I love Him, my mission of teaching my little way to souls. If God answers my requests, my heaven will be spent on earth up until the end of the world. Yes, I want to spend my heaven doing good on earth."[34] Modern realism uncovers the ordinary for its own sake, and in this sense, it intends to resist transcendent purposes. In contrast, the realism of St. Thérèse is an embrace of everyday life as the landscape of our relationship to God and a communion between heaven and earth. She expected heaven to have greater communion with the world. Here, the realism of the saints falls on the side of ordinary people, living on the near and far sides of death, in fellowship together with God.

Claiming "realism" for Thérèse does more than simply add to the muddle of competing realisms in modern and postmodern life. It is a realism of ordinary people that is intolerable to modern philosophers of the ordinary, and in this sense Thérèse is received by the people as an antidote that restores the reality of their lives. The lives of saints (particularly modern saints) share important characteristics with modern realism, but they embody a radically different purpose. Like realism, the lives of the saints, as a whole, do not depend on grand gestures. The death of martyrs might be full of extraordinary signs (like the body of Polycarp that will not be con-

32. James, *Varieties of Religious Experience*, 340, 343.

33. James, *Varieties of Religious Experience*, 347.

34. St. Thérèse, *Story of a Soul*, 263. Also, St. Thérèse of Lisieux, *Collected Letters*, trans. F. J. Sheed (New York: Sheed and Ward, 1949), 313-14, 351, 352-53.

sumed by fire), but the vast majority of the martyrs — countless numbers — are known simply to have died. The particulars of their lives are not known. We do our best to personalize representatives of the dead through figures like Miguel Pro or Maximilian Kolbe, but the overwhelming number die without notice of the details.[35] Charles de Foucault might be our best representative: he seeks to live in company with those far beyond notice (in Algiers) and is killed there as a victim of circumstance.[36] He wants to be present with Christ in the desert. Living alone, he is executed by marauding rebels. Nothing is known of his dying moments. Whether or not he is a willing victim, he willingly accepts the circumstances that lead to his death. There are no grand gestures. He dies as quietly as he lived.

Likewise, the Venerable Matt Talbot (1856-1925) lives an insignificant life much like his contemporary St. Thérèse, but as a common laborer in Dublin. A hard drinker since age twelve and supported by petty theft and deception if need be, Talbot takes the pledge of sobriety at age twenty-eight. To his own surprise, he keeps the vow for its full three months, and three months turns into forty years.[37] He works as an unskilled laborer, lives with his mother until she dies, and becomes devout in ways familiar to an early-twentieth-century Irishman, but with uncommon intensity: daily mass, fasting, daily sacrifices, quiet self-mortifications, and charitable giving.[38] His life draws little notice until after his death, when he becomes an image and hope for those with addictions. He is named venerable (as part of the process toward canonization) because, like St. Thérèse, he has become more important in life after his death. People — alcoholics — find themselves in his life.[39] Talbot is not a hero set apart. He is important because of what he shares with others.

The lives of the saints are common. They are countless, everywhere disseminated on prayer cards and daily devotionals and set as permanent fixtures through the household statue or portrait. They are all too common; as noted in chapter 2, the saints themselves are likely to be the great-

35. See Robert Royal, *Catholic Martyrs of the Twentieth Century* (New York: Crossroad, 2000).

36. See Robert Ellsberg, "Charles de Foucault," in *Martyrs*, ed. Susan Bergman (San Francisco: HarperCollins, 1996), 285-98.

37. Joseph A. Glynn, *Life of Matt Talbot* (New York: Benziger Brothers, 1930), 1-16.

38. Eddie Doherty, *Matt Talbot* (Milwaukee: Bruce Publishing, 1953), 47-54.

39. Albert H. Dolan, O.Carm., *Matt Talbot: Alcoholic* (Chicago: Carmelite Press, 1947), 42-47.

est impediment to a good, solid theory of sainthood or hagiography. Any number of saints will derail my own efforts to think of the lives of the saints in terms of a theory of realism. Yet, in terms of modern realism, the saints are fixtures of ordinary life. As fixtures, they enact — put to life in active and contemplative performance — what a theory, epistemology, or metaphysics cannot. They are constituted by, and are the instantiation of, our access to the reality of communion — to God's community of human life, to God in the lowly, to the incarnation. The saints and their lives embody an incarnational reality; they populate the borderlands between the future and now, there and here, and heaven and earth. Through their kinship, they offer an alternative to the realist attempt to circumscribe reality in particular places and times. Our desires to have saints among us, to identify them, to identify with them, and to tell their stories are desires to be part of the whole of life. They bring ordinary life and people into a real experience of *communitas*.

The saints are inhabitants of different places and times joined together as a communion. It is important that particular saints act out faith, hope, and love in their age and culture; but it is equally important that they are saints because they are members of a communion that transcends specific epochs and social forms. In his study of realism in Western literature, Erich Auerbach calls the making of these connections figural realism. It is the simultaneous signification of the historical and the transhistorical. Historical events "retain the characteristics of concrete historical reality."[40] But "every occurrence, in all its everyday reality, is simultaneously a part in a world-historical context through which each part is related to every other, and thus is likewise to be regarded as being of all times and above every time."[41] In the case of the saints, the history-bound people and events are simultaneously universal by personal association, by kinship, so that the relationship of historical and transcendent is not textual or symbolic but social and practical. On one hand, the saints are members of a heavenly communion, and on the other, they are remembered and venerated in and over time.

The veneration and the life of a saint create space where social life and faith are "challenged, interpreted, and made one's own," and amid this

---

40. Erich Auerbach, *Mimesis: The Representation of Reality in Western Literature*, trans. Willard R. Trask (Princeton: Princeton University Press, 1953), 195.

41. Auerbach, *Mimesis*, 156.

communal mode of interpretation the "site" of the saint's life represents layers of place and time.[42] In *St. Martin de Porres: The "Little Stories" and the Semiotics of Culture*, Alex García-Rivera shows that this layering is at the heart of St. Martin's role as a saint. The "little stories" are the local and time-bound accounts of his holy life that work, from below, upon the "big" story of God and creation. Born in Peru in 1579, Martin was the illegitimate child of a Spanish nobleman and a freed African slave. Martin's status as mulatto in caste, as a healer, as a lover of the poor and outcast, as a friend of animals allows the stories to cross borders, both cosmic and social. García-Rivera weaves testimony from Martin's contemporaries with the story of sixteenth-century Latin America and the continuing significance of Martin, culminating in his canonization in 1962.

We have stories of Martin's excessive humility and self-mortification as well as of his miraculous power and abundant charity. Martin is, for his contemporaries, a holy man with the power of God; in his life we can see the most demeaning elements of Iberian piety imposed upon an oppressed people of the Americas. St. Martin is remembered to have accepted his status as a mulatto dog. García-Rivera, however, sees this identification, along with Martin's self-mutilation, as an embodiment that reverses social boundaries of sixteenth-century hierarchies. At a time when the indigenous peoples of the Americas were, in the eyes of their European rulers, either not quite human or still in cultural and religious infancy, Martin invites dogs (cats and mice) into human society, into the kitchen and the friar's cell. He invites in and cares for the lowly of Peru as well. Further, through his humility, he is the dog and the brutalized mulatto that becomes the site of healing and grace. In him, social outsiders come to the center. Through miraculous events and battles with demons, he crosses the boundary between "the world of the everyday and the world of the sacred."[43] In Martin, the particular life becomes part of an expanding reality.

The saints are part of an inexhaustible web of embodiment. During his life, Martin's piety and gifts are renowned, and soon after his death, devotion to him takes hold in Lima, especially among local Dominicans.[44]

42. Alex García-Rivera, *St. Martin de Porres: The "Little Stories" and the Semiotics of Culture* (Maryknoll, N.Y.: Orbis, 1995), 20.

43. García-Rivera, *St. Martin de Porres*, 36-37.

44. Giuliana Cavallini, *Saint Martin de Porres: Apostle of Charity* (Rockford, Ill.: Tan Books, 1979), 211-23.

The canonization process fades, is taken up now and again, and fades even after Gregory XVI beatifies Martin in 1837. The successful revival of the process comes after devotion to Martin is planted in the United States by Dominicans, who are ministering to African Americans in the nineteenth century.[45] They see in Martin precisely what García-Rivera highlights. In him the African American finds a claim of dignity and justice. García-Rivera notes the obvious, that issues of race and caste are at play in prolonging the canonization process for three hundred years. However, García-Rivera sees far more at play.[46] The "little stories" of Martin take time to move from place to place, especially from the local and lowly place of Lima to the United States. Martin embodies this kind of border crossing where the mulatto enters the place of the highborn and transforms that place too. St. Martin goes to the place of nineteenth-century African Americans. The universality of the saint comes, not by the realm of forms and ideas or transcendence out of time, but by way of translation to specific places and the layering of time.

The saints converse back and forth, from divine communion to alienation in the world. Through this interaction, they form a social bridge between fragmentation of life and the whole of reality. Amid contending realisms and relativisms, hagiographic realism establishes its claim on how things are, not by theory, but by practice and performance, by a presentation of life itself in and through particular people and their relationships — both human and divine. Obviously, this incarnational realism will not meet the standards of modern rationalism, but it points us to real, deeper reasons to live. It will not claim to represent life apart from history and experience, but the logic of hagiography does require that particular lives and relations (not necessarily extraordinary ones) stand out as real evidence for what is true. The realism of hagiography will exceed the limits of modern historiography, but it will be even more bound to the history of people. The hagiographic claim is that the reality of transcendent communion is substantiated in events and relationships of the here and now.

Modern hagiography is similar to modern realism. Participation is the difference. There are many examples. Franz Jägerstätter, an Austrian peas-

---

45. Cavallini, *Saint Martin de Porres*, 226-33; J. C. Kearns, O.P., *The Life of Blessed Martin de Porres* (New York: P. J. Kenedy and Sons, 1937), 184-95.

46. García-Rivera, *St. Martin de Porres*, 6.

ant, was executed in 1943 on the charge of treason for refusing to fight in the Nazi army.[47] A short biography was issued by the Vatican when he was beatified on October 26, 2007. The biography notes that he lived the life of an ordinary peasant, "who did not draw attention to himself." When in his thirties, he "grew in his faith but was not extreme in his piety." He was "neither a revolutionary nor part of any resistance movement," but "this ordinary man began thinking deeply about obedience to legitimate authority and obedience to God, about mortal life and eternal life and about Jesus' suffering and Passion."[48] In his biography, Gordon Zahn makes clear that the qualities his community saw in Jägerstätter were impracticality, irresponsibility, and stubbornness.[49] Jägerstätter was accused by the village (rather than the Nazis) of setting himself apart by resisting the Nazis. This is the decisive question for the modern saint. Does he or she represent the people?

Other figures in the twentieth century, although well known, felt the pull of the ordinary and insignificant. As noted in chapter 1, Dorothy Day and Archbishop Oscar Romero put a modern hagiographic realism into practice. Day was a theologian of everyday life among the poor and uneducated. Her reflections on faith and faithful living are intertwined with sketches of the struggles and nobility of people in the streets.[50] Romero was archbishop of San Salvador during extraordinary times, but he took it upon himself to tell the stories of Salvadoran campesinos. Amid state oppression and violent resistance, his ministry is identification: Christ and the people. Philosophers like Edith Stein (Teresa Benedict of the Cross) and Simon Weil were also interesting, as their lives and writings were a working through and beyond the "middle realm" described by Charles Taylor — the crosscurrents of materialism and metaphysics. They lived contested identities, not only of Jew and Christian but also of mystics and philosophers of ordinary existence. They felt the pull, not to stand out, but to stand with God and a people.[51]

47. Gordon Zahn, In Solitary Witness: The Life and Death of Franz Jägerstätter (Springfield, Ill.: Templegate, 1964).

48. "Blessed Franz Jägerstätter (1907-1943), Layman and Martyr," http://www.vatican.va/news_services/liturgy/saints/ns_lit_doc_20071026_jagerstatter_en.html.

49. Zahn, In Solitary Witness.

50. See By Little and by Little: The Selected Writings of Dorothy Day, ed. Robert Ellsberg (New York: Knopf, 1983).

51. The Simone Weil Reader, ed. G. A. Panichas (New York: McKay, 1977); Simone Weil,

If they were to review the hundred or more saints canonized over the last decades, most people would likely recognize only a few names, if any.[52] The following were canonized in 2009: Arcangelo Tadini (1846-1912), Bernardo Tolomei (1272-1348), Nuno de Santa Maria Álvares Pereira (1360-1431), Gertrude Comensoli (1847-1903), Caterina Volpicelli (1839-94), Zygmunt Szczęsny Feliński (1822-95), Francisco Coll y Guitart (1812-75), Josef Daamian de Veuster (1840-89), Rafael Arnáiz Barón (1911-38), and Jeanne Jugan/Marie de la Croix (1792-1879). They represent forms of piety, virtue, and human need in various times and places. Fr. Arcangelo Tadini is known for his works of mercy during the industrial revolution in Italy. Sister Gertrude, Tadini's contemporary, dedicated her life to the adoration of the Blessed Sacrament. Marie de la Croix founded the Little Sisters of the Poor. These names come together on a list because they have a living communion with people then and now, and these people have put them forward for us all. The usual criticism of such a list is that it is too narrow, the process of canonization too bureaucratic, and the representatives not populist enough.[53] In these cases, the real life of the people provides the inescapable criteria of sainthood.

In relationship to realism, the lives of the saints imply that knowing how things really are requires a relationship with people who represent us and our relation to the world. The communion of saints does not provide an epistemology or metaphysics, but populates connections between the personal and the metaphysical, between now, people across time, and the future fullness of the kingdom of God. The saints populate the gaps between our lives and the fellowship of God. For example, the realism of Beverly Donofrio's *Looking for Mary* suggests connections between personal purposes and reality — between understanding Beverly's life as a whole and avenues of interchange with higher life. Her story is representative; it is the plight of the modern "buffered" self. It is a struggle and an active abandonment, with and through Mary, to God in the world.

This chapter began with Peter Brooks's "realist vision." He identifies a realist desire to see life and real people, and he shows that to take a realist

---

Need for Roots (Boston: Beacon Press, 1952); *Edith Stein: Essential Writings*, ed. John Sullivan (Maryknoll, N.Y.: Orbis, 2002).

52. "Saints," http://www.vatican.va/news_services/liturgy/saints/index_saints_en.html.

53. Kenneth Woodward, *Making Saints: How the Catholic Church Determines Who Becomes a Saint, Who Doesn't, and Why* (New York: Simon and Schuster, 1990), 21-49, 87-126.

view of life, we have to put it in relief. We have to raise the ordinary up to the level of spectacle.[54] This literary realism has provided an important contrast with hagiography for a few reasons. The first is that it is a spectacle of things. Hagiographic realism, in contrast, is a spectacle of relationships on a metaphysical backdrop. Nineteenth-century realism develops characteristically modern conceptions of reality, based on technological mastery and its success in making the world manageable. It tends toward a disinterested, scientific point of view, and it reflects a world of scientific and economic progress. The ordinary is bound by material determination; yet, it is full of possibilities. This world of possibilities — of "effervescent social mobility" — also brings disconnection. Ironically, the autonomy of everyday life is a source of detachment from its wholeness and meaning.

Long after the age of literary realism, Walker Percy continued to deal with this problem of autonomy and disconnection. In *The Moviegoer*, Percy's Binx Bolling sees "everydayness" as the enemy of his undefined search. "The everydayness is everywhere now, having begun in the cities and seeking out the remotest nooks and corners of the countryside, even the swamps."[55] Bolling undertakes a search for something that cannot be articulated — something like meaning, reality, connection, and freedom from restlessness. At one point, he likens this undefined desire to a "certification" of his place in life. He is obsessed with a search for "wonder" and for the real in the particular place. He wanders in what Taylor has called the middle realm, between a material landscape and a spiritual pull. It is clear that Percy has this cross-pressure in mind. At one point, Bolling explains that "businessmen are our only metaphysicians" because they know and promote the value of things.[56] The problem is that "they are one-track metaphysicians."[57] Binx is looking for something vague but more. His head spins with "the facts." He needs more.

He finds an avenue for his search by making connections through the movies and an experience that he calls "certification." "Nowadays when a person lives somewhere, in a neighborhood, the place is not certified for him. More than likely he will live there sadly and the emptiness which is

54. Brooks, *Realist Vision*, 1.
55. Walker Percy, *The Moviegoer* (New York: Vintage Books, 1998), 145.
56. Percy, *The Moviegoer*, 216-17.
57. Percy, *The Moviegoer*, 217.

inside of him will expand until it evacuates the entire neighborhood. But if he sees a movie which shows his very neighborhood, it becomes possible for him to live, for a time at least, as a person who is Somewhere and not Anywhere."[58] In short, everydayness is empty at the same time that we give single-minded attention to the value and promotion of things. Our lives need connections and confirmation from something more. Binx needs signs of meaning and purpose outside of himself. It is striking how accurately Binx still represents the loss of the ordinary in our time. Why do we want to undertake great transitions in life — courtships, marriage proposals, and weight-loss programs — on reality TV? We need the events in our lives to mean something, and meaning comes through participation on a grand scale.

So, the first reason for a comparison of the saints with nineteenth-century realism is its attempt to put ordinary life into a meaningful and realistic frame. The second is its failure to make sense of life within the limits of its assumptions about realism, that is, without depending upon transcendent meaning and participation in a whole course of things. Even Émile Zola, the naturalist author, cannot help but conjure allegory and myth. Zola's *Germinal* combines an objective, scientific point of view with epic and mythological meaning — proletarian, progressive, and nationalist.[59] The comparison, made by Brooks, between the realist vision and reality TV is exaggerated but apt. To make sense of things, we have to intensify their relations, draw the extraordinary out of the ordinary, and open avenues for participation in it. Hagiographic realism meets this challenge but in a different way: it is figurative realism, which is, perhaps, the only kind of realism that there is.

58. Percy, *The Moviegoer*, 63.

59. N. R. Cirillo, "Marxism as Myth in Zola's 'Germinal,'" *Comparative Literature Studies* 14, no. 3 (September 1977): 244-55.

✤ Four ✤

Participation

—ɯɯ—

The underlying issue of realism is participation. In chapter 1, I cited Douglas Porpora's *Landscapes of the Soul* and Charles Taylor's *Sources of the Self*. Porpora describes a malaise in contemporary life due, in part, to a disconnection between our lives and the order of things, between social and metaphysical landscapes. Is my ordinary life part of some greater whole? And does this greater whole make possible participation in the lives of others across place and over time? In *Sources of the Self*, Taylor proposes that a "disembedding" is coincident with a modern "affirmation of ordinary life." This affirmation has a direct bearing on the lives of the saints. With the modern turn, the commonplace stations of marriage and home life are asserted as more important than the so-called higher callings taken by nuns and monks. Taylor notes that this affirmation of the ordinary is fundamental (even if sometimes latent) in Christian spirituality, and that it "comes to receive new and unprecedented importance at the beginning of the modern era."[1] At the same time, however, the shared frameworks, which give ordinary life purpose and meaning, have become problematic. Modern people begin to "anxiously doubt whether life has meaning, or wonder what its meaning is."[2] Finding and articulating meaning are the objects of what Taylor calls the new modern quest. It is a heroic quest where individuals make their own way.

A quest for meaning in relationship to the saints is the subject of this chapter; but, unlike a quest to make my own personal meaning, it is a

1. Charles Taylor, *Sources of the Self* (Cambridge: Harvard University Press, 1989), 13.
2. Taylor, *Sources of the Self*, 16.

quest of communion. The chapter will not offer a philosophical resolution to the problem of meaning. Rather, it will point to a people and set of relations, through the saints, that connect our ordinary lives to a higher order. The lives of the saints populate a landscape where we can participate in the meaning of things.

In "Realism in Western Narrative and the Gospel of Mark," Charles W. Hedrick provides a treatment of narrative realism in relationship to biblical and theological claims about Christ. Hedrick's study provides a useful point of reference following the discussion of nineteenth-century realism in the previous chapter. He is as close to a nineteenth-century positivist as we are likely to find at the beginning of the twenty-first century. He seems to think (uncritically, it seems to me) in terms of late-nineteenth- and early-twentieth-century dualisms: immanence versus transcendence, science versus poetics, history versus faith, and the like. His analysis of realism is set in opposition to figurative realism as we find it in hagiography. For example, García-Rivera (discussed in chapter 3) claims that the "little stories" of St. Martin take in and transform the realities of human life. In contrast, Hedrick puts the Gospel of Mark, and no doubt would put the lives of the saints, in an otherworldly, romantic frame.[3] He holds that "Romantic realism describes the activities of superhuman beings in a supernatural world. It portrays characters like us, only much better than we are in every way, in a space similar to ours, in a time of marvels."[4] While García-Rivera develops hagiography and the saints in terms of connections between particular histories and the "big story," Hedrick's analysis puts Christ and the saints out of our world.

Hedrick notes that realism in literature is an attempt to mimic everyday life. The statement is formal; it allows a great deal of latitude about what are conceived as reality and the realities of the everyday. By ordinary reality,

---

3. Charles W. Hedrick, "Realism in Western Narrative and the Gospel of Mark: A Prolegomenon," *Journal of Biblical Literature* 126, no. 2 (Summer 2007): 345-59. Hedrick, in the main, offers an interpretation of Eric Auerbach's *Mimesis: The Representation of Reality in Western Literature* (Princeton: Princeton University Press, 1974). Given that Auerbach does little to give a universal meaning to "realism," I am considering Hedrick's claims about Auerbach to be Hedrick's view rather than Auerbach's. One of the most interesting differences is that Auerbach makes no effort to define realism in a pure form, in a form apart from narrative context. Hedrick, on the other hand, reduces Auerbach's narrative account of realism to a list of criteria.

4. Hedrick, "Realism in Western Narrative," 352-53.

Hedrick seems to mean human life from a detached point of view.[5] To this degree, his conception of realism puts our participation in the meaning of events outside of reason and real history. His account of real life, it seems, is value-free and disinterested. For example, in his *When History and Faith Collide*, Hedrick understands the collision in this way: "Theological histories are tied to the belief systems and theology of the historian doing the writing."[6] The point is undeniable. However, Hedrick's conception of nontheological or real history is harder to defend. He holds that real history (ironically) rises above the personal commitments of ordinary people.

Hedrick proposes that "modern Western historians . . . reconstruct and interpret history on the basis of objective criteria — criteria that can be measured by people of all faiths and nonfaiths as well."[7] Hedrick's practical knowledge of contemporary historiography and the disagreements among historians appears to be limited. The historian, it seems, has the ability to find a universal measure regardless of differing histories. Surely, the goal of such a measure surpasses what is actually attained by historians across the world, or even in Hedrick's own field of study on the historical Jesus. There is no agreed-upon universal history in place, but Hedrick imagines that a "placeless" historian can find a universal measure.[8] According to his own understanding of romantic realism, he appears to have a romantic conception of the historian, who heroically lifts himself above the problems of "belief systems" and the fray of convictions, commitments, and competing histories. The historian appears to transcend the human point of view. History is supposed to be a science that lifts itself above people and their storytelling.

Hedrick's contrast between belief systems and real history brings an inexorable tension to the difference between life and telling stories about it. This crisis of storytelling is parallel to the modern crisis of shared meaning and purpose. Given that stories have a plot that leads to an end,

5. Detachment, as well as the tensions of history as narrative and history as disinterested science, is developed in Hayden White, *Metahistory: The Historical Imagination in Nineteenth-Century Europe* (Baltimore: Johns Hopkins University Press, 1975).

6. Charles W. Hedrick, *When History and Faith Collide: Studying Jesus* (Peabody, Mass.: Hendrickson, 1999), 4.

7. Hedrick, *History and Faith*, 5.

8. I will identify this view of history in chapter 8, and I will cite Arthur Marwick, *The Nature of History*, 3rd ed. (Chicago: Lyceum Books, 1989). Marwick trusts only data and only professional historians with data.

they represent life and events in life for a purpose. Events unfold, coalesce, and end up somewhere. Stories have to be told by people, to people, and for a reason. Even when the purpose is merely entertainment and delight, stories require a common mind between teller and audience. What counts as delightful? In the modern context, however, the purposes of life are contested, and likewise, the stories of individuals have to be disengaged (freed) from a common and corporate purpose of human life.[9] In this context, people have difficulty telling common stories. In fact, a powerful modern narrative is the story of liberation from institutional or conventional frameworks. Individual stories are most inspiring when they communicate our convictions that common stories and institutional narratives are false. (The search for truth and meaning all come down to *The Truman Show* and *Shawshank Redemption:* the individual's escape from the prison of what our lives have been made to mean.)[10] Overcoming institutional and conventional stories is a common modern quest. The quest is heroic. We have to find a way to set ourselves apart.

The problem of modern realism is not representation per se, but fragmentation and disengagement from the whole. The difficulty of representing real life is a crisis of accounting for the relationship of parts to the whole.[11] Consider the analysis offered in chapter 3: traditional doctrines of the whole of life are overcome by nineteenth-century realism and materialism, which attempt to find the whole of life in the particular and ordinary. If ancient and medieval doctrines of life put the whole before the parts, realism puts the parts before the whole. Soon the parts replace the whole. Soon the whole cannot be conceived. Modernism (as opposed to what I have been calling modern realism) meets this fragmentation of realism by focusing on the interrelations of parts; the interdependence of parts and the interactions of signifiers take the place of representing the whole. Soon it is noticed that interactions cannot be viewed from nowhere in particular, that even the interchange of signifiers is different depending upon one's place in the con-

9. Charles Taylor, *Modern Social Imaginaries* (Durham, N.C.: Duke University Press, 2004), 49-67. One of the best accounts of this disjunction in the history of science, philosophy, and theology is Michael J. Buckley, *At the Origins of Modern Atheism* (New Haven: Yale University Press, 1987).

10. Kimberly A. Blessing and Paul Tudico, eds., *Movies and the Meaning of Life* (Peru, Ill.: Carus Publishing, 2005).

11. This point is central to the work of Hayden White. See *The Content of the Form: Narrative Discourse and Historical Representation* (Baltimore: Johns Hopkins University Press, 1990).

versation.[12] Modernism gives us the autonomous (Newtonian) text; post-modernism gives us multiple universes. Postmodernism meets the fragmentation of modernism by celebrating the fragmented text and the role of interpretation in dismantling the realist project entirely.

Ironically, postmodern disengagement has helped to clear a space for a return of nineteenth-century materialism/realism in science. People of "arts and letters" have failed to give a reasonable account of life and the whole. Scientific materialists now have authority to speak definitively about life, which they hold is entirely indifferent to us. Historians, philosophers, and cultural critics have failed to overcome what is now the problem of the "whole." We humanists are agents of fragmentation, and materialists have the authority to tell us why: the parts — our genes and genetic drives — are the real agents of life.[13] There is no "whole" of life, except competition based on genetic imperatives. Life itself is indifferent to the meaning of human life. We see meaning and purpose in our lives, but these impulses are merely accidental by-products of natural selection. Here, two claims go together. First, human beings play, at best, only a supporting role in the story of life. Second, this story of life has only a tangential relationship to how I think my life is meaningful day to day.

In short, participation is the problem of representation and meaning in life. Hedrick, as a modern realist, needs to keep real history and our investment in it apart. In his field of biblical scholarship, he distrusts narrative insofar as stories are told for a reason, and the Gospels are told so that we might believe. The effect of Hedrick's discomfort with narrative is evinced in his characterization of the Gospel of Mark. When events in Mark are lifted out of their place in the narrative, it may appear that Hedrick is correct, that the Gospel is a romantic tale about "superhuman beings in a supernatural world." We might see the binding of the strong man (Mark 3:27) as a supernatural contest in a "time of marvels." In this

12. M. M. Bakhtin, *Speech Genres and Other Late Essays*, trans. Vern W. McGee (Austin: University of Texas Press, 1986).

13. The most authoritative accounts of life's purpose are provided by evolutionary biology, which holds that human agency is trivial at best or, at worst, simply self-deception. Richard Dawkins, in his famous work *The Selfish Gene* (Oxford: Oxford University Press, 1976), argues on the first page that human agency is irrelevant; the agent of life is the gene. Also see Francisco J. Ayala, *Darwin and Intelligent Design* (Minneapolis: Fortress, 2006). Ayala attempts to account for human agency but arrives at a common solution: keep science and religion apart.

context, Jesus' healings and exorcisms seem to imagine an otherworldly place of superheroes. However, if we follow Mark's narrative, we find that it is precisely this romantic interpretation that Mark intends to challenge. The Gospel of Mark (as Gospel rather than a collection of events) unravels Hedrick's reading by setting supernatural glory outside the narrative. It is precisely a premature grasping at glory, within the narrative, that is the source of blindness for the followers of Jesus, particularly Peter, James, and John (Mark 8:31-38; 10:35-45).

In Mark, the "marvels" of the Messiah build to the inexplicable truth that he must suffer and that those who follow him will suffer as well. The romance of marvels gives way to the realities of discipleship. Mark's Gospel views the life of Jesus from the side of the resurrection, but the narrative puts us in the time of the passion and empty tomb. The flashes of glory (the transfiguration in Mark 9:2-8, for example) happen too quickly and are too puzzling to allow a coherent response. Peter falters with his words. It is Jesus' cry of abandonment (15:34), the centurion's declaration about the Son of God on the cross (15:39), and the empty tomb that wait for our response. The Gospel ends with Mary Magdalene, Mary the mother of James, and Salome fleeing in fear from the empty tomb. They are told to tell others that "He is going before [them] to Galilee" (16:7). In this way, the disciples and hearers of the word are not sent on to glory, but are called back to the beginning, called to the way of discipleship, to a way of suffering rather than divine invulnerability. They are called to live the way of the cross in the world.[14] They must travel the path from Galilee to Jerusalem anew.

This turn away from glory and romantic invulnerability is possible for the writer of Mark and for his audience because Jesus lives. The backdrop of the Gospel is our participation in God's story. Jesus is with the hearers of the Gospel even though he appears to be asleep amid the storm (4:35-41). Jesus is with the readers of Mark amid their persecution and suffering, as they wait also for the glory that can now be represented only by an empty tomb. This living in Christ is the setting of the Gospel. Without the backdrop of participation, the narrative is confined to a textual world, and it will appear perhaps, as it does to Hedrick, like a romantic otherworld of marvels and invulnerability. The most striking result of Hedrick's exclusion of a living relationship with God in Christ is that he has a shal-

---

14. Morna D. Hooker, *Endings: Invitations to Discipleship* (Peabody, Mass.: Hendrickson, 2003), 11-30.

low understanding of the Gospel of Mark at the textual level. He asserts the kind of interpretation of the Gospel that the Gospel of Mark casts off. He reads Mark as a record of a distant time, while it is in fact about the time of Jesus in the context of living with the living Christ in our time. It points our time to the future reign of God.

According to Hedrick, a realistic narrative will limit participation. The narrator, for example, will not play a role in giving meaning to events. The storyteller will introduce details and events that do not contribute to the unity of the plotline and will remain meaningless in relation to the end.[15] The narrative will not sustain a consistent point of view, and it will minimize reference to the internal states of characters. In Hedrick's view, "In 'real' life we never know what people are thinking and even if they tell us what they are thinking, we only know what they tell us they think. Hence, a narrator's explanation of the interior views of characters in the narrative is a mark of unreality."[16] This point is disputable as an accurate account of real life. For example, it is a mark of friendship that we do know what our friends are thinking. Through a shared life, we can predict what they will say in certain situations and what we will see from their point of view. We begin to feel for them what we know they are feeling at some good or bad turn of events. We can identify with them, not because we know their stories from the outside, but because we have become part of their lives. Misunderstanding this point is the basic mistake of Hedrick's version of realism. We are oriented to the real, not by stepping out, but by stepping in.

The backdrop of Hedrick's version of literary realism is an atomistic conception of life. He assumes that the reality of the particular and the parts can be known apart from reference to the whole. The Gospel of Mark, for example, requires participation, and therefore, it looks to him like an account of another world. An atomistic conception of life is at the bottom of scientific reductionism, where the real story of life is the competition of genes. It is at the bottom of the modern and postmodern: the grim and lighthearted flights from the whole of life.

Hagiographic realism aims toward the opposite. The lives of the saints call us in; they present life as anything but indifferent, and the context for remembering their lives is a living relationship. The lives of the saints offer relations of communion, so that affection and kinship form the context for

---

15. Hedrick, "Realism in Western Narrative," 346-48.
16. Hedrick, "Realism in Western Narrative," 347.

telling their stories. Textual gaps and failures of narrative representation are opportunities for identification, for filling in the gaps between protagonist and reader/hearer with further narration through participation in common life. Those who tell the story — a series of narrators and multiple layers of narration — do so out of their shared lives. It is this connection between personal and metaphysical that is necessary for a workable conception of the real, and this connection is precisely what modern forms of realism attempt to defeat and replace. Hagiography works as realism because it stands, not on its own, but amid social-metaphysical relations.

In *Mimesis*, Erich Auerbach makes a related point about realism in his famous comparison between Abraham and Odysseus. He compares Abraham's trek into the wilderness to sacrifice Isaac with a scene from the *Odyssey*, when Odysseus has returned home in disguise and is recognized by his housekeeper. The Homeric style, according to Auerbach, gives a seamless narrative. It presents "phenomena in a fully externalized form, visible and palpable in all their parts, and completely fixed in their spatial and temporal relations." The reader is fully informed. "Homer's personages vent their inmost hearts in speech; what they do not say to others, they speak in their own minds." The diverse elements of all events "are clearly placed in relation to one another. . . . [A]nd never is there a form left fragmentary or half-illuminated, never a lacuna, never a gap, never a glimpse of unplumbed depths."[17]

Auerbach shows that, in contrast, the biblical account of Abraham's journey into the wilderness is rough and unfinished. There is an "externalization of only so much of the phenomenon as is necessary for the purpose of the narrative, all else left in obscurity; the decisive points of the narrative are emphasized, what lies between is nonexistent; time and place are undefined and call for interpretation."[18] While the trials, desires, memories, and machinations of Odysseus are presented in the "foreground," the whole of Abraham's mission into the desert "remains mysterious and 'fraught with background.'"[19] While Homer gives us depth of trial, passion, and memory, the biblical story seems to leave the depths unexplored. "Abraham, receiving the command says nothing and does what he has been told to do."[20]

17. Auerbach, *Mimesis*, 6-7.
18. Auerbach, *Mimesis*, 11.
19. Auerbach, *Mimesis*, 12.
20. Auerbach, *Mimesis*, 11.

When Isaac asks about the sacrificial lamb, Abraham replies enigmatically that God will provide. If this narrative reserve were the end of the story, then we would have a realism of disconnection and the impenetrable (as Hedrick proposes). But the "unexplored depths" are not the end of the story. They are filled out by our participation.

There are obvious limits in accounting for and understanding God and, as witnessed in the incarnation, in defining and getting a full grasp on the human being. What we can say about God through analogy is governed by an infinite difference between Creator and creation. More always needs to be said, and yet, all that we say becomes complete only in silence. Likewise, the life of a saint is revelatory and yet always incomplete. The life, particularly the internal life of nearness to God, continues to unfold; yet, there is also a common sense that little needs to be said. Hagiography in its most prominent form puts the life of a saint in a single paragraph on a single page. The "lives" are usually mere introductions, meant to inspire the beginning of a practical relation. Sometimes a whole life, particularly of the martyrs, comes down to a sentence. "Jean Donovan, Dorothy Kazel, Maura Clarke, and Ita Ford were missionaries, lived among the poor in El Salvador, and were kidnapped, raped, and murdered by members of the National Guard." The lives of the saints in their standard form (the feast day liturgy and the daily reflection) are abundant in number but reserved in explanation. They invite investigation; they invite a personal journey into the depths of their inner lives.

This hagiographic participation is similar to a form of biblical realism that is outlined by Auerbach in his contrast between Genesis 22 and the *Odyssey*. First, there is the Bible's claim to truth. Auerbach calls it tyrannical. "The world of the Scripture stories is not satisfied with claiming to be historically true reality — it insists that it is the only real world. . . . Far from seeking, like Homer, merely to make us forget our own reality for a few hours, it seeks to overcome our reality: we are to fit our own life in its world, feel ourselves to be elements in its structure of universal history."[21] Those who composed and redacted the biblical narratives are bound to "the truth of the tradition." A faithful reader, likewise, is subject to its claims upon his or her world. Second, there is the crude narrative form that, by its structure, seems to demand interpretation. It demands to be filled in by what we can give once we enter biblical reality. Abraham's silent

---

21. Auerbach, *Mimesis*, 14-15.

obedience opens up a space where a believing community is required to explore the hidden depths of motive, anxiety, and divine intention. Here Auerbach notes that the interplay of interpretation and narratives depends, not so much on horizontal continuity, but on their vertical connections. One event and another distant one are both set in relationship to God.[22]

A present-day example is in order. Aharon Agus writes on the binding of Isaac. He draws on historically diverse biblical texts and talmudic interpretations of martyrdom. He begins with rabbinic commentary on the martyrdom of the mother and seven sons in 2 Maccabees 7.[23] In the midrash, the mother evokes a comparison between herself and Abraham, and in the process we learn something through her about him.[24] Through similar commentaries and interpretations, Agus fills in the story of the binding of Isaac. Drawing on the subsequent tradition for background, he is able to enrich the narrative. The silent trek with Isaac is no longer obscure, but full of meaning. When Isaac turns to his father and asks, "Where is the sheep for the holocaust?" (Gen. 22:7), we know that Abraham's "heart trembles with love and he postpones the terrible revelation of truth. He savors the moment, the love between father and son, and wants to walk like this, arm in arm, for yet awhile, short as the fleeting minutes are. Refusing to spoil the present with the shadow of the future doom, he gently brushes aside Isaac's question."[25] Abraham, here, is a real father.

Hagiographic realism functions in a space similar to talmudic commentary. Strictly speaking, however, the lives of the saints are not texts, but relationships that form the backdrop for a series of texts, oral storytelling, prayerful interchange, and visual representation. Like the binding of Isaac in Genesis 22, accounts of saints' lives often come to us in a form that requires further participation. As noted above, the standard form of the lives of the saints follows the calendar of feast days and offers an outline of the saint's life with distilled themes, prayer, and props for deeper reflection. Consider the entry on May 12 in *Saint of the Day*, edited by Leonard Foley, O.F.M. I know the entry well because my family celebrates a birthday on this feast day of Nereus and Achilleus. Foley begins by noting that almost nothing is known about the two saints, but that devotion goes

---

22. Auerbach, *Mimesis*, 17.

23. Aharon Agus, *The Binding of Isaac and Messiah: Law, Martyrdom, and Deliverance in Early Rabbinic Religiosity* (Albany: SUNY Press, 1988), 11-32.

24. Agus, *The Binding of Isaac*, 31.

25. Agus, *The Binding of Isaac*, 64.

back to the fourth century. "They were praetorian soldiers of the Roman army, became Christians and were removed to the island of Terracina, where they were martyred."[26] Foley reflects at some length on these two lives that have been described in a single sentence.

The context for the meaning of these saints' lives is a realistic reference to a shared world and a shared relationship to the living Christ. After Foley gives information about the discovery of the martyrs' tombs in 1896, he offers his own comments and then quotations from sources in the tradition, here from the fourth-century pope Damasus:

> As in the case of many early martyrs, the Church clings to its memories through events clouded in the mists of history. It is a heartening thing for all Christians to know that they have a noble heritage. Our brothers and sisters in Christ have stood in the same world in which we live — militarist, materialist, cruel and cynical — yet transformed from within by the presence of the Living One. Our own courage is enlivened by the heroes and heroines who have gone before us marked by the sign of faith and the wounds of Christ.[27]

Foley also offers the epitaph that Pope Damasus sets upon the martyrs' tombs. It expresses wonder in "what great things the glory of Christ can accomplish." Two soldiers, who are enlisted into the "cruel office of carrying out the orders of a tyrant," are converted and able to throw off their fear (which is the weapon of the tyrant) and "throw away their shields, their armor and their blood-stained javelins."[28] In each case — Foley's comments and Damasus's epitaph — the meaning of two simple events, conversion and death, is carried by a clear sense that our world and their world are the same world and marked by the same relation to the incarnation of God.

Hagiography is too diverse to make standard claims about the narrator in reference to the character's thoughts, dialogue, and action. Nereus and Achilleus are representatives of a kind of saint, where hagiographic realism is carried by external events and the history of a people. They represent a context of first-century Christians amid the persecutions of the

26. Leonard Foley, O.F.M., ed., *Saint of the Day*, rev. ed. (Cincinnati: St. Anthony Messenger Press, 1990), 101.

27. Foley, *Saint of the Day*, 101.

28. Foley, *Saint of the Day*, 102.

Roman Empire and analogous events and lives of people in the world to-day. Blessed Miguel Pro is a similar figure for the plight of the Mexican church at the beginning of the twentieth century, and Archbishop Oscar Romero's life and death speak about the poor and oppressed in El Salvador at the end of the twentieth century. Jesus' encounters with lepers (Mark 1:40-45; Matt. 8:2-4; Luke 5:12-16) provide the setting for the life of Fr. Damien of Molokai. He cares for the people on an island leper colony, contracts Hansen's disease, and dies after sixteen years on the island. Little needs to be known about his internal life or personal motives; he lives out the history of the outcast and the hospitality of God. On the other hand, the internal life of Blessed Titus Brandsma becomes important insofar as he is Carmelite. Active in the Dutch resistance, he is imprisoned by the Nazis and dies in Dachau. The circumstances of his life are enough to understand his death as martyrdom, but as the Carmelites sustain his memory, the context of the war and Brandsma's activities recede as the landscape of meaning. Carmelite hagiography draws deeper into his spiritual life and his interior path of nearness to God.[29]

Amid this diversity, the points to underline, particularly with reference to Auerbach, are narrative participation and desires for depth and intimacy in Christ. The *Odyssey* presents a whole world. In contrast, the lives of the saints are filled in by our identification and involvement in a common world. Seeing the world in Christ is at the heart of the lives of the saints. Their lives are taken into the everyday of those who remember and venerate the saints, and vice versa. Amid these interactions, the saints form a communion of vertical connections. The incarnation is the shared point of reference for hagiographic realism. If God has claimed the world through giving himself in the humanity of Jesus Christ, the lives of the saints are a participation in this embodiment and an extension of self-giving love in the Spirit of Christ. Hagiography cannot help but endeavor to reveal that God's embodied communion (not mere gnosis) is really the case. Nearness to God must make a mark on the flesh and on our world. The lives of the saints sustain what is for today a peculiar kind of realism: bodily and necessarily *in* history, yet vertical and connected to a higher order of things.

Auerbach notes that this kind of figurative and participatory realism is sustained in the medieval world. But media of knowing and standards of

29. Kees Waaijman, *Spirituality: Forms, Foundations, Methods*, trans. John Vriend (Leuven: Peeters, 2002), 614-21.

rationality change and displace it. A material-worldly realism begins to dominate appearances and the meaning of the everyday. In modern thought, hagiographic participation appears to be contrived and imaginary, full of only dreams, legends, and wishful thinking. But however unreal they may seem in terms of dominant forms of materialism and naturalism, the lives of the saints will persist because they inhabit a deeper reality ("depth" that is connected to "higher" life). In a world where hagiography is set apart as primitive and popular, it aims, with uneven success, toward a community that is considered out of bounds, a communion of divine and human and people enlivened by God across time and place. The lives of the saints narrate real connections; they are a population that links specific times and places, saints, those who name saints over time, and the fellowship of the incarnate God.

The realism of the incarnation includes the wisdom of the holy fool. Many lives of the saints, like the legends of St. Christopher, do not represent a historical person as much as a social desire, among the devout, for "the Christ carrier," for the person who enacts sacred time and establishes in the world a holy place. But the excesses of this desire for communion and the excesses of saints themselves (e.g., St. Francis and St. Rose) do not contradict the meaning of the sainthood and the roles of saints as real embodiments in the fabric of God's communion. The excesses point to the possibilities of the real thing. As exasperating as it will be for us moderns and our sense of autonomy, the saints are not self-sufficient and do not stand on their own. Hagiography draws on a web of relations and participation in the social body, where the knowing is enacted in communion. The real is not represented by a saint per se, but by their and our participation in the whole of life. The marginal and unlikely saints are carried by the lives of those we cannot help but recognize as real and true, and the ones whom we cannot help but recognize as media of what is real are likely to be the marginal and unlikely saints. The point pertains to the depths and heights, the lowliness and blessedness of the holy fool.

Enid Welsford, in *The Fool: His Social and Literary History*, describes the fool as one "who falls below the average human standard, but whose defects have been transformed into a source of delight."[30] She holds that the fool is a figure of the old, mediated order (the order of priests and kings),

---

30. Enid Welsford, *The Fool: His Social and Literary History* (London: Faber and Faber, 1935), xi.

where each person is connected to a higher metaphysical order through a social hierarchy. The possible heights of human glory and the honor of one's place require a depth of humility. The fool might be so self-effacing and such a buffoon as to give superiority to the common people, or his absurd antics might give him license to degrade the nobility. He might be ridiculed but sustains an air of indifference and invulnerability; he is outside honor and shame. With the same nonchalance, he might abuse kings and cardinals. The fool is amphibious, very much a part of everyday life but also on the margin, inviting us into comic space of action (outside the main plotline) where we see our world from the outside.

There is a long tradition of the holy fool. According to Welsford, the fool "belong[s] essentially to a society shaped by belief in Divine order, human inadequacy, efficacious ritual; and there is no real place for any of them in a world dominated by the puritan, the scientist, and the captain of industry."[31] In such a world, however, saints continue to be fools for Christ. The theological world of the incarnation assumes a hierarchy, the condescension of God for the sake of the elevation of the human being. Likewise, the holy fool goes low and receives the highest place of nearness to God. The hagiographic tradition continues to sustain a place for the serious but joyful comedy of the saints, of eccentrics and their happy end, which we will share, especially in the face of humiliation and what seem to be tragic circumstances. Some saints, who live ostensibly purposeless and dreary lives, evoke hope and delight that do not fit with the tedium, purposelessness, and anxiety of a modern world without ends.

John Saward, in his *Perfect Fools*, traces the tradition of the "fool for Christ" from St. Paul to Matt Talbot (d. 1925).[32] He cites a prayer found on a scrap of paper in Matt's room that represents, in both form (a scribbled prayer) and content, the tradition of elevation by insignificance. "Oh King of Penitents who pass for fools in the opinion of the world but very dear to you oh Jesus Christ. O Blessed Mother obtain from Jesus a share of His Folly. The Kingdom of Heaven was promised not to the sensible and the educated, but to such as have the spirit of little children."[33] Matt's prayer suggests parallels with "the simplicity, childlikeness, smallness, and weak-

31. Welsford, *The Fool*, 193.

32. Saward gives special attention to the Russian, Irish, Cistercian, and Breton traditions.

33. Cited from M. Purcell, *Matt Talbot and His Times* (Alcester and Dublin, 1976), 213, in John Saward, *Perfect Fools: Folly for Christ's Sake in Catholic and Orthodox Spirituality* (Oxford: Oxford University Press, 1980), 209.

ness" of St. Thérèse of Lisieux.[34] Saward shows that a common thread, from Paul to Matt Talbot, is a pattern of Christ's self-oblation and the "distinction between the self-centered wisdom of the world and the cross-centered wisdom of God."[35] He holds that the holy fool reveals a common way for Christians, to give themselves away and live as children of God.

In chapter 3, I presented the life of Matt Talbot in relation to St. Thérèse of Lisieux and her ordinary but theologically pliable life. Like Thérèse, Talbot is the antihero, even the antisaint, who takes the little way. He is also a holy fool. For example, he is subject to ridicule in Brendan Behan's *Confessions of an Irish Rebel*, where Behan claims that Talbot was despised by the majority of people in his own north Dublin neighborhood where he was called "Mad Talbot."[36] Behan was a successful Irish poet, playwright, and memoirist in the 1950s. At one point, he was a member of the IRA and was imprisoned. He famously described himself as "a drinker with a writing problem," and by the end of his life in 1964, he took on the role of drunken has-been. This last bit is not gratuitous information. There is a sense where Talbot and Behan are revival kinds of fools.

In his *Confessions*, Behan considers the Venerable Matt Talbot as a dupe for the middle and upper classes, Presbyterians and "Castle Catholics."[37] With his drinker's bravado, Behan questions whether this so-called reformed alcoholic really ever drank very much. Although Talbot was a dockworker, Behan establishes doubt about his purported commitment to trade unionism. This is where Talbot plays the fool to middle-class Presbyterians and Castle Catholics. Behan directs his ridicule at Talbot's asceticism. According to Behan, Talbot's piety goes too far when his self-denial manifests itself in his refusal to take strike pay, and much worse, when he refuses to take overtime pay for time spent waiting for a truck to arrive at the docks.[38] Behan does not deny that there is a local admiration for Talbot, but he is skeptical. He mocks the outsiders even from other counties in Ireland who venerate the so-called holy man.

If Matt Talbot is a holy fool, then Behan's account should not be pushed aside. We need only recognize that the stories of mockery and honor exist side by side, that ridicule by one's neighbors does not exclude

34. Saward, *Perfect Fools*, 210.
35. Saward, *Perfect Fools*, 4.
36. Brendan Behan, *The Confessions of an Irish Rebel* (London: Arrow Books, 1991), 243.
37. Behan, *Confessions*, 243-44.
38. Behan, *Confessions*, 244-45.

local veneration.[39] On the contrary, the first may very well be the source of the second. On this point, the folly of St. Benedict-Joseph Labre (1748-83) deserves attention. During his life, he is a poor pilgrim and a vagabond, and is thought by some to be mentally ill. He is denied admission into three monasteries, finds his calling as a pilgrim, sets the pace of his life by regular pilgrimages to holy sites in Europe, lives in the streets, eats scraps from garbage heaps, gives away alms that he receives, and spends hours in prayer. In life, he is subject to frequent taunting and violence, as well as threats of imprisonment and quarantine as a beggar. He is despised in life, but immediately after his death — apparently while his body still lies in a bed — he is called a saint.[40]

In *Perfect Fools*, Saward describes St. Benedict-Joseph as representative of the tradition of folly for Christ and unrepresentative of his times. He belongs in what Welsford calls an age when higher things are mediated by priests and kings. In the modern era, the fool is displaced from social life, so that the life of the fool becomes nomadic. Labre was always on the move; the fool is on a quest for a holy place. In an age of Deism and rationalism, an age that tamed religious enthusiasm for the sake of enlightened self-interest, Benedict-Joseph had no place and lived entirely apart from the material and philosophical progress of his age.[41] In her theology and history of beggars, Kelly Johnson notes that Benedict-Joseph's life as a vagrant staked out a "territory" in opposition to modern ideals. "Labre's life revolved around sacred places, the contingencies of Christian history rather than the logical efficiency of system. His vocation was physical and material: not in the sense of engineering and medicine, but the hunger and cold of a pilgrim's life, the blisters, the itch of lice, the smells of a beggar's companions. His calling was also social, though not in the orderly sense of the centralized state or an economic system. He simply could not afford the luxury of privacy because a beggar cannot survive alone."[42] By all accounts, Benedict-Joseph endured derision and violence with indifference, and his austerities with joy. He was a fool. It is hard to study his life without concluding that he suffered from mental illness. He was a saint as soon as he died. He is despised by us, but we need him when he is gone. The

39. Dublin Diocesan Matt Talbot Committee, 25 Killarney Street, Dublin (www.matt talbot.com).

40. Saward, *Perfect Fools*, 199-200.

41. Saward, *Perfect Fools*, 198.

42. Kelly S. Johnson, *The Fear of Beggars* (Grand Rapids: Eerdmans, 2007), 134.

holy fool represents, not spiritual escape, but a different kind of social and material reality.

Turning back to the question of realism, it appears that hagiography, in reference to fools like Matt Talbot and Benedict-Joseph Labre, puts a happy gloss over subjection and self-imposed suffering. Our representative modern realist, Charles Hedrick, notes that part of the worldly orientation of realism is detailed attention to the historical vernacular and artifacts as well as all the "blemishes and baser aspects" of life.[43] Yet, the base aspects of hagiography seem much too ignoble and foolish to be represented by modern realism. Modern realism is attracted to misery as long as it is meaningless. The holy fool, in contrast, suffers on a christological landscape. The realist question is whether or not the vernacular and the base aspects of life are too base and yet too easily converted to a holy image, whether or not the blemishes of everyday life can be given theological significance at all. Hedrick notes that the "reality effect" in narrative is attained when features are included that "contribute nothing to the plot or the narrative's progress. Like so many things in life, they are just there and incidental to the activity around them."[44] Further, arbitrary events may be decisive events; "unanticipated events do change the course of our lives."[45] Can such events be real if they are readily integrated and directed to the good, if the unanticipated turns and unavoidable blemishes are received as grace?

Again, the issue is whether or not the communion of saints and our participation are real. The saint's story tells the presence of God through the free motives and actions of the saint, so that divine action comes, not as intervention, but as participation — participation in Christ. For example, the martyr, like Jesus at Gethsemane, must choose his or her path. God's presence is mediated through the desire for solidarity and the freedom of the pathway. St. Lawrence (August 10) is legendary for mocking the executioners and the flames that burn his flesh. In St. Ambrose's account, he informs his executioners that he is done on one side and could be turned over. He encourages them to take a bite.[46] The point is not that God intervenes to short-circuit Lawrence's nervous system, but that the martyr's communion with Christ, through his or her mimesis, is so inti-

43. Hedrick, "Realism in Western Narrative," 348.
44. Hedrick, "Realism in Western Narrative," 346.
45. Hedrick, "Realism in Western Narrative," 348.
46. St. Ambrose, *De Officiis*, trans. Ivor J. Davidson (New York: Oxford University Press, 2002), 1.41.207 (pp. 238-39).

mate and powerful that it manifests itself physically. Fire cannot compete with the physical effects of human intimacy and the flames of desire for communion with the divine. St. Lawrence seals his death sentence through a christological act of solidarity. When (in the mid–third century) he, as a deacon, is forced to relinquish the treasures of the church in Rome to the Roman prefect, he sells all the church's possessions, gives the money to the poor, and presents them as the real treasures of the church.

The realism of the lives of the saints, therefore, is to depict the reality of God's communion, specifically in terms of a mimesis of Christ in union with the Spirit. Reality is mediated through figurative representation, and the saints are living metaphors. The death of St. Lawrence is deeply set within Catholic memory, not because of his high threshold of pain, but because through him the church as a whole, at least for a moment, is in solidarity with Christ (Matt. 25:31-46) and, as a single body, gives up all it has and follows the incarnate God (Matt. 19:21). This solidarity — which also marks Lawrence's body — is the axis of hagiographic realism. As noted above, hagiography does not fall in line with the modern tension between purposes and life. In this sense, it is holy foolishness. The stories of the saints may not look "real" to modern eyes because they look too much like stories and too much like ordinary life: motives, actions, and events are ordered to a common web of ends, which are set within a network of relationships. In this regard, historical vernacular and artifacts, blemishes, and baser realities of life are common features of hagiographic narratives. Lives are changed by unanticipated events. Tragedy looms. But all is brought into association with life in God.

Hagiography has romantic elements, but not in the sense that Hedrick outlines at the beginning of the chapter. The saints are not "superhuman beings in a supernatural world." They are not heroes who are set apart from human frailties and weakness. Rather, the lives of the saints bring together the fullness and complexity of this life. In this sense, the lives of the saints are love stories, like the return of the lost son or the foolish search for a single lost sheep (Luke 15), Charles de Foucault's hope to be the love of God in the desert, and Lawrence's solidarity with the poor in Christ. Therefore, the question does arise whether or not the romance of sinner and saint, of the lowly and the noble, of human and divine can be contained within a realistic frame of reference (as they are one in Christ). Hagiography is set within historical space, but usually introduces extraordinary events where the saint could be seen as "heroic" in the sense that she

is set apart. Ironically, however, saints distinguish themselves by their refusal to set themselves apart from the poor, the sick, everyday people, and
folly of the incarnation.

When all is said and done, the term "heroic" does not translate to the
saints. The characteristically modern saints (as portrayed in chapter 3) are
often antiheroes. They constitute a web of fellowship. They are not Homeric heroes that stand apart as though they were gods. Rather, they are
holy ones through which we might draw nearer to God in Christ. Inas-
much as the hero stands above others, the saint stands in the middle of a
network of relations. She is a sacrament — a sign and conveyance — of
love. The realism of hagiography is based on the reality of alienation in the
world and the possibility of participation in the communion of God. As
love stories, the romantic elements of the lives of the saints do not represent a flight from reason to intuition and feeling. In the marvelous and extraordinary, there is an attempt to identify the contours of the world as it
really is, to put the truth of the real and ordinary into view.

In the lives of the saints, our awakening to everyday existence comes,
not through anxiety or boredom, not through the power of the lone will,
not through the force of environment and circumstance, not through
restlessness and the abyss, but through the ordinary and extraordinary
possibilities of the good and holy in the world. Although the lives of the
saints assure us that God is all we need, hagiographic realism often challenges rather than reassures. Its upheaval comes through a passion for
the ordinary, comic pain, and a profligate joy — through Teresa of Calcutta's life with the outcasts, vision of beauty in the ugly, experience of
joy with the dying, and spiritual emptiness when alone with God.
Teresa's "dark night" of solitary prayer underlines both the joy of solidarity with the "baser" aspects of life and her unquenchable desire for nearness to God.[47] Hagiographic realism brings all the blemishes and contingencies of life into the reality of God's ever-present communion with the
world.

---

47. *Mother Teresa: Come Be My Light — the Private Writings of the Saint of Calcutta*, ed. Brian
Kolodiejchuk (New York: Doubleday, 2007).

✦ FIVE ✦

Images

—∿∿—

I n an essay entitled "The Church's Way of Speaking," Robert Wilken recommends that Christians maintain their distinctive language in order to offer to secular society a way of seeing and understanding the world. He notes, for example, the public importance of the phrase "image of God," which communicates the dignity and depth of human life as well as the idea that "there is something other than the image, the thing which the image reflects."[1] He cites several contemporary writers, nonbelievers, who draw on the Christian tradition: "Terry Eagleton on Thomas Aquinas, Jean-François Lyotard on Augustine's *Confessions*, Alain Badiou on St. Paul, and Slavoj Žižek on Christ's willing acceptance of suffering and death." He notes a commonality among these writers; they "exhibit a 'yearning' for something more than what modernity has to offer."[2] Wilken reminds us that sustaining this "more" requires us to sustain, first of all, the "thickness and density" of Christian worship and ways of life. Here, the notion of ways of "speaking" widens to images and the fixtures of a place. Wilken describes St. Patrick Catholic Church in Washington, D.C., especially its stained glass, Pietà, several statues of saints (among them Sts. Patrick, Anthony of Padua, and Thomas More), and sixteen paintings in the chancel of saints and blesseds of the Americas (e.g., Elizabeth Ann Seton, John Neumann, Frances Xavier Cabrini,

---

1. Robert Louis Wilken, "The Church's Way of Speaking," in *Handing on the Faith*, ed. Robert P. Imbelli (New York: Crossroad, 2006), 100.

2. Wilken, "Church's Way of Speaking," 101. On this point, Wilken is discussing an essay in the same volume by Paul Griffiths: "Culture's Catechumens and the Church's Task," 44-59.

and Rose of Lima).[3] In other words, a way of seeing the world is part of a landscape and language of images and objects that populate a place.

After two chapters that deal with saints in terms of texts, this chapter turns to visual images and how images of saints occupy places and help constitute connections human and divine. Chapters 1 and 2 proposed that our attraction to the saints is an expression of social desire for a kinship that bridges the gaps between our lives and life on a higher, inclusive, and personally meaningful level. In chapter 2, the main media for Beverly Donofrio's growing relationship to Mary are pictures, visual symbols, and statues. In this chapter, visual representations will be set within a framework of salvation history. The biblical landscape of alienation and return will be the context for understanding the role of images, and the logic of the image will be the context for approaching the patterns, repetitions, and living in and through others that are enacted in the lives of the saints.

Saints inhabit spaces where divine and human life are discovered together. Our desire to draw near to the saints might be simply our attraction to their abandonment to God and our hope to be part of the company that lives near to God. There are spaces to be filled, gaps and disconnections in our lives. One way of thinking about the gaps is in terms of the problems of Scripture and history: gaps made by the divide between the "historical Jesus" and the "Christ of faith," between historical data and what Jesus means for us, between modern critical methods of study and salvation history. Primarily, however, the gap to which the saints migrate is already scriptural. We could begin with Abraham as he is called out of the land of his fathers, Moses representing the people at Sinai, or David's reign, his repentance before the prophet Nathan and his cry for Absalom. We could begin on the other side with the desire of the people — to return

---

3. Wilken, "Church's Way of Speaking," 103. For a detailed description of the stained glass, paintings, and statues, see http://www.saintpatrickdc.org/guide.shtml. St. Patrick's website explains that "the sixteen niches below the Patrician stained glass windows form The Gallery of Saints and Blesseds of the Americas. Tatiana McKinney, a Russian-American working in the icon tradition, spent two years completing the semi-circular series in 1996. The saints and beatified of the New World are, from left to right: (1) Bl. Miguel Pro, (2) Bl. Andr, Bessette, (3) Bl. Juan Diego, (4) Bl. Kateri Tekakwitha, (5) St. Martin de Porres, (6) St. Isaac Jogues, (7) St. Peter Claver, (8) St. Rose of Lima, (9) St. Frances Xavier Cabrini, (10) St. Elizabeth Ann Seton, (11) St. John Neumann, (12) St. Rose Philippine Duchesne, (13) Bl. Marie Rose Durocher, (14) Bl. Junipero Serra, (15) Bl. Katharine Drexel, and (16) Bl. Damien de Veuster (16)."

to Egypt when wandering in the wilderness, to have a king and to be like other nations, to return from exile and to see the new Jerusalem. Between wandering and diaspora, there is a desire to be a people with a role and a place. Out of this desire, the ministry of Jesus is the great gathering.

A basic New Testament theme of sanctity is that to be a holy one is to belong to Christ (Rom. 1:7; 1 Cor. 1:2). But a basic mark of saints is suffering the widening gap of belonging. In this regard, Mary is our representative of communion with God. She is the daughter of the old Adam and mother of the new, and as defined by the *Dogmatic Constitution on the Church,* she is the type of the church, an exemplar of faith and love, and a sign of hope and comfort for the wandering, pilgrim people of God.[4] In praying the rosary, we join with Mary and see the life of Jesus through her eyes. In the prayers of the rosary, the joyful mysteries begin with Mary accepting God's plan (Luke 1:26-38) and conclude with losing a twelve-year-old Jesus, mistakenly assuming that he is among kin, and finding him in the temple with his true Father (2:41-52). Mary asks, "Son, why have you done this to us?" (2:48). With this scene of anxious separation, we move to the sorrowful mysteries, from Jesus' agony in the garden to the cross. Mary's presence at the cross is the context for giving her and the beloved disciple to each other; her son and her house are now found in John (John 19:26-27). Then the glorious mysteries follow the resurrection, ascension, and giving of the Spirit at Pentecost, and they conclude with Mary's return to her place as Mother of God and the daughter of Adam as the new Eve. She is crowned queen of heaven.

The story of the Blessed Virgin Mary is the story of creation, our coming from God, sojourning in the world of separation, and returning to God. It is the story of the saint's desire for communion amid our alienation in the world. It is the reason for our desire to be with the saints. This is Peter's passion. In Luke, Peter's call to be a disciple is preceded by his unease in the presence of Jesus. He is full of doubt as he follows Jesus' instructions, but with great surprise and awe he finds his nets overloaded with fish. He responds, "Depart from me, Lord, for I am a sinful man" (Luke 5:8). Later, he shows faith enough to walk on water, and then sinks (Matt. 14:22-33). He is the one to declare, "You are the Messiah" (Matt. 16:16), yet he rebuffs the idea that Jesus will be killed in Jerusalem, and in

---

4. *Dogmatic Constitution on the Church, Lumen Gentium* (1964), 53, 68. http://www.vatican.va/ archive/hist_councils/ii_vatican_council/documents/vat-ii_const_19641121_lumen-gentium _en.html.

return is rebuked by Jesus, "Get behind me, Satan!" (Matt. 16:22-23). In between Peter's declaration and Jesus' rebuke, Peter is named the rock upon
which the church will be built (Matt. 16:18). Indeed, in this one scene, he
represents both our intimacy and our disaffection. He declares his unwa-
vering allegiance yet denies Jesus three times (John 18:15-27). Like his
doubts at the beginning, his denials set up his return to the water, the Lord,
and a net full of fish (John 21:1-14). He will have to profess his love three
times to the resurrected Lord, only to have Jesus allude to his eventual
martyrdom (John 21:15-19). Like Mary, his story is one of separation and
return, and the desire in us of the communion of saints.

Mary and Peter, very different in their trials and passion, are prototypical saints of communion. We find them, as saints, at their return to
God, but we remember their separation. They enact a fundamental relationship between Scripture and the communion of saints: by accounting
for the revelation of God, the Bible also reveals our alienation, and saints
are people of communion who populate our world of estrangement. The
preceding chapters on hagiographic realism understood the saints in
terms of participation that opens up in the textual gaps. The saints come
alive in the space opened both by the promise of God and by what in us is
yet to be revealed (in Abraham's sacrifice of Isaac, for example). As a kinship, the saints fill but do not remove the gaps and divisions between our
ways and God's love for the world. The communion and the veneration of
the saints are a logical and practical consequence of a community that attends to Scripture as a gathered and pilgrim people. A people needs a
place, and in the communion of saints, that place is a network of relations.
To display this logic, I will begin with the statues and visual images that fill
the Catholic imagination and our sacred space.[5] Once a sacramental logic
is established, the chapter will give account of the saints as biblical exemplars, embodiments of interpretive performances, and sacramental types.

While Robert Wilken points to the extraordinary landscape of images
in St. Patrick Church, I will consider saints and biblical figures in stone and
stained glass and the many visual images in the modest structure of St.
Anthony Shrine Parish in Emmitsburg, Maryland.[6] It is an ordinary Cath-

5. See Andrew Greeley, "Sacred Space and Sacred Time," in *The Catholic Imagination*
(Berkeley: University of California Press, 2000), 23-54.
6. There is a photo on the parish website: http://www.emmitsburg.net/sasolmc/
directions.htm.

olic church. At the center of our attention — behind the eucharistic table and above the high altar — we have a large crucifix, wood carved, and above the side altars we have statues of Mary and Joseph. Our statues are typical figures in North American Catholic churches, and they watch over the congregation during each Mass. Mary is on the right side of the crucifix (our left), which faces us from above the altar. On Mary's right side is a statue of Jesus with a blazing sacred heart. To the left of the high altar (and our right) is Joseph. Last Sunday, one of my sons started to poke me and point to our right just before Mass was about to begin. It took me a while to understand what he was whispering. It was Father's Day and a little blue present had been placed on the base of the statue of Joseph. A little pink present had been at Mary's feet since Mother's Day. It was gone. It was Joseph's turn. My son wanted me to know that I had been included.

On each side of the high altar are two important stained glass windows. On Mary's side, we have St. Elizabeth Ann Seton, who is the patron of our town. In practical terms, she is still making her mark on Emmitsburg through the Daughters of Charity, the provincial house of the Southeast Province, their outreach programs (food, emergency housing, clothes, life insurance, assistance filling medical prescriptions, a dental program, and so on), nursing care centers, a retreat center, the Basilica and National Shrine of Elizabeth Ann Seton, and Mother Seton School (prekindergarten to eighth grade). On Joseph's side of the altar, we have the patron of our parish, St. Anthony of Padua, in stained glass. He is in his typical posture, wearing a Franciscan habit, carrying the infant Jesus, and holding a lily. Our parish literature tells us that "no church could hold the crowds that came to hear him speak. Because of what he said, parents and children made peace with each other; thieves returned what they had stolen; people who told lies admitted them publicly and corrected them. Perhaps this is why Anthony is known as the patron saint of lost items — he worked to find lost people."[7]

There are two statues at the back of the nave and several visual images on both sides. We in the pews are surrounded. The most prominent statue in the back is the Pietà, a young Mary holding the crucified Jesus in her arms. Often, toddlers of the parish are occupied for a few restless moments during Mass as their parents allow them to caress the smooth ceramic, pat Jesus' arms and legs, and touch his wounds. On the base of the Pietà is a ce-

7. "Our Patron Saints," http://www.emmitsburg.net/sasolmc/patron_saints.htm.

ramic bowl holding ceramic nails (presumably leftovers from the crucifixion). Glue marks indicate that about three of the nails are missing. I have no doubt that over the years a few kids have managed to take them home. Further in the back in the nave is a statue of St. Thérèse of Lisieux. She is holding a bundle of plastic roses. St. Thérèse died the same year (1897) that our current church building was completed and dedicated. I wonder if someone years ago made the connection. Her cult emerged quickly, and she was canonized shortly after in 1925. She is in death like she was in life — a quiet patron, taking the little way, willing to be hardly noticed in the back of the church. Again, it is the children who attend to her, usually trying to pick her flowers. On the side walls of the nave are fourteen Stations of the Cross in ceramic relief, interspersed with fifteen stained glass windows depicting biblical events, from the annunciation to the resurrection. Finally, in the north transept is another altar, with votive candles and a statue of St. Anthony, again holding a lily and carrying the child Jesus.

The statues and images in our very common church represent a long history of visual representation in the church. The style is realistic: existential, historical, and anachronistic. The stained glass scenes, the Stations of the Cross, and the statues depict the form, posture, and expressions of real people, like we congregants hope to be when we are serious about our faith. The realism could be called "existential" in the sense that it represents timeless and decisive moments that have made us who we are. But the representation signals historical realism as well. On the Stations of the Cross, the disciples as well as the Roman soldiers are in the dress of their time (or at least not our time). They are obviously distant from us, depicting real historical events. On the stained glass, props portraying biblical events — the soldier's shield, the disciples' boat, and the urns from the wedding at Cana — help place them in ancient times. Mother Seton wears her usual eighteenth-century bonnet, and St. Thérèse her nineteenth-century habit. But also, as part of the realism, there are anachronistic features — hybrid elements between existential and historical realism. The clothes of Mary and Joseph look timelessly pious; or perhaps it is best to say that the clothes are possibly ancient or medieval and, in any case, generically nonmodern. But their faces and bodies look like ours. They are kin, in a sense, from another time and place. Yet, they are in our time as well. If the historical realism sets time apart and the existential realism joins them to us, anachronisms set the saints in between as bridges between now and then.

The familiarity of the faces as well as the historical references allow realism to be maintained while the figures are clothed in symbol and metaphor. The statue of Jesus at Mary's right hand is emblazoned with the sacred heart. Mary wears her heavenly blue mantle, and Joseph carries his rod of Jesse, a staff sprouting with a lily of purity and Davidic royalty (Christian midrash on Isa. 11:1). The Stations of the Cross tend toward historical realism, except with signifying colors: hints of yellow and pink are used to distinguish Roman persecutors from frightened witnesses. Gold creates a feel of divinity amid the terrible scenes of Jesus' suffering. A similar, divine use of gold is made in the stained glass, but additional symbols are obvious in the glass, especially a liberal use of the dove and heavenly streaks of gold light. These symbols not only attach holy meaning to realistic scenes, but they also provide a grammar of significance. The colors and symbols point us to a continuous story of God's presence in the world. One can follow human and divine agency through the colors in the Stations of the Cross.

Our Mary at St. Anthony's in Emmitsburg has white skin (very white) rather than, say, the brown skin of the Virgin of Guadalupe. We are, primarily, a Caucasian congregation, and Mary's skin tells us something about God with us. The Virgin of Guadalupe, of course, tells us about God as well. Both images use a symbolic posture and blue robe, which tell us that the figure is really Mary. Mary has a multitude of realistic faces, and in our parish, especially amid our African American congregants, Mary's whiteness carries a feel of superficiality. It is the figurative elements — blue mantle, posture, serpent underfoot — that tell us who she is and remind us that the many faces of Mary are one. In this way, metaphors abound and situate the realism of our lives, other people's lives, and the historical past within a context of redemption.[8] The visual metaphors speak of the saints and biblical scenes in terms of a single salvation history. Mary is stepping on the serpent, and Anthony is carrying an infant. These are realistic (nonsymbolic) actions that put earthly life in a figurative relationship to God's time. The serpent is sin, and the infant is Jesus. In the story of salvation, Mary — the firstborn of the new creation — puts the serpent of Eden, Satan, underfoot. Anthony carries Christ to many in his time, through his eloquent words and wondrous deeds.

---

8. I am using the term "metaphor" in relationship to Janet Martin Soskice, *Metaphor and Religious Language* (Oxford: Oxford University Press, 1987).

The realism of the images follows the logic of incarnation, that is, the conviction that divine life takes on humanity in Jesus Christ for us. It is the "for us" that requires symbols and metaphors that embody the story of redemption and, along with anachronisms, place the events of redemption in our time. This logic is akin to sacramental realism. In the sacraments, the fullness of reality is made present through the concrete, here and now. Divine life is present in earthly things and events in which we participate. However, there is a concealment of the divine presence in the earthly things. The real presence of Christ is not evidence for the indifferent. He comes to us in bread, and in this way we are called to be part of the events of the making present, to witness and join the celebration of the Eucharist, to be a part of its performance. Likewise, the visual realism of statues and stained glass is part of participatory events. They populate a space of worship and discipleship. The saints, their communion, and our practices of veneration form an extension of this populated space into our world. A setting is established for sharing a place with the saints, for veneration, and for visualizing our common identity.

This layering of representation, veneration, and identity is described in its historical development, from the third to the eighth century, by art historian Ernst Kitzinger.[9] He begins his study of Christian imagery by showing a mid-third-century relief that is crowded with people and symbols but has at its center a shepherd boy carrying a sheep on his shoulders. Kitzinger calls this imagery "signitive." It does not depict the man Jesus, but shows who he is in the biblical story of redemption.[10] "I am the good shepherd" (John 10:11). Kitzinger notes that, in this early period, representation through meaningful signs, rather than portraiture, leads the way because pictorial representation is, in principle, too near to idolatry, and visual images need to be justified by the meaning they could convey.[11] In the history of Christian imagery, Kitzinger calls this justification the thin end of the wedge.

In the fourth century, when Christianity is established in the Roman Empire, representation begins to change. Christian imagery takes a public role in a Greco-Roman frame, and it shifts to epic narration and portrai-

9. Ernst Kitzinger, "Christian Imagery: Growth and Impact," in *Age of Spirituality: A Symposium*, ed. Kurt Weitzmann (New York: Metropolitan Museum of Art, Princeton University Press, 1980), 141-64.

10. Kitzinger, "Christian Imagery," 142.

11. Kitzinger, "Christian Imagery," 144.

ture. If signifying imagery is organized by themes like the good shepherd, now images of biblical events and persons are ordered chronologically and realistically. The depiction of salvation history becomes monumental in its grandeur, its location in the city, and its role in public testimony and remembrance. The signifying style has an obvious meaning-giving quality; it is communal in the sense that it requires interpretation. Epic narrative, in contrast, is "impersonal and objective." The artist has the task of bringing biblical scenes to life.[12] Here is where Christian imagery starts to acquire its sacramental realism. "The Christian world order is palpably and factually presented to the faithful both in its historical unfolding and in its present reality."[13] This manner of representation survives in the Stations of the Cross, statues, and stained glass of St. Anthony Shrine Church. It is historical realism for the here and now.

The shift from signifying imagery to historical realism opens the way for practices of devotion centered on the image. Kitzinger moves forward in his history by suggesting that there is interplay between an objective representation of the biblical record and the "need for a more direct and intimate communication with the heavenly world."[14] In a third stage of development, the image becomes "a conduit or receptacle of divine power."[15] Kitzinger notes that this kind of devotional shift occurs in both the sixth and the fourteenth centuries, and a dominance of epic (didactic) narrative lies in between, beginning in the ninth century. In the first devotional period, portable images become popular. They are close at hand and tend toward representation "in the literal sense . . . to make present that which is absent." They often represent the saint as inactive and receptive, "ready to accept homage and listen to pleas."[16] By the late Middle Ages, visual piety becomes part of the intimacy between the physical body and redemption. Christ, in his physical suffering, is shown in communion with us in order to enact our redemption. The saint is depicted in postures and situations of empathy with Christ's passion, and by drawing the saints near, the devout find a connection to Christ's suffering along

12. Kitzinger, "Christian Imagery," 146.
13. Kitzinger, "Christian Imagery," 147.
14. Kitzinger, "Christian Imagery," 148.
15. Kitzinger, "Christian Imagery," 156.
16. Kitzinger, "Christian Imagery," 149. When biblical events are shown (such as the crucifixion), anachronisms ("such as pilgrims genuflecting at the foot of the cross") serve "as a means of relating the events depicted to the here and now" (153).

with sympathy and real solace for their own.[17] In short, the visual image, along with the tangible relic, is able to hold and convey the power of what it represents.

The power of the relic and image has an obvious connection to the cult of the saints — to gathering in fellowship with holy bones and calling upon their power. More attention will be given to this form of fellowship in chapter 9 on hagiography. At this point, I want to point to the parallel between the depictions of biblical events and the lives of the saints. In our memory of the saints and our theories about them, there are similar shifts back and forth from an emphasis on instructive representation (the public monument) to images of living near the events and people here and now (the portable icon). As a narrative form, the lives of the saints function to enliven faith, give hope, and show exemplary ways of life. As images and statues, the communion of saints dwell among us — not merely where we worship, but possibly where we live, work, and go to school. The fact of the matter is that most of us will not join the communion of saints through lives worthy of canonization and veneration. The saints live out a passion for Christ that is not likely to be sustained in us, but we can share in their lives through prayer, memory, and friendship. Sharing in the communion of saints through remembrance and prayer is the route to sharing their passion.

The prototypical defender of the devotional image is St. John of Damascus (d. 749). Contemporary icons of St. John usually have him holding parchment and quill. His long page of writing, facing out to the viewer, is likely to reveal quotations from a treatise in defense of holy images. St. John's defense of icons is precipitated when, at the beginning of the eighth century (726-730), Emperor Leo III bans the use of images throughout the Byzantine Empire. The rise of iconoclasm can be attributed, not only to external factors like the rising power and influence of Islam and "a new outburst of perennial Hellenic 'spiritualism,'" but also to long-standing disputes within the church about the use of images.[18] St. John writes three treatises in defense of images between 726 and his death in 749. The reign of iconoclasm will last until 787 when the empress Irene convenes the Second Council of Nicea, which reinstates the validity of images and their veneration. A reign of iconoclasm comes again between 813 and 843, and con-

---

17. David Morgan, *Visual Piety* (Berkeley: University of California Press, 1998), 60-73.

18. Alexander Schmemann, "Byzantium, Iconoclasm and the Monks," *St. Vladimir's Seminary Quarterly* 3, no. 3 (Fall 1959): 18-34.

cludes with the final restoration of icons, which is celebrated in the East on the first Sunday of Lent at the feast of the Triumph of Orthodoxy.[19]

The Second Council of Nicea (787) is often cited for putting definite terms to a long-established distinction between veneration as honor/reverence given to the saints (*dulia* in Greek) and veneration as worship rendered to God (*latria*).[20] In a few long and spirited sentences, the council recommends that churches, sacred vessels, vestments, houses, and roadsides should be filled with images of Jesus, Mary, the angels, saints, and pious people, so that we might be lifted up by their memory and "to a longing after them."[21] In his treatises in defense of images and their veneration, St. John of Damascus makes these same points and offers arguments from Scripture and the principles of the Christian faith. For our purposes, St. John is interesting not only for his defense of images, but also for his move from a justification of biblical images to a call for the visual (sensual) representation and veneration of the saints.

St. John begins his *Defense against Those Who Attack the Holy Images* by arguing that our use and reverence of images are unavoidable. We humans cannot help but give reverence to things, times, and places that are near to God, and Scripture directs us to do so. If we give honor to what is close to God, how can we deny honor to a holy image? Images are simply part of our world and our relationship to God. St. John defines "image" in reference to the relations of the Trinity. "An image is a likeness depicting an archetype, but having some difference from it.... The Son is a living, natural and undeviating image of the Father, equal to him in every respect, differing only in being caused."[22] From here, St. John accounts for images of God in the natural world and, more decisively, in the worship and sacrifice of the Old Covenant — "as Israel venerated the tabernacle and the temple in Jerusalem."[23] Veneration as worship is for God alone, but the veneration of images such as the tabernacle is an act of obedience and honor "on account of God ... to the places of God."[24] Later, speaking of the life of Je-

19. Schmemann, "Byzantium, Iconoclasm and the Monks."

20. See Augustine, *City of God* 22.10.

21. Norman P. Tanner, S.J., ed., *Decrees of the Ecumenical Councils*, vol. 1 (Washington, D.C.: Sheed and Ward, 1990), 136.

22. St. John Damascus, *Three Treatises on the Divine Images*, trans. Andrew Louth (Crestwood, N.Y.: St. Vladimir's Seminary Press, 2003), 25.

23. St. John Damascus, *Three Treatises*, 28.

24. St. John Damascus, *Three Treatises*, 27.

sus, John points to matter as the medium of God's presence. He will ask, "Is not the thrice-precious and thrice-blessed wood of the cross matter? Is not the holy and august mountain, the place of the skull, matter?" He will ask the same about the tomb, the "all-holy book of the Gospels," and the altar, bread, and vessels of the Eucharist. With faith in the incarnation, he proclaims, "I reverence the rest of matter and hold in respect that through which my salvation came, because it is filled with divine energy and grace."[25]

Up to this point, John admits that he has justified only the veneration of biblical images and persons associated with Christ: the cross, Mary, the apostles, and so on. Following the logic of the incarnation, it seems clear to him that human beings, the "friends and servants" of God, are suited to be the more honorable image — as we are made and redeemed in the image of God. In the incarnation, "God has been seen in the flesh and has associated with humankind."[26] Here he turns to the apostle Paul for a theology of participation. God's association with us has the effect of our sharing in the life of God. He notes Galatians 4:6-7: "God sent the spirit of his Son into our hearts, crying out, 'Abba Father!' So you are no longer a slave but a child, and if a child then also an heir, through God." Romans 8:17 is a key text as well: "And if children, then heirs, heirs of God and joint heirs with Christ, if only we suffer with him so that we may also be glorified with him."

Following Paul's theology of participation, St. John links saintly imitation of Christ to the saints' role as exemplars, and their role as exemplars to our reverence for the "image." The saints are joined in divine life, and venerated "as the friends of God, who, struggling against sin to the point of blood, have both imitated Christ by shedding their blood for him, who shed his own blood for them, and lived a life following his footsteps."[27] As the saints imitate Christ, they become apt images. As we celebrate their example, we celebrate the type in reference to the archetype. We give glory to Christ, the one that is the form of their lives.[28] The Christian faith is that Christ offers reconciliation and life with God, and if this is the case, then we cannot help but to venerate the saints. John of Damascus puts the point in a

---

25. St. John Damascus, *Three Treatises*, 29.
26. St. John Damascus, *Three Treatises*, 29.
27. St. John Damascus, *Three Treatises*, 35.
28. St. John Damascus, *Three Treatises*, 35. Here, John cites Basil's *On the Holy Spirit:* "For the honor given to the image passes to the archetype."

creedal form. "For from the time when God the Word became flesh, and was made like us in every respect save sin, and was united without confusion with what is ours, and unchangingly deified the flesh through the unconfused co-inherence of his divinity and his flesh one with another, we have been truly sanctified."[29] We venerate the saints through the image because, in Christ, it is through us that salvation comes.

This idea of the embodied image follows a biblical logic of "witness" as the "imitation of Christ." When Paul and Barnabas are in Lystra (Acts 14:8-20), they are thought by the Greeks to be gods. Despite *and* because of the awe of the Greeks — evinced by the error and idolatry of the Greeks — Paul and Barnabas have the power to point with authority to the true God. The misrepresentation of the apostles as gods reveals, ironically, a truth. The Lycaonians call Barnabas "Zeus," and Paul they call "Hermes" ("because he was the chief speaker"). They make preparations to offer sacrifice. Paul has just healed "a crippled man, lame from birth" by only his word, "Stand up straight on your feet" (14:9-10). Such is the wonder of apostolic power, and the authority of the apostle's word, and this healing of the one "who had never walked" seems to fulfill (at least) two purposes for Luke in his Acts of the Apostles. First, divine life is identified in Paul and Barnabas (in their personal presence), and second, the apostles' speech is invested with divine authority.

Luke sustains the connection between divine presence and apostolic testimony by the interplay between word and response. The apostle speaks and the deed is done: the man is healed; the malady obeys. Then, the power and authority of the apostolic word refer back to Paul and Barnabas (as they are thought to be gods), and by this same authority they denounce their divine status, tearing at their garments and shouting, "We are of the same nature as you, human beings." They become the focus of awe so that they can deflect it and proclaim the true God. "We proclaim to you good news that you should turn from these idols to the living God, 'who made heaven and earth and sea and all that is in them'" (14:15). Paul and Barnabas are like icons; they are images that point to the power and presence of God.

Luke presents a parallel scene earlier with Peter and John in the temple (Acts 3:1-10). In Jewish environs, Peter and John are not called gods, but they do inspire awe and draw the crowds near. When they heal a man who

29. St. John Damascus, *Three Treatises*, 35.

is unable to walk, "people [hurry] in amazement toward them." The crippled man spends his days begging at a gate of the temple, but once healed, he walks, jumps, and finally clings to Peter (3:11). The Acts of the Apostles is not known for its subtlety: there is little nuance when the man is "walking and jumping and praising God." But Luke crafts a fine point in the drama. The crippled man is carried daily to the temple, but he is stuck at the entrance in order to beg. He finally enters through the gate as a whole man as he hangs on to Peter. Peter, in his apostolic power, is the healed man's conveyance into the temple. Peter restores the son of Abraham, and like Paul before the Gentiles, he attracts attention and then redirects it to how the God of Abraham has glorified Jesus, the Messiah, "whom heaven must receive until the times of universal restoration of which God spoke through the mouth of his holy prophets from of old" (3:21).

In the words and deeds of Peter and Paul, Luke provides an argument for inspiration. It is not the early modern assertion that miracles verify that the Bible is revelation (if for no other reason than there is no New Testament canon for Luke to defend). Rather, Luke's concern for the power of the Spirit in the apostolic word is based on his claim that people and their testimony are inspired in Christ. He offers assurance to the "friends of God," so that they can know with confidence the teachings that they have received (Luke 1:1-4). Instead of a textual proof, Luke provides something more like an argument for tradition, especially since the Acts of the Apostles begins with reference to the instruction that the apostles receive from Jesus both before his crucifixion and after the resurrection (Acts 1:1-5).

However, it is probably more accurate to say that Luke focuses on the working of the Spirit in people and their testimony, only with special attention to the apostolic witness. For example, when Jesus is presented at the temple, the word of fulfillment and redemption comes through Simeon and Anna rather than the prophetic books as in Matthew (Luke 2:22-38). Simeon and Anna enter only briefly, to the effect that continuity of agency is sustained through the Spirit as it enlivens witnesses to God's work. Likewise, at the beginning of Acts, the inaugural signs of inspiration are clearly and widely communal (Acts 2), and to this movement of the Spirit, Peter and the apostles serve as witnesses. They experience something happening to others through them, but not at their initiative. In the same way, Stephen is commissioned by the apostles to care for widows, but is actually called by the Spirit to perform signs and wonders that lead to his martyrdom (Acts 6:1-8). The Spirit's call to Cornelius, the centurion, is needed to make sense of why Peter has a vision of all creatures (mammals, reptiles, and birds) pronounced by God to be clean (Acts 10:17). Like Paul and Barnabas at Lystra and like Peter and John in the temple, the Spirit-filled person becomes a conveyance as much as an agent. There is, in the Spirit's work, the creation of embodied media, a peopled-christological relationship in our place and time.

A similar kind of presentation is offered by Paul throughout his letters: Look at me as I am in Christ. Philippians 3:4-21 provides an extended example. Paul presents himself as a Jew "circumcised on the eighth day, of the race of Israel, of the tribe of Benjamin, a Hebrew of Hebrew parentage, in observance of the law a Pharisee" (3:5), who considers everything a "loss . . . not having any righteousness of my own based on the law but that which comes through faith in Christ" (3:8-9). He will conclude the reference to himself by instructing the Christians of Philippi to "join with others in being imitators of me, brothers, and observe those who thus conduct themselves according to the model you have in us" (3:17). Here, the exemplar is reproductive. In the same letter, when Paul presents Timothy as an exemplar, he attaches Timothy to himself: "as a child with a father he served along with me in the cause of the gospel" (2:22).[30] Likewise with Epaphroditus: "for the sake of the work of Christ he came close to death, risking his life to make up for those services to me that you could not perform" (2:30).

Paul's use of himself as an example is commonly attributed to his use of Greco-Roman rhetoric. While syllogistic reasoning applies to forensic questions, exemplification is, in Greco-Roman rhetoric, the manner of deliberation about how to live.[31] Seneca, for example, holds that "the crown of life lived in accordance with virtue is to become an example oneself. . . . [Exemplars] allow the audience to conceptualize virtue with the remembrance of great men as powerful as their living presence. Examples show that the virtuous life is possible."[32] Similarly, Paul's reference to himself as an example to be imitated serves "both as a pedagogical technique and as an implied assertion of authority."[33] Paul points to himself as a kind of image that points to the truth of Christ.

---

30. See also 1 Cor. 4:17.

31. Benjamin Fiore, S.J., "Paul, Exemplification, and Imitation," in *Paul in the Greco-Roman World: A Handbook,* ed. J. Paul Sampley (Harrisburg, Pa.: Trinity, 2003), 228-57.

32. Fiore, "Paul, Exemplification, and Imitation," 235.

33. Fiore, "Paul, Exemplification, and Imitation," 238.

However, being an "image" of Christ, for Paul, is a place of suffering rather than invulnerability and glory. In Paul's rhetoric, the self-possession of the great Greco-Roman man is turned on its head in faith, suffering, poverty, and self-emptying. Recall that, in Philippians 3, Paul directs attention to himself only insofar as he disavows his pedigree of righteousness and depends upon faith in Christ. He claims that he does not already possess spiritual maturity, "but I continue my pursuit in hope that I may possess it, since I have indeed been taken possession of by Christ" (3:12). Paul is an exemplar "for the community because they, like him, are all 'in Christ.'"[34] The authority of exemplars is held together in the self-emptying of the Son,

> Who, though he was in the form of God,
> did not regard equality with God something to be grasped.
> Rather, he emptied himself,
> taking the form of a slave. . . . (2:6)[35]

Through the christological turn, Paul dislocates the typical rhetoric of the exemplar. Self-sufficiency is brought low, and dependence is raised up. In 1 Corinthians 4:6-21 and 10:1–11:1, Paul contrasts pride and boasting with the virtues and status of an exemplar. "You have already grown rich; you have become kings without us. . . . [But] God has exhibited us apostles as the last of all. . . . We are weak, but you are strong. . . . I urge you, be imitators of me" (4:8, 9-10, 15-16). The Christian exemplar is not set apart by his nobility and self-sufficiency, but set within by service and self-giving. In Galatians 4, Paul calls the community to task through an interesting twist of solidarity. He calls them to follow their own example as they, in days gone by, have been a guide for Paul. "I implore you, brothers, be as I am, because I have also become as you are" (Gal. 4:12). Noting their former hospitality to Paul and to the gospel, Paul asks, "Where now is that blessedness of yours?" (4:15). In their "strength," they look to the strong, and they are no longer open to the exemplar from below.

This reversal of exemplification is comparable to the embodiment of

---

34. Fiore, "Paul, Exemplification, and Imitation," 241.

35. In Galatians, Paul presents himself as an example because he is "a slave of Christ" (1:10) in contrast to those who teach circumcision for the Gentiles and, in the process, "might enslave us" to the law (2:4-5).

the Spirit in Luke and Acts. The sign of healing in Acts 3:1-10 leads to a drama where Peter and John are taken into custody and must answer to the Sanhedrin (4:1-2). The question put to the apostles is one of power and authority. The interrogation, of course, is an occasion to witness to Christ; threats and efforts by the Sanhedrin — the ruling body — to silence Peter and John show that their words and deeds have their source in the authority of God (4:19-20). The drama comes full circle, from power to subjection to power, and concludes how it began: people "praising God for what had happened. For the man on whom this sign of healing had been done was over forty years old" (4:21-22).

Likewise, the drama in Acts 14 moves from power to subjection to power. Here, events shadow Christ's death and resurrection. At the beginning (14:11), Paul is mistakenly called a god, and at the end he rises, as if from the dead, in the pattern and image of the true God. After his display of healing power and witness to the true God, the crowds quickly turn against him. Luke has prepared us for this turn of events. We know that Paul and Barnabas arrived at Lystra from Iconium where "there was an attempt by both the Gentiles and the Jews, together with their leaders, to attack and stone them" (14:5). After his testimony in Lystra, Paul is stoned, dragged out of the city, and left for dead (14:19). "But when the disciples gathered around him, he got up and entered the city. On the following day he left with Barnabas for Derbe" (14:20). Along with Paul's rising, this conclusion includes two delightful details. The first is the gathering of disciples around Paul. They seem to come out of nowhere; their identities are unspecified, but their role as gathered followers of Christ is clear. Jesus is raised and gathers his disciples, while the inverse is the case for Paul — as he is type rather than archetype. The gathering is the context for his rising like Christ. The second detail is the departure of Paul and Barnabas on the following day. After being thrown out of the city and left for dead, Paul's entrance back into the city serves a clear purpose. He will reenter only to leave again, but on his own initiative, for the purpose of witnessing elsewhere. As Peter must speak when he is silenced, Paul must reenter because he was thrown out.

In Acts 14, Paul is the exemplary outcast, the central figure of the edge. He is part of the reimaging of human life. Pivotal stories in the Gospel of Luke carry similar themes. Jesus' ministry in Galilee begins in the synagogue with his pronouncement of good news to the poor and his declaration that Scripture is fulfilled "today." It concludes as he is driven out of town to be thrown from a hill, only to pass through the people and go on his way (Luke 4:14-29). Zacchaeus, the despised tax collector, is accompanied from the edge of the crowd to the center, to be the gracious host (Luke 19:1-10). Jesus calls out to Zacchaeus in hospitality so that he can entertain Jesus in his home. In receiving hospitality, Zacchaeus heeds the call to perform it. His household becomes a place of redemption. Prosperity that was once directed inward is disseminated out, and Jesus announces, "Today salvation has come to this house" (19:9). In short, the image and type are necessary for a continuing embodiment of salvation as a reversal and redirection of the world to God.

If human beings are the image of God, the communion of saints is a restoration of the image that points us back to God and to the future perfection of community in the kingdom of God. This chapter began with Robert Wilken's example of "ways of speaking" through the visual images in St. Patrick's in Washington, D.C. We conclude with his experience of being reimaged by the place, and reimagining what it means to be in a church in the capital of the United States. Recall that he is describing statues and stained glass and directing our attention especially to sixteen portraits of saints and blessed of the Americas (painted by Tatiana McKinney in 1996). "These saints represent Christian holiness of the most varied sort — a religious woman, a bishop, a Native American, a missionary, for example — and they all come from the New World. They present models of the Christian life for the faithful to admire and emulate, but they also help forge a Christian identity that is distinct from the natural cultures. By combining saints from North and South America, Canada, the United States, Peru, and other countries, one is reminded that as Christians we are part of another city."[36] The people gathered with the saints at St. Patrick's are called to be a similar image (an image of the image) of God's communion.

---

36. Wilken, "Church's Way of Speaking," 103.

Six

Miracles

—⟋⟍—

The relationships examined in the book so far — relationships that join the bodily, personal, and metaphysical — include the possibility of miracles. Consider the signs that communicate the personal commitment and bond between Mary and Beverly Donofrio in her memoir *Looking for Mary* (discussed in chapter 2). One sign is miraculous and unambiguous. There is an unmistakable change in a statue (a vanished tear), which shows no evidence of a natural explanation. The supernatural character of the event, however, is subordinate to its meaning and Beverly's response. The removal (purging?) of the tear is understood as a gesture of friendship and solicitude from Mary. The second sign is an ordinary, even expected, occurrence. A hand of the statue breaks off while the statue is being carried around in a shopping bag. This ordinary occurrence, like the extraordinary one, invites interpretation. In each case, extraordinary or ordinary, the miraculous quality of the event is carried by what it means. The supernatural event means that Mary is present and making an overture of communion. The ordinary event means that Beverly has a role to play in Mary's communion with the world. She will give Mary a "hand," and her solicitude and friendship as well. Such miracles are the subject of this chapter. As Donofrio's approach suggests, miracles are convincing because of the personal meaning they convey. Keeping the priority of meaning in view, this chapter will emphasize bodily, physical, and metaphysical questions. Can miracles really happen?

Kenneth L. Woodward, in *The Book of Miracles*, asks us to put in the background this question, "Did it really happen?" He invites us to ask,

"What does it mean?"[1] In his epilogue, after discussing modern miracle stories, Woodward concludes that "in each case the miracles are recognizable as such because the stories are interpreted within the ongoing narratives sustained by communities of memory and understanding — that is, by traditions."[2] Within traditions, miracles make sense and confirm the order of things. When viewed from the outside, they "demonstrate the postmodern principle that truth (especially religious truth) is always embedded in social constructions."[3] If we turn this statement around, we can say that the communion of saints forms a constructive social-metaphysical network of meaningful relations. Here, Woodward rightly focuses on the "meaning" of signs and wonders. His *Book of Miracles* speaks to a world where shared meaning is lost (confined to the private) and where "God" has become a mere reflection of each individual self.[4] In short, miracle stories narrate social and metaphysical connections where questions of truth will have a home.

The question of "meaning" is Woodward's way of sustaining the importance of miracles in a modern context, where miracles are very much a part of life yet are also alien. In such a context, miracles are sustained by their meaningfulness. However, "meaning" needs a home. The social-metaphysical fabric of miracles and saints falls apart if we entirely disregard the question, "Did it really happen?" For miracles to mean something, they must be real: a claim of a miracle is that extraordinary things and events have significance, not merely in a postmodern sense of "how things are" *for us* or *for me*, but for how things really are. Although Woodward's meaning-based approach has limitations, it is a good one, and it has been successful in making sense of miracles in the modern world. On a social level, the sheer weight of meaning and the amount of personal associations with miracles steadily overcome modern rationalism and cultured skepticism. The convictions and investments of the people spill over the constraints of modern thought. In this sense, there is an implied argument in Woodward's broad survey of world religions: Christianity, Judaism, Buddhism, Hinduism, and Islam. The overflowing meaning of miracles in living traditions buoys and carries the question, "Did it really happen?"

1. Kenneth L. Woodward, *The Book of Miracles: The Meaning of Miracle Stories in Christianity, Judaism, Buddhism, Hinduism, and Islam* (New York: Simon and Schuster, 2000), 26.

2. Woodward, *The Book of Miracles*, 383.

3. Woodward, *The Book of Miracles*, 383-84.

4. Woodward, *The Book of Miracles*, 384-85.

For example, when considering Christianity, Woodward's attention to the "meaning" of miracles draws together a biblical framework with traditional and modern stories of the saints. After appraising Jesus' miracles, Woodward points to the logic of the incarnation — the presence and power of God in human life in Christ, which heals and elevates us, so that we share in the life of God in Christ.[5] Later, in his discussion of medieval hagiography, he shows that the meaning of miracles follows the same reasoning. Miracles have "much to do with the Christian belief in the resurrection of the body . . . the idea that Christ can and should be imitated, the belief in the power of the Holy Spirit that makes this possible, and the continuing presence of Christ in his church, which the saints and their miracles — like the Eucharist itself — make manifest."[6] By asking the question of meaning, Woodward turns to the context of a social body and social practices, extended over time, that sustain the life of miracles in our world.

In the preceding chapters, I have followed a similar strategy. I have tried, a bit more deliberately than Woodward, to keep the metaphysical questions in view; however, my first line of inquiry has been in the field of literary realism and its materialist assumptions, rather than scientific materialism itself and its hold on real explanations. Materialism has great success in explaining things, but has failed to account for the meaning of human life, especially our day-to-day practices and relationships. When human meaning is the strong hand, narrative is the way to make an advance beyond narrow, naturalist explanations. Chapters 1–5 followed a narrative line. This sixth chapter goes a step further. It moves on to metaphysics and modern science. The claim is this. The miracles of saints are a challenge to scientific materialism, and the possibility of the miraculous is a test case for a metaphysics that is hospitable to the human being. Miracles happen in a way that requires us to extend critical realism toward the distinctive, personal, and social ways that human beings perceive and know the real. Chapters 1 and 2 developed a realism of the communion of saints as a set of relationships (a kinship) rather than a theory: a population that connects the social and metaphysical and offers avenues of participation. Miracles are a form of exchange that is native to this network of associations. An indisputable proof for miracles, for or against, is not desirable. It would bind the free, thinking human being, who is not a passive

5. Woodward, *The Book of Miracles*, 136.
6. Woodward, *The Book of Miracles*, 170.

observer in the world, but part of the meaning and "coming to be" of things. That is, the real, contingent possibility of miracles is a reflection of the real human, social and historical, yet metaphysical connections that constitute life in the world.

Given this social and metaphysical claim, there is no necessary dispute with physicists, biologists, or other scientists on the relationships of things and creatures in the world. There are, however, disputes within and among these scientific disciplines. These internal debates are not our direct concern, but they do impinge upon the big questions. In short, there is no unified or seamless "scientific" worldview. The fundamental relationships of life — how the particular things are connected to the whole — are seen differently by scientists trained as zoologists, biologists, paleontologists, biochemists, physicists, and theoretical physicists. The biochemist's world is within the cell.[7] The evolutionary biologist appeals to the fortuitous and mystifying possibilities given by a near infinite expanse of time.[8] The physicist, when puzzling over the laws of matter, is likely to inquire about the relationships between matter and the transcendent, meaning-giving habits of the human mind.[9] Biologists who begin with materialist assumptions give philosophical naturalism extensive scope and set the human mind within the laws of natural mechanisms.[10] In contrast, physicists, by and large, tend to be less reductionist in their understanding of matter. This diversity of approaches is good for science and human beings. Physics, biology, and other disciplines create difficulties for how we view meaning, purposes, and the person only when they delineate narrowly materialist metaphysics, that is, when they reduce the human being to material causes. By doing so, materialists are also proposing a social doctrine and a claim (a restrictive and controlling claim) about the meaning of life and what links us to life as a whole.[11]

The study of things in the world inevitably leads to broader questions.

7. Arthur Peacocke, "Biological Evolution — a Positive Theological Appraisal," in *Evolutionary and Molecular Biology*, ed. Robert John Russell, William R. Stoeger, S.J., and Francisco J. Ayala (Notre Dame, Ind.: University of Notre Dame Press, 1998), 357-76.

8. Richard Dawkins, *The Blind Watchmaker* (New York: Norton, 1996), 46-51; Kenneth B. Miller, *Finding Darwin's God* (New York: HarperCollins, 1999), 243-45.

9. Paul Davies, *Cosmic Jackpot: Why Our Universe Is Just Right for Life* (Boston: Houghton Mifflin, 2007), 228-39.

10. E. O. Wilson, *On Human Nature* (Cambridge: Harvard University Press, 1978), 66-68.

11. K. B. Miller, *Finding Darwin's God*, 175, 182.

The study of the "physical" naturally tends toward metaphysical ideas, and among scientists, the disagreements are plain. Christopher G. Langton, a biologist and expert in artificial intelligence, holds that, in theory and within the limits of materialism, the origins of human consciousness not only can be known but also can be reproduced. "[O]ne can be both a vitalist and a mechanist at the same time. . . . It is hard for people to accept the idea that machines can be as alive as people. . . . [Biology] is the science of the possible. Biology is consequently much harder than physics but also infinitely richer in its potential, not just for understanding life and its history but for understanding the universe and its future. The past belongs to physics, but the future belongs to biology."[12] The ambition to create the "living" machine is bold, but not as bold as it may seem if we keep in view two of Langton's presuppositions. First, as a materialist, he believes that life, as humans typically understand it, is essentially pointless. Second, what is "real" about human life can be understood in terms of natural mechanisms. These two assertions are not facts as much as they are convictions that help Langton organize and interpret data. They do not follow from research as much as they are inferences that depart from research. From these two convictions, it follows deductively, not empirically, "that machines can be as alive as people." Machines can be as "alive" as people because, in Langton's world, our distinctively human purposes in life are essentially pointless. Machines can be as alive as people because squirrels and DNA are as alive as people. Langton's claim about living machines is striking, not because of what he expects machines to do, but because of how little he thinks human beings are really doing.

In contrast, Paul Davies, a theoretical physicist, is interested in how human consciousness matters for how we understand matter.[13] He does not reduce the mind to a mechanism, but he is no theologian: he tries to understand what the distinctiveness of human knowing tells us about the material world. He is not looking to some world beyond. He struggles with the insight that mere materialism cannot entirely explain matter. The quantum physicist must make sense of the physical world given that, at the most basic level, matter is governed by probability rather than invari-

12. Christopher G. Langton, "A Dynamical Pattern," in *The Third Culture*, ed. John Brockman (New York: Simon and Schuster, 1995), 350, 354-55.

13. Paul Davies, "Teleology without Teleology: Purpose through Emergent Complexity," in *Evolutionary and Molecular Biology*, 151-62.

ant law, that the components of things have a level and a range of interaction and movement that are indeterminate. This indeterminacy is cause for physicists to use the language of "possible worlds." In principle, and not as a mere lack of knowledge, matter "behaves" with a degree of unpredictability. Given this limitation to the ideas of "law" and "mechanism," Davies and other scientists find that their task is to think more broadly than the materialist will allow. In contrast to biologists who are "strongly and evangelically reductionistic," he holds that the complexities of life cannot be answered with simple answers and single, all-encompassing physical mechanisms.[14] Davies recommends that scientists think more freely about complex systems of life. He dares to talk about the purposes of things. He dares even to ask why there is a world and life at all.[15]

Davies represents a scientific dispute with scientific materialism. The dispute is about, not the validity of material explanations, but how much the material explanations can explain about the human being and the kinds of explanations we need to fully account for life. The fundamental flaw of the reductionist/materialist framework is that its proponents expect to be able to explain everything by natural mechanisms, but they cannot explain themselves, their quest for what is real (for its own sake), and the purposes of their science (in an otherwise purposeless world).[16] The basic disagreement, according to Stephen M. Barr, hinges on the human intellect and free will — our capacities for abstract thought, purposeful choices, free action in our very human and historically bound way, our ability to distinguish physical reactions from reasoned responses, our convictions in ascribing praise and blame to human behavior, and so on. Barr, a physicist, argues that quantum indeterminacy "allows" or "provides an opening" for free will, but does not explain it.[17] If the mechanics of human choices were fully explained, they would not be free. When we human beings attempt to give account of our lives and our place in the world, human self-consciousness and freedom are not so much explained as fundamental to our explanations.

We (philosophers and ordinary folk) have developed complex distinctions and categories to account for our freedom in a way that avoids think-

14. P. Davies, "The Synthetic Path," in *The Third Culture*, 308.

15. P. Davies, *Cosmic Jackpot*, 256-59.

16. Ian G. Barbour, *When Science Meets Religion* (New York: HarperCollins, 2000), 122-29.

17. Stephen M. Barr, *Modern Physics and Ancient Faith* (Notre Dame, Ind.: University of Notre Dame Press, 2003), 178.

ing about human action as though we were dogs (responding by instinct and training) or gods (absolutely transcendent and free). In the face of the invariant laws of eighteenth-century physics, philosophers sometimes have asserted a dualistic vision — where the human body is bound to nature and the spirit (godlike) is absolutely free. The extremes make things simple, but they fail to account for the distinctiveness of our embodied freedom, our reasoning and choices in time, place, community, and culture. Among scientific materialists, simple clarity wins the day. They claim that the human body and spirit are determined by known and yet-to-be-fully-explained material causes. The materialist analogy, in the twenty-first century, has shifted from the machinery to the computer. The claim is that we have "internal programs" that determine choices, and because these operating systems are opaque to us, we develop the illusion of free will.[18] In contrast, Barr and a host of other scientists propose that the human mind defies material explanations because "it is not reducible to or explicable in terms of something more basic than itself."[19]

Science, in itself, offers only possibilities, not proof: either (a) the human intellect and will are entirely determined by physical components and events, or (b) human thinking and choosing are not reducible to physical causes.[20] Barr argues that if *a* is true, then we cannot, in principle, know with certainty that it is true.[21] If we are determined by and within a physical mechanism, we would not be able to stand apart from the mechanism to observe it working upon us.[22] However, if we transcend natural mechanisms in some way (however slight), then we would be able to see ways that our lives are bound to natural causes. In sum, the nonmaterialist is able to account for scientific discovery, while the materialist is caught in a mechanical loop. The materialist mistake is to detach the part from the whole and then to reason from this detached part to the whole. The hand is detached from the body, and then the hand becomes the basis for understanding the whole body. It can't be done. One arrives at a whole body that works like a hand. Likewise, the materialist begins with the ways that we

18. Barr, *Modern Physics*, 185.

19. Barr, *Modern Physics*, 205.

20. Barr, *Modern Physics*, 205.

21. Barr cites the work of John R. Lucas, *Freedom of the Will* (New York: Oxford University Press, 1970), and Roger Penrose, *Shadows of the Mind* (New York: Oxford University Press, 1994).

22. Barr, *Modern Physics*, 197.

are clearly bound to material mechanisms, and then reasons to the "whole" and claims that we are entirely bound to material mechanisms. Barr notes the irony of such a view: materialism proposes great heights of human thinking (explaining everything) by undermining how we naturally think about human life — by hollowing out human purposes and our sense of place and role in the world. As noted above, some like Christopher Langton believe that living machines can be reproduced because they have a machine-like view of human life. Barr maintains that "there is not a shred of positive evidence that a material system can reproduce the human abilities to understand abstractly and will freely."[23] He attributes scientific materialism to a kind of dogmatism, to metaphysical suppositions rather than empirical evidence.[24]

When Barr turns to the facts, he holds that the materialist account of free will (that it is an illusion) "does not correspond to our intuitions and experience. Most people believe that when faced with a choice they have real alternatives. That is, they believe that it is physically and actually possible for them to do either the one thing or the other thing."[25] Likewise, when we come to a reasoned conclusion, we see ways that we could have thought otherwise — or that we could have willfully resisted our conclusions. These are facts of human experience. Robert Pollack (biologist), in *The Faith of Biology and the Biology of Faith*, provocatively calls this freedom of thought and action the "irrational component" of human life. The irrational, in Pollack's sense, is a constituent of life that is operative in scientific thinking as well as in how we reason through and act on the meaning and purpose of our lives.[26] Pollack, here, defines rationality narrowly; it would be better to refer to his "rationality" as "scientific rationality" and his "irrational" as "other ways of knowing."

At the end of a lengthy discussion of the science of evolution, biologist Francisco Ayala puts it simply, "Science is a way of knowing, but it is not the only way. Knowledge also derives from other sources, such as common sense, artistic and religious experience, and philosophical reflection."[27] We

23. Barr, *Modern Physics*, 226.

24. Barr, *Modern Physics*, 220-26.

25. Barr, *Modern Physics*, 186.

26. Robert Pollack, *The Faith of Biology and the Biology of Faith* (New York: Columbia University, 2000), 18-19, 32-34.

27. Francisco J. Ayala, *Darwin's Gift to Science and Religion* (Washington, D.C.: Joseph Henry Press, 2007), 177.

might want to add to or reorganize the list. But Ayala's comment does highlight the point that ways of thinking, such as everyday moral choices, faith, and our traditions of philosophical inquiry, are different from each other, have distinctive elements, and interact (along with science) with other ways of knowing. None is isolated as a world unto itself. Our investigation into things (whether by common sense or the physical sciences) leads us to consider metaphysical questions and the meaning of the human being. The issue of realism in science is whether or not rational inquiry suited to material causes should contain and limit human thinking or open out to wider questions and ways of knowing.

If we insert the question of miracles, we might say that the primary issue is not the existence of God per se, but making sense of the human being, beyond what materialism can provide. The question is whether or not everything, in principle, can be managed through explanation and prediction. Miracles cannot be proven or reproduced, predicted or managed. This makes the possibilities of miracles an interesting test case. Certainly, in a theological sense, miracles evince God's ever-present creativity and utterly distinct relationship, as Creator, to the world: God's activity, for example, does not inhibit or constrain, but makes possible human freedom. But when approaching the question of whether or not miracles really happen in this-worldly human terms, they are, first of all, about possibilities in life and about meaningful events that cannot be reduced or reproduced. The real possibility of miracles says something about the human being that is indeterminate, that cannot be managed by scientific materialism or its mechanisms of prediction and control. The argument for miracles is not disinterested proof, but human testimony — testimony about human life in relation to specific events in the world. Testimony requires convictions, and testimony in a world open to miracles offers an understanding of reality that might promise to explain less about nature and yet will make more sense of the human being and creation.

Miracles are about people and the world we inhabit. Like the scientific materialist, the most determined critics of miracles and the religious mind are also impatient with how people naturally think. David Hume (1748) sets out to deny that miracles provide proof of religious truth. But his arguments exceed his purposes; he tends toward arguing against the possibility of miracles in order to reject their use as proof. At points he discounts human testimony almost entirely and identifies the sources of miracle stories as "ignorant and barbarous nations" and the "ignorant and barbarous ancestors" of civilized peoples. According to Hume, these primitive sources find fertile ground in the natural inclinations of human beings to believe and be captivated by the miraculous.[28] Hume observes that the credulity of the people is wide and deep, but not (or never?) wide and deep enough to have authority over the regularity of nature.[29] Hume, it seems, ignores his own skepticism about rational induction, so that he can argue that the laws of nature will trump natural religious sentiments.[30]

A similar line of thought is taken by zoologist/ethologist Richard Dawkins (2006). Dawkins holds that the ignorance and barbarism of belief are not only the inheritance of peoples, but are also hardwired in the human being. "Religion" is a natural, adaptive trait that is driven by the survival drive of the gene — something like the blind obedience of children for their own good and safety or the irrational power of romantic love.[31] In religion, however, an adaptive trait (Dawkins is not sure which adaptive trait) spins off into worthlessness; it is a product of natural selection, but it is a maladaptation and is socially and morally destructive.[32] With this claim, Dawkins, ironically, puts himself in a position where he is smarter than natural selection. His ideological commitments put him at odds with pure science.[33] While religious hopes are natural, Dawkins is convinced that he can expose and defeat this bit of nature. By judging an adaptation as maladaptive, he assumes he can see into the future and determine which adaptations are necessary for human genetic survival.[34] In other words, Dawkins has a purpose in life that he cannot include in his own theory. He believes, as a matter of moral conviction rather than scientific evidence, that religious belief is a maladaptation; he marshals what he claims as disinterested science to constrain human nature.

Dawkins can be placed within a political and philosophical tradition

28. David Hume, *An Enquiry concerning Human Understanding*, ed. Tom L. Beauchamp (New York: Oxford University Press, 1999), 10.20 (p. 176).

29. Hume, *Enquiry concerning Human Understanding*, 10.35-36 (pp. 183-84).

30. William L. Portier, *Tradition and Incarnation* (Mahwah, N.J.: Paulist, 1994), 306-12.

31. Richard Dawkins, *The God Delusion* (Boston: Houghton Mifflin, 2006), 172-79.

32. Dawkins, *The God Delusion*, 279-308.

33. Alister McGrath, *Dawkins' God: Genes, Memes, and the Meaning of Life* (Oxford: Blackwell, 2005), 53-60.

34. Dawkins's conclusions contrast with the positive effects of religion in Andrew Newberg's research, in *How God Changes Your Brain: Breakthrough Findings from a Leading Neuroscientist* (New York: Ballantine Books, 2009).

traced through Hume, as both a reaction to Newtonian law and an application of it to human life. The tradition includes such figures as Adam Smith, T. R. Malthus, and Herbert Spencer. For Dawkins, Charles Darwin is the centerpiece where he finds an arrangement of their ideas. Although they might argue the details, they set human nature within a Newtonian framework where natural mechanisms (like sentiments or the market) are thought to operate with autonomy; human life is atomized (divided into parts without reference to the whole), so that social relations are reduced to individual interests. Reasoned human purposes, especially common purposes, are understood as epiphenomena.[35] In a brief line, Michael Hanby, a theologian and philosopher of science, goes straight to the point of setting Darwin (and Dawkins) within a tradition: "Darwin's Malthusian mechanism produces happy, Adam Smithean outcomes."[36] The social philosophy comes before the science: Darwin develops his framework of thought by drawing on moral philosophy, demography, and economics. Malthus, the demographer and economist, argues that "positive checks" of scarcity and competition among poor laborers form a disinterested mechanism for limiting the population. He also develops a natural theology where the suffering of the poor serves the overall good, and it all comes to a good, Smithean end that is somehow both an equilibrium and progress.[37] That is, economics, philosophical anthropology, and theology provide Darwin with a structure with which to interpret his data. What we now call "social Darwinism" can be found prior to Darwin in Malthus and Spencer. "Social Darwinism" is the historical precursor to Darwin.[38]

By the time Dawkins begins his inquiry into human life, human purposes and human reasoning itself are considered adaptations of natural selection that (may or may not) aid survival. Genes have no purposes; they simply replicate. Natural selection, a blind mechanism, becomes godlike: it determines everything. Things are created randomly, but survive by natural determination. From the assertion that genes are the real but pur-

35. Christopher Dawson, *Progress and Religion* (New York: Sheed and Ward, 1933), 19.

36. Michael Hanby, "Creation without Creationism: Toward a Theological Critique of Darwinism," *Communio* 30 (Winter 2003): 666.

37. The point on equilibrium and progress is made by Christopher Dawson in *Progress and Religion*. Also see Hanby's "Reclaiming Creation in a Darwinian World," *Theology Today* 62 (2006): 476-83, and Anthony D. Baker, "Theology and the Crisis in Darwinism," *Modern Theology* 18, no. 2 (April 2002): 183-215.

38. Hanby, "Creation without Creationism," 657.

poseless agents of human life, Dawkins invents the concept of the "meme" to be the gene's analogy as the mechanism (the replicator) of human culture — of ideas, values, the arts, and so on.[39] Like genes, memes start to "care" only about their own survival. "Once the genes have provided their survival machines with brains that are capable of rapid imitation, the memes will automatically take over."[40] In his analysis of Dawkins's meme, Alister McGrath notes that there is no evidence that culture evolves in a way analogous to Darwinian theory. There is no evidence that something like a meme functions like a gene. The meme is an imaginative idea that becomes interesting only if we are already disposed to conceptual monism — if we are captivated by a single idea or mechanism that explains everything. The fact of the matter is that we have lots of complex and interesting, historical and natural explanations of human culture, and the meme concept turns out to be "redundant or wrong — and quite possibly both."[41] Dawkins, like Darwin, infuses his interpretation of data with social philosophy and an atomistic view of the human being: we are parts, but purposeless as wholes.

This critique of Dawkins and his scientific materialism is not a denial of evolution. On the contrary, scientific advancement and a fuller understanding of evolution are implied in the critique. Scientific materialism carries philosophical presuppositions that require the scientist to overlook facts and to extend mechanical analogies beyond their reach. Ironically, in Dawkins's reduction of the mind to matter, he consistently uses metaphors of human consciousness and agency to describe mechanisms of matter. Natural mechanisms take charge of human life. As Stephen Barr explains, "Scientific materialism exalts human reason, but cannot account for human reason. . . . The materialist is thus driven to deny empirical facts — not the facts in front of his eyes, but, as it were, the facts behind his eyes: facts about his own mental life."[42] As biologist Kenneth R. Miller puts it, the history of evolution — "natural history shaped by descent with modification" — is a fact; evolution as "the detailed mechanism of change" is a scientific theory — a set of explanations, some of which are rival explanations, that are studied and debated by the scientific commu-

39. Richard Dawkins, *The Selfish Gene* (New York: Oxford University Press, 1989), 1, 192.
40. Dawkins, *The Selfish Gene*, 200.
41. McGrath, *Dawkins' God*, 135.
42. Stephen M. Barr, "Retelling the Story of Science," *First Things*, March 2003, 20.

nity.[43] A critique of scientific materialism is part of the debates and advancement of scientific explanation.[44] Scientists (like Davies, Barr, and Miller) who reject the presuppositions of materialism are free to ask broader questions about life and human purposes.

Like the reductionism of scientific materialists, there are "religious" reductionists as well. Some people of faith seek to use theological presuppositions to overcome scientific data or to extend the analogy of the mind (from the human to the divine mind) to frame a scientific theory of matter. The first theory is creationism, and the second is the theory of intelligent design. Each reduces God — similar to the way that materialism reduces human being. Creation science is committed to dating creation no more than six thousand years ago. In so doing, it imposes a distinctively modern interpretation on the creation accounts in Genesis, and it rejects the facts of evolution. God and what we know of natural creative causes are set in competition. Ironically, creation science puts God utterly outside natural processes of the ever-changing and evolving world. In the argument from intelligent design, God is grasped within the operation of a natural mechanism. Intelligent design points to the existence of complex natural systems (like the eye), which defy incremental evolution by natural selection.[45] The next step is to argue from the inadequacy of evolutionary theory on this point to the existence of a designer — to God. However, insofar as God is understood as the conclusion to a scientific argument, God becomes graspable by science and bound within the mechanisms of design. If materialism leads to narrow science, intelligent design, as an attempt to find data of the divine mind in science, narrows the being and action of God.

To reflect divine agency, miracles must be outside empirical or scientific explanation but within human experience and observation. Francis Collins, former director of the Human Genome Project, gives a two-part definition for a miracle. In the first part, "a miracle is an event that appears inexplicable by the laws of nature and so is held to be supernatural in origin."[46] Collins argues that, because miracles are inexplicable, our first response ought to be skepticism. We know that appearances can be

43. K. B. Miller, *Finding Darwin's God*, 53-54.

44. K. B. Miller, *Finding Darwin's God*, 165-91.

45. Michael J. Behe, *Darwin's Black Box* (New York: Free Press, 1996).

46. Francis S. Collins, *The Language of God: A Scientist Presents Evidence for Belief* (New York: Free Press, 2006), 48.

deceiving. We should add that our own wishful thinking can be self-serving and self-deceiving as well: I might want to think that the clouds and sun will be put to the purposes of my Sunday picnic. On the one hand, we have an error in observation; on the other, we have an error of injustice in the ordering of our relationship to God (i.e., we assume that the universe is at our service). On the basis of the regularity of nature and mistakes in observation, Collins argues that miracles should be considered improbable but not impossible. On the basis of justice (not only science), it should be argued that God's grace is more likely to change us than to change the movement of the clouds. In each case, miracles are not part of the ordinary course of things or our ordinary (ordered) relationships to God and the world.

However, Collins's phrase "inexplicable by the laws of nature" means much more than that miracles will be out of the ordinary. "Inexplicable" means neither a "violation of nature" nor a failure of science. It does not mean that nature is defeated, and it does not mean that someday our understanding of nature will catch up to the extraordinary event so that it will be explained. On the one hand, "inexplicable" (rather than violation) means that God is not on the "outside" as though he would have to intervene to get in. On the other hand, it means that God is not on the "inside" as though God's relation to the world could be explained like a cause in the world (scientific explanation). To think of miracles as a violation or intervention in nature implies (wrongly) that something is added, as though God butts into the natural chain of events. On the contrary, miracles "occur when something is *not* present (i.e. a created cause or a collection of created causes)."[47] This appeal to something missing is not the "God of the gaps"; it is not inserting God into gaps in natural explanations. God does not intervene to fill the gaps of material causes; God is ever-present. We could say that miracles are about, not so much a difference in God (God is ever-creative), but a difference in the world. God is always active and creative, and miracles are events where ordinary causes and explanations do not follow their usual course. Miracles are events where we find ourselves and the world extraordinarily permeable, porous to God in a way that is inexplicable (in principle) to our knowledge of creation and the regularities of life. In this sense, we would not say that "nature is violated," but it

47. Brian Davies, O.P., *An Introduction to the Philosophy of Religion* (New York: Oxford University Press, 1993), 195.

might be appropriate to say that "our laws of nature" have been violated and God has "intervened" in our lives.[48]

If miracles are not some change in God, then there must be some inexplicability in the world and some plausibility to God's action in the ordinary course of things. Quantum physics accounts for indeterminacy and inexplicability as a principle of things. Kenneth Miller holds that "the indeterminate nature of quantum events would allow a clever and subtle God to influence events in ways that are profound, but scientifically undetectable to us."[49] Further, God, as Creator, is outside of time — God's action is not constrained by time — so that God's relationship to natural causes is beyond our perception. "Locked into a single point in time and moving in a single, unchanging path from the present to the future, we wouldn't have a clue."[50] If quantum indeterminacy leaves room in our explanations for the ever-present causality of God, the plausibility of God's ever-present relationship to the world is outside of science. Miller is not using quantum physics to make scientific claims, but to indicate their limits.

Stephen Barr approaches the question of God's causality by turning to Thomas Aquinas and his account of simultaneous and cooperative causes (e.g., primary, secondary, instrumental causality and so on).[51] The Thomist point is that God's relation to the world is unlike the relationships of things in the world.[52] God does not have to compete for space, time, or influence. The Creator "causes" in a way that does not undermine or compete with this-worldly causes. Indeed, natural causes depend upon the very-present creativity of God. "God does not move the sun; he makes the moving sun to be."[53] The same holds for human freedom. "[J]ust as by moving natural causes [God] does not prevent their acts being natural, so by moving voluntary causes He does not deprive their actions of being voluntary; but rather is He the cause of this very being in them; for He op-

48. B. Davies, *Introduction*, 199.

49. K. B. Miller, *Finding Darwin's God*, 241.

50. K. B. Miller, *Finding Darwin's God*, 242.

51. Barr, *Modern Physics*, 257-67.

52. Michael R. Miller, "Freedom and Grace," in *Gathered for the Journey: Moral Theology in Catholic Perspective*, ed. David Matzko McCarthy and M. Therese Lysaught (Grand Rapids: Eerdmans, 2007), 183-86.

53. James Ross, "Creation II," in *The Existence and Nature of God*, ed. Alfred J. Freddoso (Notre Dame, Ind.: University of Notre Dame Press, 1983), 130, cited in M. R. Miller, "Freedom and Grace," 187.

erates in each thing according to its own nature."[54] These arguments do
not prove that God is the cause. Rather, they show consistency between
natural causality and the willingness of the Creator, who is revealed in the
self-emptying and reconciling life and death of Jesus Christ. God's non-
competitive and cooperative causality is plausible (but not proven) because it is consistent both with the God who is revealed and with how we
know the world works. Miracles, then, are not isolated moments of God's
agency, but extraordinary signs of God's ever-present relationship to the
world. In miracles, things in the world have a different relation to each
other in such a way that we are able to see the agency of God.

This difference in the world leads to the second part of Collins's definition: miracles are meaningful and purposeful. They are not "supernatural acts of a capricious magician, simply designed to amaze."[55] We should
add that they are not the payoff from a divine insurance policy. God's
grace does not make human beings invulnerable and safe. The "interven-
tions" of God accord with who we know God to be, with Jesus' reconciling
mission (self-emptying), inauguration of God's reign, teaching, poverty,
and cross. They accord with the call of discipleship, to go and do likewise.
In other words, they are consistent with God's relation to the world, yet revealing for us (ordered to God yet extraordinary for us). The inexplicable
character of a miracle means, not only that our ordinary explanations are
not enough to account for an extraordinary event, but also that the event
itself is illuminating.[56] A prayer for a miracle is a petition to open real
events and people to be a sign of grace; we are asking to be transformed.
To this degree, a miraculous event becomes not so much something to be
explained, but itself a kind of explanation. This takes us back to our discussion of meaning at the beginning of the chapter. Science needs only to
admit, however slightly, inexplicability and plausibility, but the reality of
the event is carried by its meaning and purpose. A miracle gives us a
deeper understanding of God's ever-present relationship to the world.

Saints are signs of the presence and communion of God. They form a
communion, which joins this world of social relations with metaphysical
ones (chapters 1–5). In this context, miracles of the saints point to an em-

---

54. Thomas Aquinas, *Summa Theologiae* I.83.I.ad3, cited in M. R. Miller, "Freedom and Grace," 190.

55. Collins, *The Language of God*, 53.

56. Collins, *The Language of God*, 52-53.

bodiment of grace (the unity of body and spirit) and a social miracle — God's far-reaching friendship, which is expressed through the sharing of burdens and joys among us.[57] The saints are the change in the world that accompanies miraculous events. Their lives are laid open and porous to God. The spiritual porousness of the body is a basic theme of the lives of martyrs, ascetics, and mystics. The asceticism of desert holy men and medieval mystics produces robust bodies and opens new networks of fellowship.[58] Polycarp (d. 155) endures the flames of execution with grace, and afterward, the faithful desire fellowship with his holy bones.[59] Serenity of spirit, grace of the body, and fellowship also characterize the deaths of twentieth-century martyrs like Titus Brandsma, Edith Stein, and Maximilian Kolbe.[60] In medieval and modern times, the pilgrimage and shrine are sites of fellowship (with the saint and fellow pilgrims), healing, and what we, in modern times, might call personal and social "empowerment."[61] The common theme for the pilgrim and petitioner is, in Jesus' words of the Gospel, "Your faith has saved you. Go in peace and be cured of your affliction" (Mark 5:34).

The saints' relationship to the social body and the restoration of the body is extraordinary, but certainly plausible. In recent empirical research, the spirit (i.e., mind/brain) and social relations are considered under a single heading, the "psychosocial," which is observed to have a clear connection to the body. Studies on psychosomatic aspects of health indicate that the body is porous — that "expectancies about the external world" and "intrusive positive thoughts" have an effect on the body, on

57. John Bossy, *Christianity in the West, 1400-1700* (Oxford: Oxford University Press, 1987), 11-12.

58. See *Life of Antony by Athanasius*, in *Early Christian Lives*, trans. Carolinne White (London: Penguin Books, 1998); Caroline Walker Bynum, *Fragmentation and Redemption: Essays on Gender and the Human Body in Medieval Religion* (New York: Zone Books, 1991); and Caroline Walker Bynum, "Bodily Miracles and the Resurrection of the Body in the High Middle Ages," in *Belief in History: Innovative Approaches to European and American Religion*, ed. Thomas Kselman (Notre Dame, Ind.: University of Notre Dame Press, 1991).

59. *Martyrdom of Polycarp*, in *The Apostolic Fathers: Greek Texts and English Translations of Their Writings*, trans. J. B. Lightfoot and J. R. Harmer (Grand Rapids: Baker, 1992), 239, 241 n. 3.

60. Robert Ellsberg, *All Saints* (New York: Crossroad, 1997), 318, 343, 350.

61. See Jacobus de Voragine, *The Golden Legend*, vol. 1, trans. William Granger Ryan (Princeton: Princeton University Press, 1993); Mary Lee Nolan and Sidney Nolan, *Christian Pilgrimage in Modern Western Europe* (Chapel Hill: University of North Carolina Press, 1989).

health in general, and on responses to medical treatment in particular.[62] Even more obvious are the alternative effects on the body of depression, anxiety, and despair.[63] Likewise, social networks and support systems, particularly ones that pray, have observable effects (although the nature of the causal mechanism is a matter of speculation).[64] Alternatively, the body is resistant (impermeable to healing) and therefore more vulnerable when marked by isolation and "social inhibition."[65] As one study put the matter, it is difficult to distinguish spirituality and social networks, and both have an obvious relationship to the body.[66] On an empirical level, therefore, it should be uncontroversial to say the communion of saints is healing, whether of mind or body, or mind and body. On a theological level, we see and touch the presence and friendship of God. Saints are where the world is open to God.

62. Irving Kirsch, "Placebo Psychotherapy: Synonym or Oxymoron," *Journal of Clinical Psychology* 61, no. 7 (2005): 791-803; Luanna Colloca and Fabrizio Benedetti, "Placebos and Painkillers: Is Mind as Real as Matter?" *Nature Reviews Neuroscience* 6 (July 2005): 545-52; M. Michelle Rowe and Richard G. Allen, "Spirituality as a Means of Coping with Chronic Illness," *American Journal of Health Studies* 19, no. 1 (2004): 62-67; Debra A. Marshall, Elaine Walizer, and Marina N. Vernalis, "Optimal Healing Environments for Chronic Cardiovascular Disease," *Journal of Alternative and Contemporary Medicine* 10, supp. 1 (2004): S-147-55; Rachel Sherman and John Hickner, "Academic Physicians Use Placebos in Clinical Practice and Believe in the Mind-Body Connection," *Journal of General Internal Medicine* 23, no. 1 (2007): 7-10.

63. Kathryn Senior, "Should Stress Carry a Health Warning?" *Lancet* 357 (January 2001): 126.

64. Michael J. Breslin and Christopher Alan Lewis, "Theoretical Models of the Nature of Prayer and Health: A Review," *Mental Health, Religion and Culture* 11, no. 1 (January 2008): 9-21; Kevin S. Masters and Glen L. Spielmans, "Prayer and Health: Review, Meta-Analysis, and Research Agenda," *Journal of Behavioral Medicine* 30 (2007): 329-38; Alex Cahana, "The Placebo Effect and the Theory of the Mind," *Pain Practice* 7, no. 1 (2007): 1-3.

65. Johan Denollet, "Personality, Emotional Distress and Coronary Heart Disease," *European Journal of Personality* 11 (1997): 343-57.

66. Sandra E. Sephton et al., "Spiritual Expression and Immune Status in Women with Metastatic Breast Cancer: An Exploratory Study," *Breast Journal* 7, no. 5 (2001): 345-53.

SEVEN

Pilgrimage

—ᗰ—

The communion of saints is a social miracle. In the lives of the saints, miracles are not primarily extraordinary events in relation to nature, but principally signs and expressions of communion in God and with people living and dead. Saints represent human life in body and spirit as united and open to God. The miracles of the saints are primarily intercessory. Intercession points to the social miracle: social relations are constituted as a metaphysical communion. For this reason, the lives of the saints establish gathering places of interaction and interchange. By the fourth century, ascetics like Antony of Egypt (d. 356) go out into the desert to retreat from and defy the allure of worldliness in the city and to live only with God.[1] But the recluse often becomes the center of a community. His or her desert dwelling becomes the destination for pilgrims seeking a place to be near to God in the world. The lives of saints establish gathering places, and pilgrimage is a basic practice of devotion to the saints. This chapter will attend to the pilgrimage as a movement of communion — a progress toward a place where heaven meets the earth.

For several decades pilgrims have been making their way to visit Padre Pio, whether at San Giovanni Rotondo while he was alive or, after his death, at his shrines — whether in San Giovanni or some other part of the world. Many reports of healing have been recorded, and they

---

1. See Laura Swan, *The Forgotten Desert Mothers: Sayings, Lives, and Stories of Early Christian Women* (Mahwah, N.J.: Paulist, 2001).

tend to combine miraculous events with a description of Padre Pio's down-to-earth yet holy presence.[2] Padre Pio (d. 1968) is well known for carrying the stigmata, his aroma of sanctity, reports of bilocation, the power of his intercessory prayer, his role as confessor, his blessing the sick, and the building of a thousand-bed hospital (the "Home to Relieve Suffering").[3] He has roused suspicions and accusations of fraud from within and outside the church. During two different stages of his life, his contact with laypeople and his ministry were restricted by his superiors. Many have objected to his "medieval" view of himself as one who shared Christ's suffering.[4] Nonetheless, San Giovanni Rotondo hosts millions of pilgrims every year.[5] In 2002 he was canonized a saint before a gathering of 300,000 people at the Vatican, in an atmosphere and Mass that seemed to a *New York Times* reporter to be "more carnival than canonization."[6]

There are countless stories of Padre Pio's intercession for those who suffer. I will include two. The first might relieve the modern mind. The other is likely to be troubling. Both emphasize the body as the medium of spiritual unity, integrity, and faith. Both portray Padre Pio as merely an intercessor. Indeed, his body, as a stigmatic, is understood by himself and

2. "In 1967, my mother-in-law took her dying eight year old son, five thousand miles to meet Padre Pio. The doctors at the children's hospital where he had been treated for years, told her to take him home and enjoy him — he only had a little time left. He had a cancer which at that time had a 2% survival rate. Instead, she took him to San Giovanni Rotondo to meet Padre Pio. The friars escorted him up to Padre Pio's cell while she waited. When they brought him back to her, Padre Pio said something to her in Italian and one of the friars translated it for her and he said, 'The boy will be alright.' Her son, my husband's brother, just recently turned 40!" http://www.padrepio.com/in-10.html.

3. Christopher McKevitt, "San Giovanni Rotondo and the Shrine of Padre Pio," in *Contesting the Sacred: The Anthropology of Christian Pilgrimage*, ed. John Eade and Michael J. Sallnow (London: Routledge, 1991), 88.

4. Even the editor of his letters seems a bit troubled by Padre Pio's language. Pio explains to his spiritual director, "When the whole world troubles and weighs on me, I desire nothing other than to love and to suffer." The editor offers a footnote to the effect that "He does not desire suffering in and for itself but only insofar as it unites him intimately with Jesus and allows him to share in Christ's mission." Padre Pio, *Secrets of a Soul: Padre Pio's Letters to His Spiritual Director*, ed. Gianluigu Pasquale (Boston: Pauline Books and Media, 2002), 17.

5. Peter Jan Margry, "Merchandising and Sanctity: The Invasive Cult of Padre Pio," *Journal of Modern Italian Studies* 7, no. 1 (2002): 101.

6. John Tagliabue, "Vatican City Journal; The Friar, Miraculously, Marches into Sainthood," *New York Times*, June 17, 2002, A4.

those devoted to him as a particular result of a universal relationship between Christ's passion and the suffering of the world.[7]

The first miracle story is about a pilgrim who stays in San Giovanni for almost a year seeking a cure for throat cancer. He does all that a pilgrim is supposed to do (confession, Mass, prayer), but with no effect on the cancer. His voice has been reduced to a whisper, and breathing is difficult. Late one evening he is at the breaking point both physically and emotionally. Like the desperate friend of the parable in Luke 11:5-8, he goes to the monastery in the dark of night and pounds on the door. He interrupts the friars while they are praying the office. Padre Pio lays his hands on the man, who experiences a profound, mystical moment of grace, a momentary release from physical suffering, and an enduring sense of well-being. Later, Padre Pio gives him instructions to go to a surgeon in Bologna, where he is treated and cured.[8] The narrator of the story closes with a comment that concedes little to the wonders of modern medicine. "The next time I saw [the man who had cancer] was in my office in Milan.... So far as he was concerned, the surgeon had merely been an instrument used by Padre Pio, for whatever recondite reason, and I for one would certainly not disagree with him."[9]

The second story is about a man who pleads with Padre Pio "to restore his sight 'even if only in one eye.' After repeating questioningly 'Only in *one* eye?' Padre Pio [tells] him to be of good heart and that he would pray for him." Weeks later the man returns to San Giovanni and reports to Fr. Pio that his sight has been restored in one eye. With a bit of surprise and recognition, Padre Pio responds, "Only from *one* eye? Let that be a lesson to you. Never put limitations on God. Always ask for the big grace!"[10] The story is distressing to the degree that Padre Pio's attitude can be seen as callous and pedantic. Rather than full physical restoration, the power of prayer seems to be put to a moralistic point about faith. Yet, from a different angle, the story puts the "power" in the hands of the one who is healed rather than Padre Pio, and it indicates a higher purpose to intercession and healing. The "lesson" about faith puts body and spirit in unity. The body is the medium for the spirit, and the spirit is the medium for the wholeness

---

7. This theme is consistent throughout his letters in *Secrets of a Soul,* but see pages 42-45.

8. John McCaffery, *Tales of Padre Pio* (Garden City, N.Y.: Image Books, 1981), 114-16.

9. McCaffery, *Tales of Padre Pio,* 116.

10. McCaffery, *Tales of Padre Pio,* 117-18.

of the body. In the first account, an experience of spiritual unity opens the way for the effectiveness of a medical cure. In the second, physical restoration comes in the measure of faith.

Life-changing experiences of grace, "lessons" of faith, and healing are common enough on the landscape of the modern pilgrimage, whether we are making our way to Lourdes, Medjugorje, the Basilica of Our Lady of Guadalupe, the Carmelite convent of St. Thérèse in Lisieux, or the Mother House of the Missionaries of Charity in Calcutta. Shrines dot the countryside; they are settings of touch. They are spaces to draw near to sanctity. Travelers through central Maryland might stop at the Basilica and National Shrine of Elizabeth Ann Seton (d. 1821), and visit the National Shrine Grotto of Our Lady of Lourdes as well. The grotto began to be used as a replica of the shrine in Lourdes in about 1875. A little way down the hill is the site of the first Catholic church in Emmitsburg, where St. Elizabeth Ann Seton first stayed with her new community of sisters in 1809.

Hundreds of thousands of pilgrims come to Emmitsburg each year to take home water from the mountain spring, to pray the rosary, and to be in a place "away from the world, isolated from strip malls and market places, off the beaten path, in the woods, 'half in the sky' as Mother Seton described it in 1809."[11] A former grotto chaplain, Fr. Jack Lombardi explains the sense of the "place": "I was recently giving blessing with a relic of Mother Teresa after Sunday noon Mass to all the children gathered. I came upon a little boy in a wheelchair. His family gathered around him and asked for God's healing. The little boy, age five, said, simply, point blank: 'I want to walk.' The Grotto is above all a place of healing and prayer, where all souls can come, like that little boy, and ask for God's strength, grace and love."[12] Again, in this statement, we find the body and spirit united. We have the blessing with a relic and request for physical healing. The physical object associated with the holy person meets a physical need, and the petition, "I want to walk," takes on meaning for "all souls." There is more to Fr. Jack's imagery. The pilgrimage site is a place "half in the sky." It is a real place where a personal journey connects with

11. Fr. Jack Lombardi, "Inspiration," Mount St. Mary's University, Grotto of Lourdes, http://www.msmary.edu/grotto/.

12. Fr. Jack Lombardi, "About the Grotto," http://www.msmary.edu/grotto/about/index.html.

divine life, where our lives in time meet with eternity through the physical media of the body and a place.

The biblical story of salvation is a history of pilgrimage, embodiment, and place. It is a story of gathering and dispersal, liberation and wandering, captivity and longing for home. It begins with the itinerant life of Abraham and God's promise of an heir, a people, a land, and a blessing (Gen. 12:1-3). Joseph is cast out to Egypt, where he becomes part of the royal house and salvation for the sons and daughters of Jacob. Egypt turns out to be a land of captivity from which the people are liberated. They are liberated but wander in the desert before they are set toward the Promised Land. This pilgrimage of Israel is the history through which the world will come to know God. Jerusalem will be the place where the nations are drawn to God's holiness (Isa. 2). The story of Israel becomes fully universal through events where all seems lost, where judgment has come — in the sacking of the holy city and captivity in Babylon. In captivity, Israel's call to be holy is understood anew to be *for* the nations. This is also the point when Israel's history (as its people) becomes diffuse, when the way forward is not entirely clear.[13] In being a Jew, one is on pilgrimage and waits for God's great gathering and restoration. One becomes part of the meaning of things precisely by being a Jew, whether at home in Judah or in diaspora.[14] It is in the pilgrim character of Judaism, on the path to be holy as God is holy, that the Jews represent human history.

Christianity takes on this biblical history and its connection between being a representative people and the call of human life in relationship to God. The New Testament begins with the call and gathering of Israel, in John's call to repentance; in Jesus' eschatological act of calling out the Twelve; in the good news to the lame, blind, and imprisoned; and in the return of the leper, once made whole, to the temple (Matt. 8). While the destruction of Jerusalem means the diaspora of Israel, the death of the Christ means dispersion and return. There is, first, the dispersion of frightened disciples, then their gathering by the resurrected Lord, and finally the story of dissemination (going forth to the nations) and the hope of Christ's return and eschatological gathering.[15] The church is a social sacrament, a

13. Hans Urs von Balthasar, *The Glory of the Lord: A Theological Aesthetics*, vol. VI, trans. Brian McNeil, C.R.V., and Erasmo Leiva-Merkakis (Edinburgh: T. & T. Clark, 1991), 215-98.

14. Michael Wyschogrod, *The Body of Faith: Judaism as Corporeal Election* (New York: Seabury Press, 1983), 238-43.

15. Gerhard Lohfink, *Jesus and Community* (Philadelphia: Fortress, 1984).

people of God, constituted not by their own nobility or virtue, but by God's righteousness and reconciliation.[16] In other words, the church in time is constituted by the Eucharist, by the self-giving presence of God in Christ and the procession of motley pilgrims to the table.

The communion of saints sustains the biblical history of journey and gathering and, like Scripture, does so amid the trial and error of social life. As set in time and place, the saint's shrine is unavoidably a site where issues of order and power are posed and rearranged. The holy places, near the bones of the dead, are at first in cemetery zones outside the city. As the West is Christianized (in the fourth century and Constantine's reign), the holy sites begin to redraw "almost every community's internal boundaries."[17] Holy places redraw the contours of the city. "By the early fifth century, the old [pagan] trajectories of urban topography and civic identity were being pulled out of orbit by the gravity of the new stars being elevated by popular acclaim as well as episcopal patronage."[18] The shrines of the saints will be an environment for the gathering of pilgrims to the feast, to benefaction, devotion, and economic activity. Power and patronage are given a "gentle reverse side" where "justice, mercy, and a sense of solidarity might spring."[19]

The cult of the saints plays an important role in giving shape to Christendom. The saints are part of a network of social functions and relations: a hierarchical social order permeated with a sense of biblical origins, relations of solace in the face of unavoidable suffering (the shared suffering of the saint), and guides for passage into a new life among the saints and friends of God.[20] The relics of the saints mark the coming redemption of our bodies and the continuity of our passage from this life to the next.[21] The saints become part of the structure of the city, as their relics are trans-

16. Augustine, The City of God, trans. Marcus Dods (New York: Modern Library, 2000), book 19.

17. Dennis Trout, "Saints, Identity, and the City," in Late Ancient Christianity: A People's History of Christianity, vol. 2, ed. Virginia Burrus (Minneapolis: Fortress, 2005), 167.

18. Trout, "Saints, Identity," 167-68.

19. Peter Brown, The Cult of the Saints: Its Rise and Function in Latin Christianity (Chicago: University of Chicago Press, 1981), 126-27.

20. Trout, "Saints, Identity," 184-85.

21. Caroline Walker Bynum, "Bodily Miracles and the Resurrection of the Body in the High Middle Ages," in Belief in History, ed. Thomas Kselman (Notre Dame, Ind.: University of Notre Dame Press, 1991), 68-106.

lated to the seats of bishops and as shrines become a legitimate source of power. The cult of the saints is vulnerable to abuse, as is any potent social practice, but it is also open to wide social participation. The saints and their shrines become media for the dispersion of wealth and privilege, for the setting aside of social divisions, and for the miracle of community. The pilgrimage to the shrine of a saint "takes people out of their established places, mixes social strata and the sexes, allows individuals to wander like vagabonds."[22] The modern categories of sacred and profane do not apply; the so-called "liminal" or threshold experience of the shrine is also opportunity for various kinds of ordinary forms of exchange.[23] The pilgrim is a role and status shared by all.

The saints, with relics and shrines as physical signs, are intertwined in social relations.[24] They are not "spiritualized" but share the fate of the body both physical and social. Relics and shrines are brought into the city, but also sustain a pathway out on the periphery and in the countryside. In other words, the saints in the Christianized world become not only part of the structure of things, but also a regular manner of finding an alternative space. Their memories and cults become media to express tensions and contradictions in the social order. They sustain the pilgrim character of a biblical people amid various stagnating elements of medieval society. The saints have taken the way of God and to God, and we have opportunity to draw near to them, to become a people that shares in divine life.

Although the cult of the saints becomes part of the medieval order of things, the saints' relationships to us are just as important in a modern world. If the cult of the saints coheres with the enchantments and otherworldly aspirations of premodern life, communion with the saints and their holy places continues to be important in our disenchanted world (or so-called disenchanted world). Consider a study by a team of anthropologists in the 1980s. Mary Lee Nolan and Sidney Nolan researched the activity in over 6,000 Christian pilgrimage sites in modern western Europe and estimated that these pilgrimage centers host between 60 and 70 mil-

22. Stephen Wilson, introduction to *Saints and Their Cults: Studies in Religious Sociology, Folklore, and History,* ed. Stephen Wilson (Cambridge: Cambridge University Press, 1983), 14.

23. Victor Turner is used by moderns to explain pilgrimage. See *Image and Pilgrimage in Christian Culture* (New York: Columbia University Press, 2011).

24. Bynum, "Bodily Miracles," 81. Bynum argues that the relic was not thought (among ordinary folk) to be the saint, who was believed to reside in heaven.

lion pilgrims every year.[25] The Nolans analyze the sites and the practices of the pilgrims in detail. For example, they indicate that often, but not always, modern sites distinguish religious activities from profane festivals and celebrations. However, this setting apart of the sacred rituals and practices may actually maintain and even heighten an ancient sense of the holy place — a place of power, conversion, patronage, and exchange. The saints offer benefaction. The pilgrims sustain the shrines economically and by spreading and telling the stories of the saints. To modern ears, the exchange of favors and devotions and the flow of euros might sound crude. The authors, however, conclude with what they present as an anthropological observation. A modern view that "strips the earth of sanctity and leaves us no place truly sacred during our earthly sojourn . . . [is perhaps] an unacceptable condition for ordinary humans."[26] It may be liberating to use money in a holy place.

The logic of the modern economy requires an independent sphere of the marketplace. The market is understood to be an impersonal set of mechanisms based on the premise that individual self-interest will order the common sphere of economic relationships.[27] Liberal economic theory hopes for a natural equilibrium and distribution of goods through continual growth that is spurred by impersonal market forces and self-interest.[28] To make this claim, theories of economic progress have to hide a contradiction. It is not that self-interest moves us in a common direction that we understand as good and rational. Rather, the theory is that self-interest moves individuals in different and competing directions, which ultimately form counterweights in the system. We participate in a whole by being against each other as individuals. The whole is ordered by fragmentation. Because the system requires rival and counterbalancing inter-

25. Mary Lee Nolan and Sidney Nolan, *Christian Pilgrimage in Modern Western Europe* (Chapel Hill: University of North Carolina Press, 1989), 1-10.

26. Nolan and Nolan, *Christian Pilgrimage*, 338.

27. Charles Taylor, *Modern Social Imaginaries* (Durham, N.C.: Duke University Press, 2004), 79; Nicholas Xenos, "Liberalism and the Postulate of Scarcity," *Political Theory* 15, no. 2 (May 1987): 226.

28. Nicholas Xenos shows the historical roots of the concepts of scarcity, unlimited desire, and choice in "Liberalism and the Postulate of Scarcity." These are also the basic principles in a contemporary textbook in economics. "Human wants are unlimited, but resources are not. Limited, or scarce, resources force individuals and societies to choose." Karl E. Case and Ray C. Fair, *Principles of Economics* (Upper Saddle River, N.J.: Prentice-Hall, 2002), 25.

ests, self-interest is rational precisely because it is not a common interest or end.[29] No one takes interest in the whole.

The science of commerce begins with the problem of scarcity in relationship to unlimited desire. As the market economy develops further and further, there seems to be no end to desire or limit to what might become a commodity. One rational interest must compete with another. Because desire is considered unlimited, progress means that new places and spheres of relations, new and expanding markets, will have to be rationalized in the same way. This conception of market rationality leaves us, the beneficiaries of progress, in an ambivalent but comfortable position.[30] We are likely to have misgivings about our own materialism, misplaced priorities, the ruin of the environment, or the degeneration of social trust.[31] Regardless, it is assumed that we cannot help it. We human beings are naturally bound to growth through the market. The social trust and common purposes required to overcome the mechanisms of the market have been systematically excluded.

Among the multitude of saints and holy ways of life, a persistent theme cuts across modern progress. It is the desire to share suffering, to go to the lowest place with Christ and the least of our brothers and sisters (Matt. 25:40). Padre Pio is representative in this regard. His excessive desire to share Christ's suffering in the world forms a destination of pilgrims and a communion of intercession and healing. The signs of his desire — his tireless commitment to the confessional, his stigmata, and the building of a hospital — have established a shared place. Modern progress, as ceaseless change, sets up an antagonism between the passage of time and the continuity of a place. The cult of the saints, in contrast, is the establishment of the holy place through time. The communion of saints does not form a utopia. Utopia in its religious mode requires perfection and a view from the end of time, and in its secular sense, it attempts to transcend suffering and disability through technological means. A history of saint-

29. The judgment that rationality coheres with a narrow view of individual self-interest is so ingrained in much of social science that it is not necessary to argue for it. From this assumption practical rationality can be managed mathematically. See Paul Weirich, *Equilibrium and Rationality* (Cambridge: Cambridge University Press, 1998).

30. Xenos, "Liberalism and the Postulate," 232-33, notes a similar ambivalence of David Hume and Adam Smith.

31. See "The House Divided," the new introduction in Robert Bellah et al., *Habits of the Heart*, updated ed. (Berkeley: University of California Press, 1996), vii-xxxix.

hood, in these terms, is antiutopian. The history of sainthood is not a story of progress. If utopia represents the high point of history, the saint goes low. She may communicate eccentric visions and otherworldly delight, but the presence of God and the vision of life are shared, typically, by way of suffering and poverty, alienation and anguish. The depth of our humanity comes to us by way of the cross.[32]

The end of sharing and imitation — this-worldly suffering and otherworldly delight — gives the communion of saints a typological and sacramental (rather than progressive) history. The narration of modern Christian history tends to either attach faith to the modern story of progress or see progress as the fall from a primitive, biblical ideal.[33] Progressive Christianity attempts to rationalize faith and disentangle the human being from intimate but retrograde social bonds. Disinterest and detachment begin to characterize true Christian love.[34] This argument for the priority of disinterested love accords with a view that God's work in the market is done by individuals and through disinterested economic relations.[35] Primitive religion, in contrast, assumes a conception of history shared by the fundamentalist and the skeptic. We are separated from the biblical world and need to return to it by force of will (the fundamentalist) or leave it behind by force of the intellect (the secular skeptic). In contrast to linear progress or decline, the lives of the saints move vertically from the surface to the depths. At times our lives are dominated by the desires of the surface, like the desire to be free of human frailties and limitations. But often the depth of meaning in human history comes to the surface in the saints — the extraordinary image points to our alienation and our destiny of sharing in divine life and communion with neighbors.

As a constant and excessive critic of progress, Ivan Illich offers a challenge to the modern *homo economicus* and the reign of utility. He gives us a

---

32. Ivan Illich, "The Institutional Construction of a New Fetish: Human Life," in Ivan Illich, *In the Mirror of the Past: Lectures and Addresses, 1978-1990* (New York: Marion Boyars, 1992), 225.

33. Richard J. Callahan Jr., Kathryn Lofton, and Chad E. Seales, "Allegories of Progress: Industrial Religion in the United States," *Journal of the American Academy of Religion* 78, no. 1 (March 2010): 1-39.

34. See the definition of love given by Anders Nygren in *Agape and Eros: The Christian Idea of Love* (Chicago: University of Chicago Press, 1982).

35. Jacob Viner, *The Role of Providence in the Social Order* (Princeton: Princeton University Press, 1972), 80-85.

suitable orientation to pilgrimage and progress as lived through the saints. Illich, it seems safe to wager, will never be declared a saint even in a popular sense. But his life does reflect the eccentric pattern and passion of the communion of saints. He is a prophet in the biblical sense. He cannot help but speak against the achievements of a godless age and puts the incarnate word of God at the center of history. He is silenced for a time by the church, and he is ridiculed by secular liberals and conservatives.[36] Illich's orientation to modern progress is shaped by his life with poor and so-called undeveloped peoples, by his faith in the incarnation of God in Jesus Christ, and, as a medieval historian, by the bodily contact that is characteristic of the cult of the saints — by contact with the relic and by the smell, touch, and warm breath (the conspiracy) of the somatic gift.[37]

Throughout Illich's work, there is a stark contrast between socioeconomic management and bodily intimacy, between technical conceptions and "vernacular" life, between the rule of experts and the relationship of persons.[38] He contrasts the smell of the traditional city with an ideal new to the modern era — the Enlightenment's "utopia of the odorless city" and its "avant-garde of deodorizers."[39] Odors from the shallow graves of the dead and from human waste have been replaced by the smell of industrial pollution and the automobile. The contrast is extreme, but undeniable. We deodorize ourselves so that we smell like manufactured soaps and perfumes. Yet, the amount of machinery, energy, and waste required to keep the city in operation fills the city with smog and the outlying land with trash and garbage. Much of our trash will pollute because it cannot properly decompose. It doesn't properly stink. According to Illich, economic progress, technological solutions, and social management are now as much problems as they are solutions.

Illich is not against comfort and progress per se. Rather, he sees the standard and limit of technological and industrial advances to be convivi-

---

36. See David Cayley's introduction in *Ivan Illich in Conversation* (Concord, Ontario: House of Anansi Press, 1992), 1-58.

37. Ivan Illich, *The Rivers North of the Future: The Testament of Ivan Illich as Told to David Cayley*, ed. David Cayley (Toronto: House of Anansi Press, 2005), 47-70, 205-19; "The Cultivation of Conspiracy," in *The Challenges of Ivan Illich*, ed. Lee Hoinacki and Carl Mitcham (Albany: SUNY Press, 2002), 233-42.

38. Ivan Illich, *The Church, Change, and Social Development* (New York: Herder and Herder, 1970), 17-22.

39. Ivan Illich, "H2O and the Waters of Forgetfulness," in *In the Mirror of the Past*, 145-58.

ality — hospitality, interdependence, and freedom. He is not against free economic exchange, but against economic ideologies, capitalism or socialism, which set out to define the human being. The ideology of the so-called free market is the view that the market ought to be free from prior and imposed standards of human goods and needs. The market is supposed to establish needs. In contrast, Illich argues that the measure of progress is whether or not technology is directed toward the good of persons and whether or not economic life increases opportunities for noneconomic endeavors (e.g., avocations and play), enhances personal intercourse, and satisfies desires (rather than producing unlimited economic desires).[40]

In industry, medicine, transportation, and communications technology, he shows that progress does provide great social benefits, but that it hits a saturation point. Technological progress passes through a stage of clear benefit to a point where the human and environmental costs of advancement are far greater than what is gained. He points out that technological progress has become a conceptual good, so that scientific or industrial benefits of an earlier age (in transportation or communications, for example) are used as evidence that technological progress is always the answer. He notes, in 1973, that "it has become fashionable to say that where science and technology have created problems, it is only more scientific understanding and better technology that can carry us past them. The cure for bad management is more management.... [T]he cure for polluted rivers is more costly nonpolluting detergents.... [T]he attempt to overwhelm present problems by the production of more science is the ultimate attempt to solve a crisis by escalation."[41]

One reason for the intensity of Illich's analysis is that he hopes to gain a perspective on our "practical certainties" and the "radical otherness of our twentieth-century mental topology."[42] In this regard, the medieval world and the lives of the modern poor serve as vantage points from which to see who we have become. Illich looks to the past as a way to see a better future. He looks to the lives of the so-called underdeveloped peoples to find examples that might guide first-world development. Illich is critical of economic progress and technological progress because both

40. Illich, *Tools for Conviviality* (New York: Harper and Row, 1973), 10-14.
41. Illich, *Tools for Conviviality*, 8-9.
42. Illich, introduction to *In the Mirror of the Past*, 9-10.

have increased the need to manage people, to limit their freedom and interdependence, and to create in them the identity of the consumer.[43] The technological structure of modern life limits our options. Automobiles, for example, promise greater freedom, but we have created a way of life that is unimaginable without the car. "Man has developed the frustrating power to demand anything because he cannot visualize anything which an institution cannot do for him. Surrounded by all-powerful tools, man is reduced to a tool of his tools.... The blackout of reality in the smog produced by our tools has enveloped us. Quite suddenly we find ourselves in the darkness of our own trap."[44] Other reasons for Illich's harsh perspective on progress, it seems to me, are simply a profound sense of being uprooted and a powerful desire for home. He expresses a profound faith in the incarnation and the personal, bodily self-giving that it lets loose in the world.[45] The incarnation produces a kind of uprootedness — a radical call to community in God and beyond establishes boundaries of human separation. Illich's faith in the incarnation produces a deep sense of alienation; wandering pain and passion are evident in his words.[46]

There is a clear parallel between Jean Vanier's establishment of L'Arche communities and Illich's concerns for "the experience of life" over utility and for human relationships over social management. In contrast to the medical triumph over disease, Illich dares to speak of the art of suffering, to challenge the pathology of institutionalizing illness, and to discourage making an enemy of disease.[47] Likewise, L'Arche takes the dis-

43. These are persistent themes in Ivan Illich, Deschooling Society (New York: Harper and Row, 1971), Medical Nemesis (New York: Random House, 1976), and Tools for Conviviality. For contemporary accounts that show the relationship between the free market and social management, see Juliet Schor's discussion of the management of time required for the emergence of industrial production in The Overworked American (New York: Basic Books, 1993). Also, Michael Perelman's study, The Invention of Capitalism: Classical Political Economy and the Secret History of Primitive Accumulation (Durham, N.C.: Duke University Press, 2000), shows that so-called laissez-faire policies and the growth of nineteenth-century industry required the management of labor, to force peasants from a subsistence, but self-sufficient, economy to wage earning in industrial production.

44. Illich, Deschooling Society, 109.

45. Illich, Rivers North, 207. Also see Lee Hoinacki, "The Trajectory of Ivan Illich," Bulletin of Science, Technology, and Society 23, no. 5 (2003).

46. See Illich, "Silence Is a Commons" and "Dwelling," in In the Mirror of the Past, 47-64.

47. Illich, "Twelve Years after Medical Nemesis: A Plea for Body History," in In the Mirror of the Past, 211-17. Illich suffered for a decade with a tumor in his face, which "he chose to treat

abled out of institutions and professional care so that they might share an ordinary home life with ordinary people. Illich and Vanier share a conception of common life and bodily presence — based in belonging, hospitality, touch, the smell of food cooking, but also the odor of sweat and feces, the slow pace of time, the rhythms of housework and bodily care, human (as opposed to technological) resources, fasting, the feast, and celebration. L'Arche communities, Vanier hopes, "are signs that it is possible to live on a human scale, even in the present world."[48]

For Illich, the incarnation establishes the possibility and the completion of human history as radical, personal communion, "free, and therefore vulnerable and fragile, but always capable of healing."[49] It is not an end found at the conclusion of a linear progression, and it is not the endless desire of progress. However, it is instantiated in time, specifically in the unbearable intimacy of the Eucharist where "the fellow conspirators" share union with the Spirit and, by eating, are transformed into a "we" that "is somebody's 'I' . . . the 'I' of the Incarnate Word."[50] This conception of history is metaphysical. It moves from surface to depth, and from depth to higher life. In Illich's analysis of progress we can see that modern development is often a flight from the depth of existence. It is a flight from the fragilities of our bodies, the personal exposure of intimacy, and risks of human community. All these have to be managed and buffered through technological media. The lives of the saints respond to the same human anxieties, but in an entirely different way. The excessive desire and alienation of the saints, as well as their openness and bodily conveyance of the extraordinary, are responses to the incarnation and expressions of its depth in human life. Sainthood forms a history of embodied representations (types) of God's relationship to the world in Christ.

In a lecture titled "Hospitality and Pain," Illich tells a short history of compassion.[51] He examines experiences of pity, compassion, and pain in terms of what the incarnation gives to human history and the evil that is

---

as a difficult friend rather than an enemy." Carl Mitcham, "In Memoriam Ivan Illich: Critic of Professional Design," *Design Issues* 9, no. 4 (Autumn 2003): 26.

48. Jean Vanier, *Community and Growth*, rev. ed. (Mahwah, N.J.: Paulist, 1989), 310.

49. Illich, *Rivers North*, 54.

50. Illich, "The Cultivation of Conspiracy," in *The Challenges of Ivan Illich*, 240.

51. Ivan Illich, "Hospitality and Pain," lecture at McCormick Theological Seminary (Chicago 1987), 1-17; http://www.davidtinapple.com/illich/1987_hospitality_and_pain.PDF.

opened up through its perversion.[52] He tells the story of hospitality in the West and the creation of the hospital as a social institution. The effects of the hospital are ambiguous: it uproots hospitality from the home but also gives new status to the poor and the sick of the city. Institutions of care (hostel and hospital) develop through "successive generations . . . who believe that God in his mercy wanted to be compassionate with us."[53] In the twelfth century, for example, lepers (including those with Hansen's disease and other maladies of the skin) were no longer set apart in a community of nonpersons, but were welcomed into a fraternity of care.[54] In the modern world, however, the same desire to manage and relieve pain develops into the reign of technique, where professional management and technology "invade" the human condition and come to define it. With the integration of suffering into the dignity of human life, Illich sees two possibilities beginning to emerge. On one hand, there are possibilities for deeper human intimacy and sharing suffering. On the other, there are new opportunities for a technological disassociation of suffering from common life and its management by experts.

Illich's historical narrative culminates in the emergence, at the beginning of the modern era, of a new conception of the self: personal individuality. Referring to social and theological changes beginning in the twelfth century, Illich holds that "the new separateness of the *I* from the *we* provides these first modern Europeans with a new kind of skin in which experience can be embodied in a new way."[55] On one hand, he has in mind Francis of Assisi's stigmata, Elizabeth von Schoenau's visions of Christ's passion, and Angela of Foligno's burning tears. "Compassion *with* Christ, for these late medieval mystics, is faith so strong and so deeply incarnate that it leads to the individual embodiment of the contemplated pain."[56]

---

52. "My subject is a mystery of faith, a mystery whose depth of evil could not have come to be without a corresponding and contrary height in the history of salvation. . . . I want to speak about the cross, about the crucifix in history. I shall describe how this cross was transmogrified from a memorial to the bloodiness of God's Incarnation — and thus a guiding image of the consequences for each of the faithful — into a symbol for the myriad evils that western society's organization and technology seek to eliminate." Illich, "Hospitality and Pain," 2.

53. Illich, "Hospitality and Pain," 17.

54. Illich, "Hospitality and Pain," 13.

55. Illich, "Hospitality and Pain," 16.

56. Illich, "Hospitality and Pain," 16.

On the other hand, Illich is thinking of a whole host of ways the modern self comes to be managed, shaped, and fragmented for the sake of mastering the self. His historical example is the flip side of the medieval saint's compassion; it is the inception of inquisitorial torture that "seeks to destroy the world of the victim, and to objectify this destruction in confession."[57] Illich quickly moves from the thirteenth century to the twentieth, referring to George Orwell's 1984, "when he [Orwell] makes the betrayal of love the necessary condition for the extinction of self." Illich adds that "the confession at which torture aims is the act of recognition that the tools of the state have created a new reality that the individual must be conformed with to find him- or herself."[58] This shift to the totalitarian tendencies of the modern state is uncharacteristic of Illich, whose work emphasizes the radical monopoly of technology and the social sciences. Technological monopoly is "radical" because it not only markets but also defines and controls the structure of life and death. In each case, state or technological expertise, Illich is concerned with modern forms of the control and management of the self.

Along with this history of control, Illich tells a short history of the suffering saint. He begins with martyrdom in the first centuries of Christianity. "Martyrdom became the visible horizon within which a new kind of this-worldly existence was lived. Baptism meant leaving the fleshpots of Egypt for the intensely experienced presence of the desert.... On the skyline rose the cross."[59] Illich follows the standard history of martyrs and saints: he indicates that, after Constantine and the Christianization of the empire, the way of the cross is sustained through monastic asceticism, through the mortification of the flesh and forbearance amid the spiritual trials of the world. At this point of redefined martyrdom, Illich picks up his narrative of compassion. Illich highlights Hildegard of Bingen's vision of water and blood "spurting from the heart into the chalice held by the *Ecclesia*, figured as a woman standing next to the Crucified."[60] For Hildegard, Illich notes, the body of Christ is central to redemption. Hildegard's signitive style soon gives way, in later generations, to "the realistic representation of a tortured man." The pain of the world begins to be

---

57. Illich, "Hospitality and Pain," 16-17.
58. Illich, "Hospitality and Pain," 17.
59. Illich, "Hospitality and Pain," 14.
60. Illich, "Hospitality and Pain," 15.

seen in Christ's body. Among the saints, the way of the cross will be felt and followed, not in martyrdom, but in prayer and in relationship to the neighbor. The way of the cross becomes an intimacy and personal identification with Christ in sharing the suffering and healing of the world.

At this nexus of suffering and redemption, we find Padre Pio. The stigmata, real and figurative, are at the core of his identity. His hope for sharing the sufferings of Christ might seem simple and maudlin; but there is a complexity that comes from the intimacy of sharing life with another, sharing both joys and burdens. The simplicity of St. Pio's piety is produced, not by a desire to suffer for the sake of suffering, but through a straightforward and steady desire for friendship. The beloved is the suffering God. Padre Pio simply desires to share the burdens and delights of Christ's love for the world.[61] He describes his desire for intimacy with God in letters to his spiritual director. "It is all summed up in this: I am devoured by the love of God and by the love of my neighbor. For me God is ever fixed in my mind and imprinted on my heart. I never lose sight of Him. I have to admire His beauty, His smiles, and His agitation, His mercy, His retribution or, rather, the rigor of His Justice."[62] When a desire is that simple, life becomes both quiet and deep. An "ever-active volcano," Pio explains, has been poured into his very small heart.

Illich's description of the suffering saints applies to Pio. Padre Pio desires to share compassion *with* Christ, and his body becomes a site of this union. He is marked by the stigmata in 1918, during the final months of World War I and amid the Spanish flu epidemic. The epidemic is estimated to have killed at least 50 million people worldwide.[63] It is also important that he stayed in San Giovanni Rotondo; the town became a place of pilgrimage as early as 1919. It became a place of confession, prayer, and medical care (the hospital opened in 1956).[64] In this regard, reports of the saint's bilocation have a dual effect. They show the intensity and importance of his bodily presence to others and how practically bound he is to the friary in San Giovanni. He is bound to a place. Among the bodily wonders, his greatest miracle is recognized as the funding and building of the hospital, Casa Sollievo della Sofferenza. The signs of Pio's body and the economy

61. Pio, *Secrets of a Soul*, 44.
62. Pio, *Secrets of a Soul*, 192.
63. John M. Barry, *The Great Influenza* (New York: Penguin, 2005).
64. McKevitt, "San Giovanni Rotondo," 81.

and hospital of San Giovanni are marked by controversy from within and without, and it is undoubtedly clear that judgments about his sanctity will be made according to how one views the signs of communion on his body and the spiritual and corporeal unity of the place.

In his study of social life and the economy of the town, Christopher McKevitt divides the inhabitants of San Giovanni Rotondo into three groups: (1) pilgrims, (2) resident devotees who settle there to be near Padre Pio, and (3) longtime residents of San Giovanni. He notes clear divisions between these groups. The pilgrims experience San Giovanni as liminal time and place. They are on retreat. They are drawn out of their ordinary lives into a prayerful place, and they expect to see things differently, to find meaning and purpose, to experience God's presence, and to return to their ordinary lives anew. McKevitt notes that members of the second group seek to relocate their lives from secular places to San Giovanni as a sacred place. The liminal becomes the ordinary. "The pilgrim journeys from the outside to a place regarded as sacred by virtue of the holy person who lived and died there and whose spirit is felt to be still present in the place."[65] The resident devotees are pilgrims who settle. They are most often unmarried women who attempt to sustain "the ritual time and space of the pilgrim" and sustain their lives by means of the shrine, managing "to live on pensions or private incomes, however small, or to work for the friars or the Casa Sollievo in the promotion of Pio, or they might run boarding houses."[66] They see their real work as sharing Padre Pio's life of prayer and healing.

The traditional residents of the town consider themselves outsiders to the religious activities of the pilgrims and resident devotees. They experience their hometown as ordinary and secular. They see Padre Pio as a holy man, but they are more likely than the other groups to point to the benefit of the holy man's worldly transformations of the town. "[Padre Pio] founded the hospital because he saw their need. He also established nursery schools and schools for handicapped, and started workers' cooperatives. He spoke on their behalf to people of power. . . . Pio remains for them a man who entered *their* historical time and space and acted upon these to transform them."[67] They have received great benefit from the hos-

---

65. McKevitt, "San Giovanni Rotondo," 92.
66. McKevitt, "San Giovanni Rotondo," 93.
67. McKevitt, "San Giovanni Rotondo," 92.

pital and shrine, but they are not on the inside of the town's religious, economic, and administrative institutions. Outsiders are at the center of the shrine and hospital. Most of the town's people lay stress on the very human role Pio has had in relation to the town. They live in an ordinary world that has been touched by the attraction of the sacred.

San Giovanni is certainly not a place of seamless social harmony. But its divisions are about where and how God's love and presence meet with our world. Its conflicts represent the desires and struggles of pilgrimage. People establish places with a vertical as well as a horizontal topography. Life is mapped out not only on the surface, but also by the depth of suffering and the elevation of communion with God. This is how we tell the history of the saints.

Eight

History

—ᚙᚙ—

The historical event "is more similar to the miracle than to the natural event."[1] In contrast to the natural event, the historical event — as a happening in the passing of time — is contingent and unrepeatable, and it can be understood as an event because it can mean something for people. Possibilities of what something can mean are the environment for historical facts. The historical event or person has meaning for how we (e.g., American or Mexican or Christian or secularist) understand the course of things. When a scientist refers to a natural event, the agent of the event is law, such as laws of physics, physiology, or evolution. For instance, the flora of a region might be unique, but they are created by laws of adaptation. Natural selection is "a powerful molding force" that takes chance events and makes them conform to necessity.[2] In contrast, the historical event is constituted in time by relations that could be different, by the agents of the events, and by those who scrutinize the data and tell the story about the agents. Like the miracle, the historical fact is linked to life through human meaning rather than mechanisms.

History depends upon relationships across time, through connections that are sometimes explicit but usually tacit and part of the common ground of historians and readers. If history were a science, it would be like quantum physics: disciplined examinations of the smallest details and facts reveal that the course of things is indeterminate, so that to be an

1. Ewa Domanska, "A Conversation with Hayden White," *Rethinking History* 12, no. 1 (March 2008): 3-21, 4.
2. Jerry A. Coyne, *Why Evolution Is True* (New York: Viking Press, 2009), 119.

event *in* or an object *of* history, facts must be already in a context of representation, that is, as facts they are already "under a description" and within meaningful contexts of language and representation.[3] The telling of history connects events without natural necessity. The historical event is like a miracle, not because divine cause replaces material causes, but because events are conveyed by persons rather than by disinterested law. We witness and record historical data; we find them in the past; we bring them to light in the present.

The key issue for understanding the saints in history is how we understand the parts (events, artifacts, people, places) in relationship to the course of history, that is, the particulars in place and time in terms of a conception of the whole across place and time.[4] A conception of the whole — whether tacit or explicit — assumes the centrality of certain kinds of social agents (e.g., rulers, workers, or nations). It is important that the social center provides a means to understand the place and future of outliers (barbarians, peasants, foreigners). Empires define civilization. In Marxism, the industrial worker defines the place of the agrarian peasant. The narrative of global progress sets the terms for telling the history (the potential or impotence) of underdeveloped peoples (i.e., who will history leave behind?). The historical survey offers ways to understand the central features of what is happening in the world, as well as the integration and exclusion of things on the edges.

Likewise, the main question, for this chapter, is about the relationship of the lives of saints to a social and historical whole. The lives of the saints are full of contingencies that offer an orientation to life as a whole — to communion with God and neighbor — to the unity of human beings. The *lives* embody our desires to have a meaningful place in time — for the edges and outliers (our ordinary lives) to find the center in the community of saints. The communion of saints is not a progressive movement in history, but it is connected to "the fullness of time." The lives of the saints have a history; hagiography varies according to time and place. But in these different times, the saints embody connections with a common future that makes its way, time and again, into the pres-

3. Hayden White refers to "events under description" as understood by Arthur C. Danto, *Narration and Knowledge* (New York: Columbia University Press, 1985).

4. This task of putting part to whole is a central theme of Hayden White's *Metahistory: The Historical Imagination in Nineteenth-Century Europe* (Baltimore: Johns Hopkins University Press, 1973).

ent. The communion of saints is a diffusion of instantiations, in time, of the kingdom of God.

In the saints, the particular is joined to the whole, not by historical proximity (one age following the next as in a progressive narrative), but by analogy, specifically by typology.[5] In the lives of the saints, the presence of the whole of life in time comes to us through the media of "types." Typology is metaphor with an embodied, relational telos. Metaphor is used, here, not in merely a grammatical sense, but in terms of intersecting fields of meaning where two subjects stand on their own, "infant" and "linebacker," and yet one is spoken of "in terms that are suggestive of another."[6] She is a little linebacker. The metaphor works when the stout two-year-old and Ray Lewis of the Baltimore Ravens have their own histories and fields of agency. Typology, in relation to the saints, is not a classification of "types," for instance, of confessors or prophets or saints as persons with specific moral qualities.[7] Rather, typology enacts an intersection of agents and their distinct locations. People in time join persons of another time; hagiographic typology is metaphor with a relational goal and purpose; its telos is communion. Our little Abigail (so many years ago) was called a linebacker, but the metaphor did not imply friendship between her and Ray Lewis. With saints as types, the possibility of "knowing one person in terms suggestive of another" is carried by the possibility that the "one person" is in communion with "the other." A communion is implied when we speak of God in Christ and the saints. In effect, history can be told through the saints because the "intersecting semantic fields" are part of real social relations in the communion of saints. One time is connected to another insofar as each is in communion with Christ.

Typology is liable to the accusation that it disregards the historical particular — for example, that it bypasses the meaning of words and deeds of the Hebrew patriarchs and prophets in their own time for the sake of some other time (the life of Jesus) or no time at all (ahistorical doctrine). Although this accusation holds true for many traditional uses of typology, it need not be true and, in the lives of the saints, it usually is not

5. This analysis of typology as a trope is inspired by Hayden White, *Tropics of Discourse: Essays in Cultural Criticism* (Baltimore: Johns Hopkins University Press, 1978).

6. Janet Martin Soskice, *Metaphor and Religious Language* (Oxford: Clarendon, 1985), 23.

7. Catherine Brown Tkacz, *The Key to the Brescia Casket: Typology and the Early Christian Imagination* (Notre Dame, Ind.: University of Notre Dame Press, 2002), 52.

the case. Typology need not diminish the particular historical event; on the contrary, the historical particulars and the unrepeatable elements of the "types" (the saints) are likely to be highlighted for reasons that any distinctive historical events will be highlighted — to show the signs of the times.[8] For example, Franz Jägerstätter's resistance to the Nazis ends in martyrdom, and his witness is analogous to a long line of martyrs, but the historical specificity of his martyrdom tells us also about the struggles of the Austrians under Nazi occupation and specifically about Jägerstätter's struggles and his unique life. Jägerstätter is a solitary witness.[9] Yet, he is a type. Being "in Christ" in life and death gives more significance to his particular history rather than less. Jägerstätter is not mentioned in a history of modern Austria.[10] But he stands out in the history of the church because he stands with Christ.

In her study of early Christian typology, Catherine Brown Tkacz notes that "quite early the Christians found a new role for typology."[11] The received use was to understand "focal past events . . . [as] predictive of future events in salvation history. . . . Typology was used by rabbinic exegetes as they considered how the Hebrew Bible forecast what the Messiah would be like and what his coming would bring about."[12] This mode of interpretation is prominent in the New Testament and the early church, as a means to "demonstrate that Jesus was the Christ, the fulfillment of the prophecies about the Messiah."[13] Tkacz cites examples: Romans 5:14 where Paul calls Adam a type of Christ and the Letter to the Hebrews where Moses, the priesthood, Melchizedek, and the sacrifices and faith of the patriarchs all point to fulfillment in Christ. Along with this interpretation of the pre-Christian past, typology was also used to understand the present. This use of typology, specifically in reference to the saints, joined the Christian to Christ. "The Christian was to imitate Christ, to live so to

8. Hans Urs von Balthasar, *The Glory of the Lord: A Theological Aesthetics,* vol. 6, *Theology: The Old Covenant* (San Francisco: Ignatius, 1991), 402.

9. Gordon Zahn, *In Solitary Witness: The Life and Death of Franz Jägerstätter* (New York: Holt, Rinehart and Winston, 1965).

10. Barbara Jelavich, *Modern Austria: Empire and Republic, 1815-1986* (New York: Cambridge University Press, 1987).

11. Tkacz, *The Key,* 56.

12. Tkacz, *The Key,* 53.

13. Tkacz, *The Key,* 53.

recreate the events of salvation history." This form of typology was used "to recognize God's actions among men."[14]

In the lives of the saints, the terms "type" and "typology" are not used. But a typological means of connecting historical events and persons to Christ is clear. Countless examples can be cited.[15] Certainly, ancient martyrs like Stephen (Acts 6:8–8:2) and Polycarp (ca. 155) are types in this sense of the typological recurrence of Christ's self-giving and reconciling death. Modern martyrs like Maximilian Kolbe (d. 1941) and Edith Stein (d. 1942) enact this "presence" as well. Kolbe takes the place of a condemned man at Auschwitz. He dies so that another might live. Edith Stein also dies in Auschwitz, but the meaning of her death and its typological connections are contested. Is she executed as a Jew? Or does she suffer in relationship to Christ? It seems that she would say "yes" to both, redoubling rather than resisting a typological understanding of her death.[16] Who she is in life and death is defined by intersections of identity and communion in God.

The typological connections among the saints are not merely repetitions. It was true with Franz Jägerstätter, and now with Stein: the unrepeatable elements of their lives are of equal importance to the repetitions of embodiment of life in Christ. It matters for Edith Stein and for us that she is executed by the Nazis as a Jew. She calls us to account for our anti-Semitic history rather than to ignore it. Additional examples are numerous, but allow the theme of the unrepeatable type to stand with a final illustration. Catherine of Siena (1347-80) is a singular figure who rejects the two social options available to her, marriage and the convent. She makes her own way as a recluse and then as a servant of the poor. She inserts herself in political and spiritual gaps created by papal mismanagement in Italy and the church. She is a unique historical figure. As singular, she is also a bridge across time in union with Christ. "That which she was to her disciples — teacher, mother, friend, counselor — Jesus was to her. . . . Her fol-

14. Tkacz, The Key, 56.

15. David Matzko McCarthy, "The Gospels Embodied: The Lives of the Saints and Martyrs," in The Cambridge Companion to the Gospels, ed. Stephen C. Barton (Cambridge: Cambridge University Press, 2006), 224-44.

16. Boniface Hanley, O.F.M., No Strangers to Violence, No Strangers to Love (Notre Dame, Ind.: Ave Maria Press, 1983), 55-60; Edith Stein, The Science of the Cross: A Study of St. John of the Cross, ed. Lucy Gelber and Romaeus Leuven, O.C.D., trans. Hilda Graef (Chicago: Henry Regnery, 1960).

lowers fed upon her wisdom, warmed themselves at her love; they lived in her as in a living host offered for the love of men."[17] She is singular in history precisely because, like others, she is a type of Christ.

Hagiographic typology is anachronistic; that is, persons and events appear in the present from a different place and time — usually joining past and future in the fullness of time. We tend to think about history as a time line. In our modern political and cultural imagination, history is either an ascending or descending line (a rise or fall). Hagiography, in contrast, is not linear; it does not imagine links in time in a linear progression of past to future. It is future-oriented without progress. From the point of view of progress, the histories of the saints will appear to be repetitions of the past — pious patterns that go nowhere. For this reason, the lives of the saints also might be confused with a cyclical view of history. But rather than a straight line or turning wheel or historical dialectic, the history of saints has triangular shape. It is a ceaseless triangulation of one time and place joined to others through divine life. Events and people in time are linked with each other, not immediately, but through their common end in God, who is ever-in-the-present. Or, to triangulate in a different way, our future — the reign of God — has come to us in time in Jesus Christ, and he will come again, and we see, through the saints, in various times and places in between, that the future is also now.

In Christ, the whole of history comes to us "in the fullness of time"; that is, the end to which we are drawn "is an advent, that which 'comes' of its own accord."[18] "[The future] is not an evolutionary derivative or a technological goal toward which we march in well mapped stages. We have to deal with it as something that outbids all plans and normative development, something in fact which, while making such foresight possible, always makes it questionable and provisional. The future . . . is not amenable to man's power."[19] Because the coherence of the whole of history comes to us as advent, human history and its "power," as it were, are hardly diminished. On the contrary, the significance of human agency in specific times and places, when freed from managing the outcomes of the whole, takes on greater importance. Although this point may appear to be incon-

17. Igino Giordani, *Catherine of Siena: Fire and Blood*, trans. Thomas J. Tobin (Milwaukee: Bruce Publishing, 1959), 111.

18. Adolf Darlap, "Time," in *Sacramentum Mundi*, vol. 6, ed. Karl Rahner et al. (New York: Herder and Herder, 1970), 260.

19. Darlap, "Time," 260.

gruous from the side of progress, the triangular nature of Christian time frees us for history in the particular, for the single life and its meaning for all time. Christ has died and risen, Christ will come again, and in between, God-with-us is embodied in time. Hagiography highlights the historical particular in terms of this always-present possibility of the future happening now, of the whole of life in God.

Several years ago I was set on the wrong historical road by my reading — perhaps my misreading — of Dorothy Day's *Loaves and Fishes*. In the second chapter she explains that Peter Maurin had taken upon himself the task of giving her a Catholic education, specifically a "Catholic outline of history." Peter believed that "one way to study history was to read the lives of the saints down the centuries."[20] I understood this approach to history in a linear sense (that is, Peter's "down the centuries") as a means to link time and to tie together the whole. After considerable study and frustration, I found that one could perhaps illuminate historical eras by studying the saints, but one could not see the coherence of history by simply connecting together the lives of the saints from one decade or century to the next.[21]

The lives of the saints, I discovered, are like the various kinds of chronicles written throughout the Middle Ages, for the most part, by monks.[22] The chronicles are compilations of events but not narratives that link events over time.[23] They are collections of annual records, but they do not provide the history of an age. Their orientation is local; the records read something like the memories that are passed around our kitchen table. "Remember that snowstorm last January when school was closed for a week? Yes, and in March, we went to Ireland." Consider, for example, the *Royal Frankish Annals* of the eighth and ninth centuries. One event, such as the resumption of war between the Franks and the Spaniards, is followed by another set of events, such as the activity of Italian pirates, and then another, such as excessive rain that creates unfavorable conditions for farm-

---

20. Dorothy Day, *Loaves and Fishes* (Maryknoll, N.Y.: Orbis, 1997), 12.

21. A good example of using the stories of saints to illuminate the ages is Joanne Turpin, *Women in Church History: 21 Stories for 21 Centuries* (Cincinnati: St. Anthony Messenger Press, 2007).

22. Ernst Breisach, *Historiography: Ancient, Medieval, and Modern*, 3rd ed. (Chicago: University of Chicago Press, 2007), 126-30, 144-52.

23. See Hayden White's analysis in "The Value of Narrativity in the Representation of Reality," *Critical Inquiry* 7, no. 1 (Autumn 1980): 5-27.

ing.[24] The impact of the events on us, rather than any wider social or political effects, is enough for the story to be told. God is the unifying agent of history, so that significant events are recorded without need for temporal connections. According to most modern historians, the medieval chronicles "lack the elements of reflection or analysis which would make them history."[25] Often, the chroniclers are unable "to distinguish between sacred and profane matters."[26] They "give only a bare outline of the world in which they live."[27]

These statements are true about medieval hagiography. Consider, for example, Gregory of Tours's *Life of the Fathers* (written in the sixth century) and the compilation of lives in Jacobus de Voragine's *Golden Legend*, which was written in the thirteenth century and was the most popular collection of saints' lives for hundreds of years. A key theme for both Gregory and Jacobus seems to be that events in the lives of the saints leave a lasting impression and can happen anytime and anywhere. The lives of the saints are timeless but always, possibly, near to us in our time and place. Gregory describes the lives of the fathers in the singular, *Life of the Fathers*. His accounts of saintly lives reveal their different gifts and characters, but all these represent "the one life in Christ."[28] One life simply follows another with little reference to the wider world in which the saints live. The theme that ties the lives into a whole is that the saints represent the real possibility of holiness in Gaul and among people that share our lives — our very relations (that is, Gregory's relations). The unifying context of *Life of the Fathers* is a common faith.

Likewise, in Jacobus de Voragine's *Golden Legend*, communion with and through the saints is woven into the narratives. The common faith is clearly institutional and conveyed by bishops and priests, the Eucharist, the veneration of saints, and the power of their relics. For example, St. Agatha (third century) is executed by a Roman consul, but she becomes the patroness of the very city that ejects her. A year after her death, a "mul-

24. Gregory of Tours, *The History of the Franks*, trans. Lewis Thorpe (New York: Viking Penguin, 1974), 107-8.

25. Arthur Marwick, *The Nature of History*, 3rd ed. (Chicago: Lyceum Books, 1989), 30.

26. Marwick, *The Nature of History*, 31.

27. *Carolingian Chronicles: Royal Frankish Annals and Nithard's Histories*, trans. Bernard Walter Scholz (Ann Arbor: University of Michigan Press, 1970), 8.

28. Edward James, introduction to *Life of the Fathers*, by Gregory of Tours (Liverpool: Liverpool University Press, 1991), xiii-xiv.

titude of pagans" gathers at her grave, tears the veil off her tomb, and spreads it out at the foot of an erupting volcano (Mt. Etna). The flow of lava is stopped; she saves her city of Catania from a river of fire.[29] She purifies and Christianizes the place. Likewise, the story of Mary Magdalene's life (whom Jacobus identifies as Mary the sister of Martha and Lazarus) focuses on places and experiences of communion. The lengthy account of her life includes her work in spreading the gospel (sent out by Peter), her death at the moment of receiving the Eucharist from the bishop of Aix, the translation of her bones to Burgundy in the eighth century, and several accounts of her work in that new time and place. To an eighth-century pilgrim from Flanders, she promises, "I shall not forsake thee until thou be reconciled with God."[30] In like manner, Jacobus, throughout the *Golden Legend,* seems to use anachronisms and a layering of place and time, not inadvertently, to bring all together in the communion of saints. One common anachronism is the premature Christianization of the Roman Empire. The people of Catania look to the Christian martyr Agatha to save their city at a time when Christianity is suppressed by the edict of Emperor Decius. Ancient Roman magistrates put Christian holy men and women to death, and at that moment, their courts are taken over by medieval bishops, who administer the Eucharist just before the martyr's death. The point: God's eucharistic communion and representatives of the faithful (saints and bishops) have no limits to their reach; all are under the reign of God in Christ.

The historical connections of hagiography are mediated by "the fullness of time" of God in Christ. This mediated (typological and triangular) unity corresponds to the remembrance and celebration of saints within a liturgical framework of time. The remembrance and veneration of martyrs, from the beginning, establish the annual feast of the saint's day. The liturgy sets a context for the triangular pattern of the communion of saints. Consider the feasts of March 1-4. St. David, the sixth-century monk, bishop, and patron of Wales, is followed by St. Agnes, the thirteenth-century Bohemian princess; St. Katharine Drexel, the twentieth-century American heiress; and St. Casimir, the fifteenth-century Polish prince. An ascetic abbot and bishop in Wales (March 1) is side by side with a medieval,

---

29. Jacobus de Voragine, *The Golden Legend,* trans. Granger Ryan and Helmut Ripperger (New York: Longmans, Green, and Co., 1941), 157-61.

30. Voragine, *The Golden Legend,* 355-64.

eastern European princess (March 2), who is canonized on the eve of the Czechoslovakian revolution in 1989. Katharine Drexel (March 3) is a Philadelphian who lives a long life distributing her wealth to the oppressed and poor (especially Native Americans and African Americans). She is side by side with a young Polish prince, destined to be king, but who seeks God's reign, not his own, and dies before he ascends to the throne. In historical time and place, these saints are diverse. But in God's communion, they belong together and call us to belong to them.

This belonging across time and place points to the main point of the chapter: to understand how specific histories are connected to a historical whole. The typological orientation of hagiography offers mediated connections; one time meets another in Christ. In this way, the lives of the saints appear to undermine our modern understanding of historical data and narratives. According to modern historical sensibilities, the data should tell the story.[31] In contrast, consider the participatory character of hagiographic realism in chapters 3 and 4. We become part of the saint's life. The lives of the saints do not tell themselves but are told in the context of sharing life across time. Hagiography does not fit a modern historical frame. However, hagiography of any given age does use parallel methods and standards by which historical documents and events are researched and analyzed. The fundamental difference is how the historical specifics are connected to a sense of history as a whole.

Historical forms of writing about the saints are comparable to the history of historical writing. For example, Gregory of Tours's *Life of the Fathers* fits with his *History of the Franks*.[32] *Life of the Fathers* reads like a chronicle in the sense that it appears to be distinct records of persons and events set side by side without historical connections. The connections are made through the life of holiness. *The History of the Franks* (although not a chronicle) has a similar character. For example, the greed and treachery of Berthegund, the daughter of a holy woman and abbess, are followed by a long discourse on the resurrection of the body given by Bishop Gregory to a wavering priest, which is followed by the death of a recalcitrant deacon of the bishop in Paris, which is followed by a vi-

31. White, "The Value of Narrativity," 8. He notes the "artificiality of the notion that *real* events could 'speak themselves.'" Arthur Marwick argues for this view, that the data tells the story, in *The Nature of History*.

32. Gregory of Tours, *The History of the Franks*, trans. Lewis Thorpe (New York: Penguin Books, 1974).

olent revolt and looting of a convent in Portiers.[33] On one page there is a miraculous cure of a toothache, and on the next, Tours is devastated by the plague.

Gregory organizes his history by means of key events. Book I includes creation, the flooding of the earth, the Israelites crossing the Red Sea out of Egypt, Christ's resurrection, and the death of St. Martin of Tours. Books 2–10 record events from the death of St. Martin to the completion of Gregory's writing of *The History*.[34] The historical periodization shows the similarities between *The History of the Franks* and *Life of the Fathers*. Work of God in the world, from creation to the cross, comes to bear on Gaul, especially in the life of Martin of Tours, but also in many other events and holy people. *The History of the Franks* focuses all of salvation history on the workings of God — in both wrath and redemption — in Gregory's own time and place. His discussion of Noah and the flood is typological in the traditional sense; it sets the theme for Gregory's time. "[God] is moved to anger so that He may fill us with awe.... He is enraged so that He may reform us. I have no doubt at all that the shape of the Ark represented the concept of mother Church, which moves forward through the waves and between the rocks of life here below, protecting us in her maternal bosom from the evils which threaten us, and defending us in her loving embrace and guardianship."[35] In the last pages of *The History of the Franks*, Gregory provides a lineage of the good bishops of Tours. He is the nineteenth. If there were a climax to his history, then a catalogue and brief descriptions of bishops would be an anticlimax. But the review of nineteen bishops is the appropriate way to conclude because *The History of the Franks* does not progress; it is about the present — the presence of God and the church in the land.

As the standards of historical writing change, hagiography changes as well. In modern terms, Gregory's historical record can hardly be called history. But in his historical context, he "was a painstaking and accurate recorder of events."[36] For a modern historian, both his historical writing and his hagiography are too heavily laden with supernatural agents and popular legends. The transition to modern historical methods begins dur-

33. Gregory of Tours, *History of the Franks* 10.12-15.

34. Gregory of Tours, *History of the Franks*, book 1 and book 10.31.

35. Gregory of Tours, *History of the Franks* 1.4.

36. Lewis Thorpe, "The History of the Franks," in Gregory of Tours, *History of the Franks*, 33.

ing the Renaissance, generally speaking, from the fourteenth to the seventeenth centuries. Renaissance humanists develop methods of literary and linguistic analysis, a concern for primary sources and their authentication, a clearer distinction between sacred and secular, and an eye for material causes and secular institutions (i.e., political as opposed to religious history). By the sixteenth century, a periodization of history begins to emerge: the Ancients, the Dark Ages, and the Rebirth.[37] While Gregory of Tours sought to identify the work of God in the present, Renaissance historians looked to reconstruct the ancient past.

Hagiography does not keep pace with these new developments in historical study, but it does follow close behind. Critical research on the saints by the Bollandists (named after the Jesuit Jean Bolland) is set in motion by the Dutch Jesuit Héribert Rosweyde in 1607.[38] The Bollandists set out to collect and authenticate documents and to put them to the textual analysis developed by Renaissance humanists.[39] Their criticisms of popular legends, contrived saints, and spurious traditions offend popular devotion and create some controversy.[40] But their critical research sets the standard for hagiography in the church. Jean Bolland (1596-1665) lived to see the publication of volumes covering the feast days for January, February, and March. The introductory volume for December, under the direction of Hippolyte Delehaye, was completed in 1940.

Two theological features of the Bollandists' research ought to be noted. First, the lives of the saints are organized according to feast day, so that saints who are centuries apart are placed side by side. Second, the Bollandists' main worries in studying premodern saints are the intrusion of superstitions, pagan mythology, and popular legends, all of which undermine the historical particularity of the saint in question as well as an adequate understanding of the imitation of Christ. Amazing tales of miraculous deeds are often repetitions of legends, usually mixed with local, pre-Christian piety and folklore.[41] Good examples are the legends of

37. Breisach, *Historiography*, 3rd ed., 159-60.

38. Hippolyte Delehaye, S.J., *The Work of the Bollandists: Through Three Centuries, 1615-1915* (Princeton: Princeton University Press, 1922), 9-10.

39. Breisach, *Historiography*, 3rd ed., 193-94; David Knowles, *Great Historical Enterprises* (London: Thomas Nelson and Sons, 1963), 3-32.

40. Lawrence Cunningham, *A Brief History of Saints* (Oxford: Blackwell, 2005), 76-77.

41. Hippolyte Delehaye, *The Legends of the Saints*, trans. Donald Attwater (New York: Fordham University Press, 1962), 119-60.

Agatha, many of which are catalogued in the *Acta Sanctorum* (February 5) and some of which are included in the *Golden Legend*.[42] The Bollandists were concerned with making known the real saint, and "each Life of a saint is corrected in accordance with fact and established by proofs which have been tested in light of the sane and judicious discussion and criticism from which the slightest traces of triviality, weakness, superstitious fanaticism and partisanship have been thoroughly eliminated."[43]

Following the trajectory of the Bollandists, modern hagiography takes full advantage of contemporary historical methods. The methods are used, but usually without the typical modern historical mind-set. St. Thérèse of Lisieux, considered in chapter 3 on realism, serves as a good example. The basic elements of her biography and autobiography are not contested historically. There tend to be worries that her piety is too bourgeois and saccharine. But her worldview is not a historical problem. Her desires for heaven and, in heaven, to be a coworker with Christ are not disputed. The real problem of Thérèse's history is whether or not these desires can be fulfilled. After death, can she have a continuing living relationship to the world?

To be named a saint, this kind of living relationship requires confirmation by at least two posthumous miracles. It is unusual but not controversial to show that cures or other events in a person's life have no natural explanation. A person has a cancerous tumor one day and, inexplicably, does not at a later date. The controversy is not about the evidence, but about its implications. The debate is between those who claim that there is a natural explanation, even though it is not as yet known, and those who testify to the power of God and the intercession of a patron or companion long dead. This disagreement is not, strictly speaking, a historical problem. It is a metaphysical one. The two opposing sides are likely to agree that prayers for a saint's intercession could be coincident with an unexplainable cure. But modern historians (as historians) would not accept a metaphysical claim that the coincidence of prayer and cure implies a supernatural agency or cause.

St. Katharine Drexel (1858-1955) is an interesting historical case. Her father and brothers were prominent Philadelphia bankers in the early twentieth century, and the Drexel family is well known for its philan-

---

42. *Acta Sanctorum*, Februarii I (Paris: Apud Victorem Palmé, 1863), 599-662.
43. Delahaye, *Work of the Bollandists*, 108.

thropy. It is noted in the history books.[44] Educated at home with her sisters, Katharine begins writing letters, reflections, meditations, and personal notes at an early age. Her biographers have access to thousands of her letters (as well as 18,000 she received) and day-to-day ledgers such as travel diaries, notebooks, and the like.[45] In 1891, she founds the Sisters of the Blessed Sacrament for Indians and Colored People, and from that date her activities and the activities of the order are well documented. Drexel and her community establish sixty-five schools and missions in twenty-one American states.[46] She lives frugally and gives generously, putting the Drexel inheritance to the work of the Sisters of the Blessed Sacrament and the church.

Documentary evidence and eyewitness accounts indicate that Katharine is an extraordinary person. She lives a life of prayer, special devotion to the Eucharist, obedience, and humility, with a shrewd and realistic understanding of the ways of the world and how to get things done. She is tireless in her sense of mission and forceful with her entrepreneurial plans on behalf of Native Americans and African Americans. She sweetens her work for others by giving herself — by taking the good of others personally.[47] Given the amount that she wrote about her life and work, she exhibits a striking lack of self-referential concern or ill will toward others. The evidence of her character and deeds, practical talents and endeavors, spiritual gifts and pilgrimage indicates that Katharine lived a holy life.

The evidence points to her holy life only if it is supposed and expected that God will be shown to us through a person in the world. The historical question is not the empirical evidence per se, but a view of the possibilities in human life. Sainthood is not merely a Christian label for an exemplary person. The saint lives out communion with God in Christ, and she is a person through whom Christ draws near to us. She lives in unity with God and with us. Katharine Drexel is named a saint in 2000 after extensive study of her faith and virtue as well as examinations of two posthumous miracles. Both miracles are cures of irreversible deafness. In 1974,

44. Russell F. Weigley, ed., *Philadelphia: A 300-Year History* (New York: Norton, 1982), 500, 684; Randall Miller and William Pencak, eds., *Pennsylvania: A History of the Commonwealth* (University Park: Pennsylvania State University Press, 2002), 294.

45. Consuela Marie Duffy, S.B.S., *Katharine Drexel: A Biography* (Philadelphia: Peter Reilly Co., 1965), xi-xii.

46. Duffy, *Katharine Drexel*, 391.

47. Duffy, *Katharine Drexel*, 359-61.

Robert Gutherman is diagnosed with irreparable damage to the eardrum and two bones of his right ear; in 1992, Amanda Wall is diagnosed with incurable sensorineural deafness in both ears.[48] For evidence of Katharine's agency, the irreversibility is documented medically as well as the extraordinary reversal of both cases.[49] Testimony is given that the families and others who are praying for Gutherman and Wall are entreating Katharine, specifically, to intercede on their behalf.

The testimony's merit hinges on the credibility of personal relationships. Both Robert and Amanda ("Amy") are children when healed (Robert a teenager and Amy an infant), and both live in Bucks County, Pennsylvania, the home of the St. Katharine Drexel Mission Center and National Shrine. Robert and his family are already connected to Katharine and the Sisters of the Blessed Sacrament. He is an altar server at the Motherhouse in Bensalem.[50] Robert's story is retold now and again in Bucks County, and Amy's family learns of his cure twenty years later and hopes, through Katharine, to follow his path. These miracles are held together by convenient contingencies and local relations and influences, which are certainly suspect to the historian's eye. Someone knows someone who knows Katharine, and Katharine, still in relationship after death, responds. The documentary evidence and testimony are not historical problems, but the metaphysical backdrop — the relationship of the saint to life here and now — is a problem for history. The metaphysical backdrop is not tangential to modern hagiography; the possibility of living relationships with the saints is the main point.

Modern martyrs, as opposed to saints like Katharine Drexel, are likely to present a different historical problem. Posthumous miracles are not required in the naming of a martyr, but metaphysical questions emerge nevertheless. Salvadoran archbishop Oscar Romero is an interesting case. The writings about him and by him (i.e., pastoral letters, correspondence, diaries, and homilies) are voluminous in both English and Spanish. A Christian martyr dies as a witness to the truth of Jesus Christ as Lord and Savior. In Romero's case, the historical questions are who he "dies as" and what he "witnesses to." The facts of Romero's death are not contested. He

48. Mary van Balen Holt, *Meet Katharine Drexel: Heiress and God's Servant of the Oppressed* (Ann Arbor: Servant, 2002), 108-9.

49. *Acta Apostolicae Sedis*, vol. 79 (1988), 1806-10, and vol. 92 (2000), 538-40.

50. Van Balen Holt, *Meet Katharine Drexel*, 108.

is murdered on March 24, 1980, while celebrating the Mass (precisely during the homily). The assassins are off-duty national guardsmen who believe they are acting on orders from higher levels in the military.[51] Questions persist for a few decades after his death about Romero's allegiance to Marxist movements and whether or not he dies as a witness to faith or as a partisan in El Salvador's civil war. There are biographies that tend in this second direction at least to the degree that their story of Romero is that he converted from being a pawn for the government to being a champion of resistance.[52]

Why does Romero die? During the civil war the opposing sides in El Salvador have interests in making him a political tragedy: he dies either because he is taken in by the left and enters a political world where he does not belong or because he is formerly taken in by an oppressive government and then becomes its victim. Adjudicating these options and the possibility of rejecting both are the historical questions of what Archbishop Romero says and does. But even these questions, although empirical, require a theological imagination about the possible courses of action in Romero's life. The empirical questions raise metaphysical ones. He dies defending the poor and oppressed and with a consistent denunciation of violence. These facts are clear. It is clear that his message was not merely "religious." But this mix of politics and religion presents the metaphysical problem of his death.

If God's presence cannot be shown and if the kingdom of God cannot appear in time, then religious martyrdom must be about otherworldly beliefs. It must be about "beliefs" that have no "political" place. In this context, if Romero's message is not merely religious, then he must have died for some identifiable political program. However, if the communion of God in Christ does, possibly, appear now and again in the world, then the options are widened. If Romero does not die for a political program and if his death is not merely "religious," it must be that a different kind of politics was available to him. In the homily just before he is martyred, he states this possibility, citing the *Pastoral Constitution on the Church in the Modern World* (Vatican Council II, no. 39): "God's reign is already present on our

---

51. Robert Royal, *The Catholic Martyrs of the Twentieth Century* (New York: Crossroad, 2000), 270-71.

52. Plácido Erdozain, *Archbishop Romero, Martyr of Salvador,* trans. John McFadden and Ruth Warner (Maryknoll, N.Y.: Orbis, 1981).

earth in mystery. When the Lord comes, it will be brought to perfection."[53] Romero is assassinated as a witness to the kingdom of God, not as a witness to a distant future, but as a living witness to a possibility in the present. At bottom, the historical problem of Romero's death is the same as the problem with St. Katharine's posthumous miracles. Is it possible for heaven and earth to meet through a person? Romero is martyred because he challenges the powers, not as part of a political program, but because he embodies in the present the advent of God's reign in the fullness of time.

What can the lives of the saints tell us about history? In the communion of saints, the fullness of time of God in Christ is the common referent point: we are interconnected (triangulated) through a common future that comes to us time and again in the present. In the lives of the saints, particular histories are preserved and connected (typologically) to the whole of life. Through our lives with the saints, we form social relations to the whole. In chapter 1, this point was proposed in the context of *Landscapes of the Soul* by sociologist Douglas Porpora. Porpora argues that contemporary crises of social life and personal identity correspond to a lack of or disconnection from a metaphysical landscape. The lives of the saints embody these connections, but for this reason, the histories of saints do not fit with the standards of modern history. In short, the lives of the saints (as saints) are not suited to modern historiography and, in their lack of fit, they answer a modern metaphysical problem.

In a preface to modern historiography, Ernst Breisach notes that "[contemporary] Christian historiography . . . still has not found a persuasive replacement for the Eusebian model of world history."[54] Eusebius writes his *Ecclesiastical History* in the fourth century. The "Eusebian model," as Breisach uses the term, integrates sacred and profane history. Salvation history gives shape to a temporal sequence of ages, with creation at the beginning, Christ at the center, and the Last Judgment as the culmination. This kind of model, which connects church history to world history, "reverberates" well into the seventeenth century.[55] That is, echoes of sacred history remain in the background along with vestiges of Christendom.

53. Oscar Romero, *The Violence of Love*, trans. James R. Brockman, S.J. (Maryknoll, N.Y.: Orbis, 1988), 206.

54. Ernst Breisach, "A Prefatory Note to Modern Historiography (since 1914)," in *Historiography: Ancient, Medieval, Modern*, 2nd ed. (Chicago: University of Chicago Press, 1995), 326.

55. Breisach, *Historiography*, 3rd ed., 81.

Even in the first half of the nineteenth century, Leopold von Ranke — the "father of historical science" — assumes a metaphysical basis for his historical method. "Ranke found the link between the mundane and the metaphysical realms in ideas, those eternal forces which manifest themselves partially and temporarily in the phenomena of the world."[56] By the end of the nineteenth century, traditional sacred history and less particularistic, modern ideas of "eternal forces" are set outside history. Modern science (seventeenth and eighteenth centuries) begins with the presumption that God is Creator, and by the end of the nineteenth century presumes that God has been replaced — that the order of things attributed to divine providence could be found in the things themselves. Likewise, by the end of the nineteenth century, historical science assumes that the course of history is found in the data itself.

In the beginning of the twenty-first century, modern histories lack a connection to unifying world history. Various histories are written without a common theoretical or philosophical foundation.[57] The quintessential modern form of historical writing is the monograph and academic article. "They deal with one single, clearly defined topic, and . . . their contribution to knowledge, at least, is that they make available hitherto unknown or little-studied, pieces of primary source material."[58] The primary source materials and the "clearly defined topic" are not connected to the whole of history. It is becoming increasingly difficult to unify the course of narrower yet still broad "wholes" like the history of the West.[59] The nineteenth- and twentieth-century plans to gradually uncover the laws of history have created diverse interpretations.[60] A reduction of history to economic forces or to material progress has been unable to rein in the history of the modern world.[61]

The fragmentation of history matters if we believe that humanity is a whole. Christians, in particular, are called to face the alienation and to live

56. Breisach, *Historiography*, 3rd ed., 233.

57. Breisach, *Historiography*, 2nd ed., 324.

58. Marwick, *The Nature of History*, 264. Marwick adds the category "general history" as a complement to the learned article and the monograph, but he defines it as an "ambitious monograph" (264).

59. Lynn Hunt et al., *The Making of the West: Peoples and Cultures*, vol. 2, 2nd ed. (Boston: Bedford/St. Martin's, 2005), 1222.

60. Breisach, *Historiography*, 2nd ed., 324-25.

61. Breisach, *Historiography*, 2nd ed., 325-26.

for a deeper unity — to respond to a deep and broad social desire. In his *Nature of History,* Arthur Marwick holds that without a history we "would be utterly adrift on an endless and featureless sea of time." He explains that "it is only through a sense of history that communities establish their identity, orientate themselves, understand their relationship to the past or to other communities and societies."[62] We live in a time when human unity and divine life stand apart from how history is told. But the metaphysical connections that we lack in history we find in the lives of the saints. The progression of ages cannot be told through the saints. However, through communion with the saints — through memory, participation, veneration, and benefaction — our particular histories are joined to the community of the whole. Christianity cannot be adequately historical without the communion of the saints.

62. Marwick, *The Nature of History,* 14.

NINE

Hagiography

—⁓—

Histroy cannot be told by lining up the saints in a temporal progression of holiness. But the lives of the saints present both the uniqueness of historical events and the unity of this singularity to life and to history as a whole. The saints anticipate and embody the fullness of time; they are the dissemination of God-with-us as the unity of history in the present and through time. Without the constant appearance of holy people, we would have to question whether or not Christianity is historical.[1] But with the continuous appearance of the saints, our histories are lifted out of a merely historical frame and put on a metaphysical landscape. These are the tensions of hagiography. It must be historical and meet the standards of historical writing (at any given time); yet, it must transcend history. Given its metaphysical backdrop, ancient and medieval hagiography emphasizes transcendent relations and the presence and power of God. Given the modern turn to the human being as the center, modern hagiography emphasizes moral goodness and works in the world.[2] These are points of emphasis: both are needed — both sharing in divine life and marking out pathways in the world. Hagiography points to our sharing in human life in communion with God and the saints as media of grace.

Another way of stating the theme is to say that holiness, along with salvation, is social. Karl Rahner is well known for his proposal that the

1. This point is a modification of arguments made by Patrick Sherry in his *Spirit, Saints, and Immortality* (Albany: State University of New York Press, 1984), 43-48.

2. In referring to metaphysical and anthropological backgrounds, I am thinking of Hans Urs von Balthasar, *Love Alone Is Credible*, trans. David C. Schindler (San Francisco: Ignatius, 2004).

veneration of saints is based on the intimacy between the love of God and love of neighbor.[3] He begins by arguing against an "abstract monotheism" and plays out the Christian conviction that "the humanity of Jesus is the medium through which our immediate relationship with God is achieved."[4] The love of God reconciles humanity in Christ, and our love for the saints, because they are "in Christ," brings the "theological and Christological character of love of neighbor . . . clearly to the fore."[5] The other side of the relationship is also the case. In the saints' love for us, we can expect that they will "entreat the God of the living to let that light [of holiness] shine upon us too which is the manifestation of his own love and blessed eternity of his own life."[6]

In the Bible, holiness is social in this shared sense: it is nearness to and association with God. It is the character of our relationship to the world. In the Old Testament, holiness is "the mark of Israel as a group or of individuals in Israel dedicated to Yahweh and to his awesome service. It comes from the idea that God dwells in the midst of his people."[7] In the New Testament, holiness "is further applied to Christian disciples in earthly life, who now become God's people in a new, extended sense."[8] Echoes of Israel's call to holiness can be heard among Christians of the New Testament. "He who called you is holy, be holy yourselves in every respect of your conduct, for it is written, 'Be holy because I am holy'" (1 Pet. 1:15-16). This is the proposition with which Joseph Fitzmyer, S.J., begins his analysis of biblical evidence for "the veneration, intercession, and invocation of holy people."[9] The people of God are called to reflect the holiness of God.

Fitzmyer notes that the phrase "holy ones" has an ambiguous quality in Scripture. Sometimes it refers to those on earth (as noted above). Sometimes it refers to heavenly beings (Zech. 14:5; Job 5:1). Among early Chris-

---

3. Karl Rahner, "Why and How We Venerate the Saints," in *Theological Investigations VIII*, trans. David Bourke (New York: Herder and Herder, 1971), 3-23.

4. Rahner, "Why and How," 12.

5. Rahner, "Why and How," 21-22.

6. Rahner, "Why and How," 23. Also see Patricia A. Sullivan's development of Rahner's arguments, especially in terms of the invocation of the saints. "A Reinterpretation of Invocation and Intercession of the Saints," *Theological Studies* 66, no. 2 (June 2005): 381-400.

7. Joseph Fitzmyer, S.J., "Biblical Data on the Veneration, Intercession, and Invocation of Holy People," in *The One Mediator, the Saints, and Mary*, ed. H. George Anderson, J. Francis Stafford, and Joseph A. Burgess (Minneapolis: Augsburg Fortress, 1992), 136.

8. Fitzmyer, "Biblical Data," 136.

9. Fitzmyer, "Biblical Data," 135-47.

tians, the meaning of "saints" was extended to the dead, particularly in terms of the general resurrection.[10] In Philippians, Paul expounds on the meaning of living in Christ by extending it to death. "For to me life is Christ, and death is gain. . . . I long to depart this life and be with Christ" (Phil. 1:21, 23). In the New Testament, holy ones are remembered, honored, and believed to be in community with the living Christ. In Hebrews 12:1-2, for example, "famous persons of faith of bygone times are presented not merely as witnesses of what real faith is, but also as a compact throng of believers, whose company living Christians are already called to share."[11] Ephesians 2:19-20 should be noted also: "You are no longer strangers and sojourners, but you are fellow citizens with the holy ones and members of the household of God, built upon the foundation of the apostles and prophets, with Christ Jesus himself as the capstone." Fitzmyer argues that "the saints" (*tôn hagiôn*), in this context, is a reference to "holy Christians that have passed on." The passage extends Paul's image of the church as the body of Christ to solidarity with those already "with the Lord."[12]

On the basis of this solidarity with the dead, Fitzmyer hopes to show that there is a basis in Scripture for an invocation of deceased saints as intercessors before God. Traditionally, arguments against the intercession of the dead have appealed to 1 Timothy 2:5, Romans 8:34, and 1 John 2:1, which affirm that Christ is our advocate and the one mediator before God. Fitzmyer argues that 1 Timothy 2:1-6, in fact, implies that salvation in Christ is motivation to pray for others. He offers a catalogue of scriptural figures who have done so, from Abraham's intercession on behalf of Sodom and Gomorrah to Stephen's prayer for those who stone him.[13] Paul writes to the Philippians, "I give thanks to my God at every remembrance of you, praying always with joy in my every prayer for all of you" (Phil. 1:3-4). Fitzmyer concludes that the twin elements of solidarity with the dead and prayer for others are suggestive. If we are able to intercede for the living, the holy dead are able to intercede for us. The fundamental

10. Fitzmyer, in "Biblical Data on the Veneration, Intercession, and Invocation of Holy People," draws continuity with "biblical teaching about the resurrection of the dead, which emerged clearly in the last pre-Christian centuries of Palestinian Judaism (e.g., Dan 12:2) and of immortality, which surfaced in Judaism under the influence of Greek philosophical thinking (Wis 3:4, 4:1, 8:13) and which begins to pervade New Testament writings" (137).

11. Fitzmyer, "Biblical Data," 142-43.

12. Fitzmyer, "Biblical Data," 143.

13. Fitzmyer, "Biblical Data," 144-46.

point is not that intercessory prayer provides us with what we want or that the intercessions of the dead have magical power. Rather, the basic rationale for the *invocation* of the saints is our *convocation*. We pray in communion.[14]

During the persecutions of the postapostolic age, the graveside shrines of the martyrs became places of pilgrimage, gathering, and worship with the saints as fellow disciples and patrons. Recall that the *Martyrdom of Polycarp* (second century) served to indicate that saints not only display exemplary faith but also inspire a desire for communion. When Polycarp is pursued by persecutors, he is not inclined to flee. But he does so at the request of fellow Christians. When soldiers finally catch up with him, he hands himself over. He sits them down for a meal, and he requests an hour of prayer for himself. In a striking scene, he stands and prays unceasingly for two hours as the soldiers look on from the table as his guests. Later, the faithful look on anxiously as Polycarp stands in the stadium before the magistrate and bloodthirsty masses. After rejecting Caesar's authority several times, Polycarp makes clear that death is the only possible option. He prays as wood and kindling are stacked around him. He gives praise and thanksgiving to the Lord of all, and the fire is lit. Among his brothers and sisters in Christ, his faithful death sparks a desire to collect his bones and "have fellowship with his holy flesh."[15]

In the context of persecution, devotion to the martyrs, graveside gathering, and death-day piety sustain a polity of communion. The martyr's death (here Polycarp's) is recognized as entry into immortal life, where "he rejoices with the Apostles and all the righteous, and glorifies the almighty God . . . and blesses Lord Jesus Christ."[16] The Lordship of Christ is set over against Caesar, and devotion to the saints enacts Christ's victory over the powers of the world, forms a kinship with the company of heaven, and gives access to the protection and privileges of that kinship. After the age of Roman persecution had passed, Augustine would say of Perpetua and Felicity, martyred in Carthage at the beginning of the third century, "Let it not seem a small thing to us that we are members of the same body as these. . . . We marvel at them, they have compassion on us. We rejoice for

---

14. Sullivan, "A Reinterpretation of Invocation and Intercession of the Saints."

15. *Martyrdom of Polycarp*, in *The Apostolic Fathers: Greek Texts and English Translations of Their Writings*, trans. J. B. Lightfoot and J. R. Harmer (Grand Rapids: Baker, 1992), 241 n. 23.

16. *Martyrdom of Polycarp*, 243.

them, they pray for us. . . . Yet do we all serve one Lord, follow one master, attend one king . . . embrace one unity."[17]

Christ's Lordship is communion. In the fourth century, when Christianity is established in the empire, martyrdom gives way to asceticism, and the saints' contest with the powers of the world turns to the open spiritual terrain outside the city. The *Life of Antony*, written by Athanasius of Alexandria (d. 373), sets the struggles of faith on the landscape of the desert. It is the devil's minions, rather than the emperor's, that track down and test the holy man.[18] Through ascetic practices and contests with demons, Antony, like Polycarp, shows that he is willing to face death faithfully and graciously. Like the martyr's, the ascetic's bodily suffering becomes a medium of the power and communion of Christ. In reference to medieval piety, Caroline Walker Bynum holds that this connection between the body of the saint and a reversal of suffering is tied up with the patristic and medieval theology of the resurrection. In *The Resurrection of the Body in Western Christianity, 200-1336*, she shows that the continuity of our earthly bodies with our transformed and resurrected bodies is a persistent concern in ancient and medieval Christianity. How will our identities be sustained in relation to earthly suffering and the final resurrection? In relation to this problem, the martyrs and saints enter the communion of heaven, and their bodies form a bridge between earthly hardship and heavenly rest. God's nearness to the martyr in death offers "a sort of anesthesia of glory [that] might spill over from the promised resurrection into the ravaged flesh of the arena."[19] As the cult of the saints takes hold, the devout are drawn to bodies and relics of the saints because they are considered "pregnant already with the glory they would receive fully only at the resurrection."[20]

17. Augustine, *Sermo* 280.6, in Migne, ed., *Patrologia Latina*, 38:1283-84, cited in Elizabeth A. Johnson, "Saints and Mary," in *Systematic Theology: Roman Catholic Perspectives*, vol. 2, ed. Francis Schüssler Fiorenza and John P. Galvin (Minneapolis: Augsburg Fortress, 1991), 150.

18. *Life of Antony by Athanasius*, in *Early Christian Lives*, trans. Carolinne White (London: Penguin Books, 1998), 1-70.

19. Caroline Walker Bynum, *The Resurrection of the Body in Western Christianity, 200-1336* (New York: Columbia University Press, 1995), 46.

20. Caroline Walker Bynum, "Bodily Miracles and the Resurrection of the Body in the Middle Ages," in *Belief in History: Innovative Approaches to European and American Religion*, ed. Thomas Kselman (Notre Dame, Ind.: University of Notre Dame Press, 1991), 81.

The ascetic's life in the desert is hardly a rejection of the body or the earthly bonds of the body of Christ. This point is central to the *Life of Antony*. Athanasius is careful to note that ascetic discipline makes Antony's physical form youthful and robust. His presence in the desert, likewise, establishes a place alive with the Spirit. Christ's wisdom and mercy are conveyed through him. Antony disavows pleasures of the flesh, but his great sacrifice is giving up his solitude in the desert. The life of the ascetic is Christ's Lordship taken root in the soul and the fruit of victory is faithful communion. Athanasius indicates that Antony comes to be known for his austere life, his triumph over temptations, his patience and humility, healings and other miraculous deeds, and his capacity to "see" the trials of others through prayer. As a consequence, he becomes a locus and guide for many companions who gather with him in the desert.

For Antony and the holy ones of his age, desert asceticism and a desire for intimacy with God function to establish an alternative social space, a location apart from the city. The more the saint attempts to recede in prayer and nearness to God, the more would-be monks come to follow his way. His holiness makes holy space for others. His cell in the desert and the anniversary of his death become the place and time where God's power and grace are revealed and distributed. People crowd him during his life, and their devotional practices surround him after his death. The cult of the saints integrates and redraws both the late-Roman system of patronage and the topography of the city.[21] The community gathered in remembrance of the saint is the medium for "the lurching forward . . . of new forms of reverence" and "the common preoccupation . . . with new forms of the exercise of power, new bonds of human dependence, new, intimate, hopes for protection and justice in a changing world."[22]

By the beginning of the medieval age, the cult of the saints becomes an integral part of social life. The patron saint, the relic, and the pilgrimage site become conduits of social concord and the congenial use of authority; they provide a set of relationships and an embodied locus for the distribution of wealth.[23] Insofar as the cult of the saints forms a network of kinship, it also will be the medium of discord as well as the assertion of clerical au-

---

21. Peter Brown, *The Cult of the Saints: Its Rise and Function in Latin Christianity* (Chicago: University of Chicago Press, 1981), 50-68.

22. Brown, *Cult of the Saints*, 21-22.

23. Brown, *Cult of the Saints*, 93-105.

thority and resistance against it. With the integrating of saints and social life, bodies of the saints and other holy tangibles are often moved from the outlying areas to the city. This translation of the saint's bodily remains shows the dominance of a place (usually the city over the town shrine) and is cause for social disruption and conflict. Amid this tension, devotion to a patron saint will still open up alternative social spaces, outside the city and beyond civil and ecclesiological authority. A civil framework of sponsorship might be challenged, not by calls for its dissolution, but by the emergence of another center of patronage at a monastery. Likewise, access to and honor given to relics become entangled with local disputes.[24]

If the cult of the saints ought to foster a network of God's incarnate love, then failures of charity and justice will parallel the successes. Along with the social prominence of pilgrimage sites comes the fabrication of heroic deeds and relics of the saints for social and economic gain. Whether for good or for ill, whether created by popular enthusiasm or by greed, the fictitious saint becomes useful. The useful deception is ultimately self-serving and alienating. Consider this warning given at the beginning of the twelfth century by Guibert, the abbot of Nogent, near Laon, France.[25] "It is much more tolerable for you to lose trust in your own merits, than to despair of the patron through whom you have placed your hopes before God. Since you trust yourself less, you call upon the patron, but surely you know that if your advocate is convicted of falsehood, then you stand to lose all that you have gained."[26]

Guibert's treatise *On Saints and Their Relics* was not widely read in the medieval era, but it does provide a picture of typical worries about the cult of the saints.[27] Some of Guibert's criticisms resonate with modern concerns. As an educated cleric, he has little trust in the popular imagination and its oral culture. He wants to slow down and calm popular enthusiasm with a patient consideration of testimony, the authority of tradition, and especially written records. He ridicules a multiplication of relics that had come to the point where John the Baptist must have lived with two heads. His tone shifts, however, from ridicule to condemnation when he sees

---

24. Patrick Greary, "Humiliation of Saints," in *Saints and Their Cults*, ed. Stephen Wilson (Cambridge: Cambridge University Press, 1983), 123-40.

25. Guibert of Nogent, *On Saints and Their Relics*, in *Medieval Hagiography: An Anthology*, ed. Thomas Head (New York: Garland, 2000), 400.

26. Guibert of Nogent, *On Saints*, 416.

27. Lawrence S. Cunningham, *A Brief History of Saints* (Oxford: Blackwell, 2005), 54-61.

greed rather than mere enthusiasm behind the invention of relics. "Fraud-
ulent deals are frequently struck — not so much in the case of whole bodies, as in the case of limbs and parts of bodies — and common bones are
thus distributed to be venerated as the relics of the saints. These things are
clearly done by those who, according to the Apostle [1 Tim. 6:5], *suppose
gain to be godliness* and turn the very things which should serve for the salvation of their souls into the excrement of bags of money."[28] Guibert does
not question the purpose of the cult of saints but asks for clearer testimony and evidence and for a watchful eye against superstition and greed.

Guibert tells his own tales of wonder and the intercession of local
saints, and his primary standard for veracity is whether or not the acts of
the saint accord with the worship and faith of the church. He does not call
into question the possibility of the extraordinary. Rather, Guibert is wor-
ried that people are attracted to mere novelty rather than signs and wonders that serve the faith. To offer a positive example, he tells the story of
Erlebald. Erlebald is a priest who subjects himself to harsh discipline. He
fasts, wears a squalid hair shirt, and sleeps without covering or mattress.
He is a holy man, and he appears, after his death, to a bishop in order to
advise greater faithfulness.[29] Modern piety tends to emphasize internal
faith rather than pilgrimages and nearness to the bodies of the saints.[30]
Guibert sustains a medieval concern for the body of the saint. He encourages the desires of the faithful to go to the saints and to draw near to God
through them.[31] The fragmentation and scattering of the body are what
concern him. "Would not lifeless bones, if they were able, most justly
complain when they suffer dispersion in every direction?" Would not the
saints wish for their bodies to rest and turn "back into the fruitful soil" until transformed by God in the final resurrection?[32] Guibert hopes to pro-
tect good practices of veneration and prayers for intercession from the invention and crass trade in relics as well as from popular credulity. His
criticisms point to the good of communion with the saints.

The naming of saints was based on local and popular devotion, but by
the thirteenth century institutional structures were put in place for the
canonization of saints, the regulation of local cults, and the integration of

---

28. Guibert of Nogent, *On Saints*, 418.
29. Guibert of Nogent, *On Saints*, 412.
30. Cunningham, *Brief History of Saints*, 54-56.
31. Bynum, "Bodily Miracles," 77-78.
32. Guibert of Nogent, *On Saints*, 420.

feast days into the liturgy of the universal church.[33] Speaking of the cult of the saints in the fifth century, Peter Brown notes an inversion of the traditional hierarchy of the universe. Rather than from above, the intermediaries between God and human beings come from below, from the martyrs, "true servants of God [who] could bind their fellow men even closer to God than could the angels."[34] Throughout the Middle Ages, it is clear that sainthood continued to lift up from below. Lawrence Cunningham notes that by the sixteenth century only 10 percent of saints were canonized by papal decree.[35] A particular kind of saint begins to gain official recognition: clergy and founders of religious orders. But a variety of saints persist through popular recognition and devotion.

In the sixteenth century Luther denounces elements of devotion that appear to encourage external merit rather than inward trust in Christ alone. He allows for the remembrance of saints by means of images, and he promotes the veneration of the martyrs and saints for their faith in Christ alone. However, Luther rejects the idea that God's grace is disseminated through the constellation of saints, relics, and indulgences. For the reformers, this rejection turns on the biblical command against idolatry, which Calvinists take to require a complete refutation of veneration and images. Undoubtedly, the reformers (like Guibert four centuries earlier) could point to ample evidence where popular devotion had crossed the line to superstition and where the memory of a saint had become more important for the collection of offerings than the power of grace.[36]

The Council of Trent responds by defending the veneration of saints and denouncing abuses. The council condemns false doctrines, superstition, base profit through trade in relics, and disorderly feasts at a saint's shrine. However, it encourages reverence for saints and the use of images. "[T]hrough the images which we kiss and before which we uncover our heads and go down on our knees, we give adoration to Christ and veneration to the saints, whose likeness they bear." Such devotion to the saints is said to advance an imitation of them, of their virtue and their adoration of God. The council also asserts that the proper veneration of saints does not

33. Gerd Tellenbach, *The Church in Western Europe from the Tenth to the Early Twelfth Century,* trans. Timothy Reuter (New York: Cambridge University Press, 1993), 99.

34. Brown, *Cult of the Saints,* 61.

35. Cunningham, *Brief History of Saints,* 54.

36. Hubert Jedin, *Crisis and Closure of the Council of Trent,* trans. N. D. Smith (London: Sheed and Ward, 1967), 147.

contravene the work of Christ as our sole redeemer and savior. On the contrary, as living members of Christ, the martyrs and saints inhabit Christ's heavenly kingdom and offer their prayers on our behalf. "[I]t is a good and beneficial thing to invoke them and to have recourse to their prayers and helpful assistance to obtain blessings from God."[37]

Typically, the Reformation and Counter-Reformation (questions of merit and abuse) form the lens through which the medieval cult is understood. The animating themes of kinship and communion are often overlooked. John Bossy, in his *Christianity in the West, 1400-1700*, argues that by 1400 the function of sainthood depended far less on the saint's power, austerity, or extraordinary virtue and far more on his or her friendship with God and fellow human beings. The saints are "God's extensive affinity." Patient endurance and penitential practices continue to constitute the sojourn of average Christians, but this pathway holds less importance for inspiring veneration of the saints. "The congenial dogma about saints was that friendship with God was to be demonstrated by the furtherance of friendship among men."[38] Bossy tempers the common view that medieval saints become popular because Christ has become distant. On the contrary, saints such as Ann, Joachim, James, Simon, and Jude tie Jesus into a sphere of family and friends that resonates with the everyday world of the devout. These saints emerge through popular traditions as the very human family of the human Jesus. Among the saints, Christ is known with and through the members of his house.

Amid what looks to moderns to be imaginary depictions, the saints are seen to be the very imaginable, genuine, and recognizable population of the heavenly city. By the end of the Middle Ages, honor continues to be given the saints for their exemplary lives and faith. Many saints continue to be loci of restorative suffering and miraculous power. However, the meaning of sanctity is diffused. A variety and multiplicity of saints are held together not by their heroic virtue or wondrous deeds but by their kinship. They are a certain, constant, and efficacious link of communion between heaven and earth. Insofar as the Middle Ages brings a proliferation of relics and places of worship, the relic corresponds to the sanctified

---

37. "Council of Trent," in *Decrees of the Ecumenical Councils*, vol. 2, ed. Norman P. Tanner (Washington, D.C.: Georgetown University Press, 1990), 774-75.

38. John Bossy, *Christianity in the West, 1400-1700* (Oxford: Oxford University Press, 1987), 11-12.

body, and the body corresponds to the shared place. The saint, his or her body and touch, is a concrete bond. Like the sweet-smelling corpse of the martyrs and the incorruptible bodies of holy ones long dead, the communion of saints is the life of sojourners on earth enlivened and sustained by the company of heaven.

This communion with the saints is a means for ordinary Christians to become part of the media of God's dissemination of grace in the world. Lively accounts of communion and dissemination are provided by Jacobus de Voragine's *Golden Legend,* compiled in the mid–thirteenth century and circulated widely until the sixteenth.[39] The work is full of fanciful lore and magical moments. In its best moments, the *Legend*'s metaphysical excesses put important theological themes in clear relief.

Its story of Lucy, martyred early in the fourth century, carries representative themes. Lucy accompanies her mother, who suffers incessant bleeding, to the tomb of St. Agatha. Upon their arrival, they attend Mass and hear the Gospel story of the woman who is healed of the same affliction. After Mass, the two pray at Agatha's tomb. Lucy falls asleep, and she receives a vision of the saint who tells her, "My sister Lucy, virgin consecrated to God, why do you ask me for something that you yourself can do for your mother? Indeed, your faith has already cured her." Not only is her mother healed, but the vision is leverage for Lucy to announce and to impose her secret vow of virginity. She convinces her mother that she must reject her betrothal and that her dowry ought to be given to the poor.

When Lucy is free from her vow, she tricks her betrothed into helping her sell off her assets. He, in retaliation, gives her over to the Roman consul, Paschasius, who commands that she be sent to a brothel, to defile her so that she "will lose the holy spirit." Lucy stands firm. In fact, a thousand men are unable to move her. She is drenched with urine in an effort to counter her "magic." She is burned, covered with boiling oil, and stabbed in the neck. Still, she stands firm. With a dagger in her throat, she prophesies the downfall of Paschasius. She also reveals that "just as God has given my sister Agatha to the city of Catania as protectress, so I am given to the city of Syracusa as mediatrix." That is not all. Envoys arrive from Rome to drag Paschasius away in chains. Caesar had received word that the consul had been pillaging the province. At that very moment, Lucy "did not

39. Jacobus de Voragine, *The Golden Legend,* vol. 1, trans. William Granger Ryan (Princeton: Princeton University Press, 1993), xiii.

breathe her last before the priests had brought her the Body of the Lord and all those present had responded Amen to the Lord. There she was buried and a church was raised in her honor."[40]

Amid the intensity of martyrdom, Lucy's death is protracted. She persists in the place of her testimony, so that she can receive the sacrament in the company of her brothers and sisters in Christ. Even in death, she stays on the spot, keeping company where a church is built. Medieval Christians might not follow Lucy in martyrdom, but they can hope to share the same reconciling moment of death. Like the martyrologies of old, Lucy endures great suffering; however, her face is not directed heavenward. She is not like Polycarp, who stands alone on the pyre of his execution. In death, she enjoys communion with all who are gathered. Fellow Christians are not kept at a distance. Their desire for fellowship with her "in the flesh" is not frustrated, but communicated through the holy meal. Lucy stands accused by the authority of Rome. Yet, in a prolonged moment of death, it is the persecutor who is judged and condemned. His court is transformed into a place of worship. The authority of Caesar is put in service to the Lordship of Christ. The unity of spiritual and social life is nearly seamless.

Lucy's relationship to Agatha is also revealing. Agatha is no distant patron, who takes the honor of conveying the healing power of Christ. She calls Lucy a sister and discloses what she, Lucy, can do for her mother. This turn in the narrative calls attention to the character of Lucy's faith, but also points to the character of Agatha as a patron. Her benefaction produces democratization of heavenly power.[41] Agatha and Lucy are sisters in the manner of their martyrdom, but their kinship is connected to larger themes of affinity and conviviality in *The Golden Legend*. The companionship and support of the saints are intertwined with the liturgy and sacraments of the church.

Companionship and a dissemination of grace are prominent in a central anecdote in the life of St. Basil.[42] In a household under Basil's care, a slave contracts with the devil in order to enchant and marry a nobleman's daughter, who is destined to be set apart as a virgin. The slave's relationship with the devil is not secured unassisted. He gains access to the devil

---

40. Voragine, *The Golden Legend*, 1:27-29.
41. See Brown, *Cult of the Saints*, 48.
42. Voragine, *The Golden Legend*, 1:109-12.

by a sorcerer's letter of recommendation, which promises a favorable return of souls for the favor done. The young man indentures himself to the evil one, and he is required to give a written statement to seal their agreement. The young woman falls hopelessly in love, and she badgers her father for his consent to marry. He agrees reluctantly and gives her what wealth is due to her, saying, "Be on your way, my poor, poor daughter."

Bishop Basil enters the narrative when the man's contract with the devil is exposed. The young husband draws notice to himself by never going to church or making the sign of the cross, neither praising God nor entrusting himself to God in any visible way. Friends and associates start to talk. When confronted by his new wife, his denial is met with her challenge to go to church. Caught by the truth, he admits the full details of his scheme. She turns to Basil. Basil asks the young man if he wants to turn back to God. He does, but in despair he tells Basil of the written contract. "Don't worry, my son!" says Basil. "The Lord is kind and will accept you as a penitent."

After the husband expresses his desire for God, a process unfolds that is oddly comparable to delivering an addict to a rehabilitation facility. The spirit is willing, but the demons are entrenched. Basil marks the man with the sign of the cross and then shuts him in a cell, where he is taunted and terrorized by demons. Basil continually reassures him, and prays for him. Again and again, Basil returns with food and the sign of the cross. Days go by. The torments weaken, and finally the young man sees a vision of Basil fighting for him and beating the devil. "The bishop then led him out of his cell, summoned all the clergy and religious and the whole populace, and urged all to pray for the man." On the way to church, Basil struggles with demons as they try to wrestle the young man from his grasp. As penitent and saint are being dragged away by the demons, the bishop announces that all the people will not stop praying till the devil gives up the former slave's contract. Immediately, the contract falls from heaven as it has been ransomed by Christ. "Whereupon Basil destroyed the script, led him into the church, made him worthy to receive the sacrament, instructed him and gave him rules for right living, and restored him to his wife."[43]

In this account and in the story of Lucy, the saint's agency is sustained through the community and the practices of the church. Lucy's testimony

43. Voragine, *The Golden Legend*, 1:111-12.

and victory over the Roman consul are not sufficient. The happy death of the martyr depends upon communion with those gathered in God's name and through sharing the body of Christ. Likewise, Basil is not an independent agent. In his contest with demons, a miracle of grace is received, but it cannot be attributed directly to the saint. St. Basil's agency is diffused through the practices of penitence and the prayers of the people. Like Lucy's death, the exorcism is protracted, and the demons are not defeated until all the people pray as one. There is an echo of Agatha's encouragement to Lucy, "My sister Lucy . . . why do you ask me for something that you yourself can do?" The possessed young man is not helpless; in fact, he shows strength of spirit as he endures his torments. In a world where God's presence can be seen and touched, he is never without hope. Basil stands apart as a saint only insofar as he brings the sacrament and the common work of the faithful into relief. The saints are a common trust, through which the dissemination of God's power and mercy comes through the people — accessible to all. Certainly, this grammar of sainthood has been open to excess and abuse, but the depth at which it sets God's power and grace within common life and common faith also helps explain the enduring cult of the saints.

The cult of the saints endures today, but not without its own problems. The problems, in the main, are metaphysical. Certainly there are places where people embrace superstitions and legends, but these excesses are not typical modern or postmodern problems. In chapter 1 the modern approach was characterized by its focus on our memory and textual evidence, rather than the personal and living reality of the saints. The modern approach looks to saints almost exclusively as moral, primarily social and political, exemplars. They are stories to be put into practice by us. Postmodernism disrupts the modern meaning of moral, social, and political. The postmodern approach to saints focuses on the variability of interpretations and the multiple worlds of the text. The life of the saint collapses into the worlds of various interpreters. Each approach, modern and postmodern, attempts to find a place for the saints apart from a network of relationships that spans across the living and the dead. I have attempted to show, in each chapter, that the saints are important precisely because they connect us to a metaphysical landscape of relationships. The cult of the saints endures because the saints are relational openings where our lives become porous to life as a whole.

The communion of saints comes to us through the inner life and outward movement of God's Trinity. The inner life of Father, Son, and Spirit is beyond precise explanation. In *The Three-Personed God*, William Hill outlines errors and oversimplifications that result when we base our understanding of the Trinity either on the unity of God or on the distinctions of persons. The Trinity is a unity of divine nature and a communion of persons. When the "one nature" is the point of departure for our thinking, "the identities of the persons become blurred and their distinct roles outside God lost sight of."[44] When the agency of three divine persons is considered first, the distinctions of Father, Son, and Spirit are explained "at the cost of unity and equality."[45] Hill recommends that we give neither "oneness" nor "threeness" logical priority. Rather, he recommends that we allow one point of view to interact with and balance the other.[46] Hill's recommendation is especially important when we emphasize the role of saints as embodiments of communion and the possibilities of sharing life with God.

The distinctive relations, operations, or "appropriations" of Son and Spirit tend to be emphasized when thinking about the saints. But we ought not to lose sight of the essential unity of God. Giving account of holy people requires appeal to the activity of the Spirit who gathers and joins and draws us up into the love of Father and Son.[47] In *The Three-Personed God*, Hill begins his discussion of appropriations or distinctions in agency with "the ancient Greek formula that spoke of all things being 'from the Father, through the Son, and in the Holy Spirit'" and by which we pray "*to* the Father, *through* the Son, *in* the Holy Spirit."[48] Hill summarizes these appropriations of God in relationship to creation, history, and our salvation as Source, Word, and Bond. In relationship to the saints, we can say that the Father is the one who sends the Son. The Son is the one who is sent, who is God in the flesh, the creator who is the "exemplar of creation," the self-communication of God — the Word and Truth — who is sent into history, the particular history of Jesus of Nazareth.[49] The Spirit, as the love that binds Father and Son, is our bond, our advocate, the

---

44. William J. Hill, O.P., *The Three-Personed God: The Trinity as a Mystery of Salvation* (Washington, D.C.: Catholic University of America Press, 1982), 280.

45. Hill, *The Three-Personed God*, 279.

46. Hill, *The Three-Personed God*, 281.

47. Hill, *The Three-Personed God*, 281; Sherry, *Spirit, Saints, and Immortality*, 60-61.

48. Hill, *The Three-Personed God*, 282.

49. Hill, *The Three-Personed God*, 282-84.

"prolongation of the Father's love for his eternal Son," and "the expansion of God's love for his adoptive children."[50]

The Christian confession of faith in Father, Son, and Holy Spirit is the basis of hagiography and its identification of holy people who are the sharing of human life in communion with God. When Hill refers to the appropriations of God in terms of Source, Word, and Bond, he also notes that in our human sphere these relations of God are likely to be received as power, knowledge, and love.[51] The Trinitarian economy is the basis for understanding the saints in terms of loving, knowing, and ruling. Saints are exemplars who imitate Christ in particular times and places. They embody God's love and are media through which we can know, in some small measure, the pathways of fidelity to God and the power of God's self-giving love. Their appearances among us anticipate the fullness of time, when the rule of God's love, the kingdom of God, is completed for all time. Through Christ and in the Spirit, we are and will be constituted "as the New Creation of God."[52]

As we confess faith in a Trinitarian God, we cannot help but expect to find saints among us. We will fail to do so; we will reduce them to mere exemplars, and we will exaggerate their holy power. But, I dare say, we cannot help but name and draw near to the saints as living members of God's communion. Our persistent desire to have saints is a desire for the human sharing of God's good company. The saints populate a metaphysical landscape of this profoundly social desire.

50. Hill, *The Three-Personed God*, 286.
51. Hill, *The Three-Personed God*, 283.
52. Hill, *The Three-Personed God*, 287.

Conclusion

—m—

When I set out to research and write this book, I had no intention of confirming the work of sociologists. However, Douglas Porpora's social research and his analysis in *Landscapes of the Soul* do offer terminology and spatial metaphors to understand the role of saints. Porpora claims that "we are who we are not just in social space, not just in moral space, but in metaphysical space as well. If to know who we are is always to know our position in space, then part of who we are is our position in the cosmos."[1] The embeddedness of social relations within metaphysical space encapsulates this book's concern with both the saints and social desire. The use of the word "desire" is certainly a play on modernism and postmodernism, but for the most part, it is a theological emphasis on the character of love. Too often, saintly love is thought to be dispassionate and perfectly altruistic. Such a view is a product of ignorance about the saints. God's love overwhelms them and makes most of them eccentric if not foolish (for Christ). God's love in Christ is perfect passion. An astounding mark of God's self-giving is that we are wanted by God. *Agape* is the fulfillment of *eros* (Benedict). God's love is social both in the intrarelation of the Trinity and in the Trinity's outward relations to us. The saints are the social bonds among us of God's rule of love.

In *The Catholic Imagination*, sociologist Andrew Greeley studies and analyzes sacramental sensibility among Catholics. He is not attempting to prescribe the kind of worldview we should have. He holds that data on religious

---

1. Douglas Porpora, *Landscapes of the Soul: The Loss of Moral Meaning in American Life* (New York: Oxford University Press, 2001), 20.

169

attitudes and habits indicate that Catholics already live "in an enchanted world."[2] Peoples, places, and things are media for God's presence and love for the world. Saints "are sacraments of God's love, of God's immediate care for humans, and of the response of some humans to that love."[3] How, Greeley asks, can these claims be made from a sociological point of view? Has not the world been "demystified and demythologized? Does not disenchantment rule the modern world? Or could it be that the enchanted Catholic imagination is indeed a manifestation of post-modernity?"[4] Greeley's answer corresponds to my approach to the saints. Or, to put it accurately, *Sharing God's Good Company* is a product of the world Greeley describes.

Is the metaphysically porous world of saints impossible in the modern world? Is our veneration of the saints a kind of postmodern playacting borrowed from another world?[5] In chapter 1, I put the questions this way: Are saints otherworldly as in the modern view? Or, are they "other" in the world as postmodernists are likely to propose? The simple alternative is that the saints share with us God's world. Greeley replies, "I don't believe in either modernity or post-modernity. I find no persuasive evidence that either modern or post-modern humankind exists outside of faculty office buildings. Everyone tends to be pre-modern."[6] His example is the so-called antagonism between religion and science. He says, "I find ample evidence that most humans (other than philosophers and theologians) see little inconsistency between science and religion in their ordinary lives."[7] Greeley's comment brings to mind Padre Pio (chapter 7). Healing through intercessory prayer and founding a hospital are all the same to him. *Sharing God's Good Company* deals with the saints in terms of realism, progress, miracles, and history. In doing so, I have tried to undo various modern and postmodern buffers and tangles and to settle in the place where our lives are connected to life as a whole.

2. Andrew Greeley, *The Catholic Imagination* (Berkeley: University of California Press, 2000), 1.

3. Greeley, *The Catholic Imagination*, 38-39.

4. Greeley, *The Catholic Imagination*, 2.

5. See Fredric Jameson's discussion of pastiche in *Postmodernism or the Cultural Logic of Late Capitalism* (Durham, N.C.: Duke University Press, 1991), 17-26.

6. Greeley, *The Catholic Imagination*, 2.

7. Greeley, *The Catholic Imagination*, 2.

Index

Abraham, 67-69, 80, 92, 119
Agatha, St., 141-42, 146, 163-64, 166
Agus, Aharon, 69
Alienation, 55, 78, 80-82, 124, 127-28, 151
Ambrose, St., 76
Analogy, 49, 68, 103, 108-9, 136
Anthony of Padua, St., 79, 83
Antony of Egypt, St., 113, 115, 157-58
Aquinas, St. Thomas, 79, 111-12
Athanasius of Alexandria, St.: *Life of Antony*, 157-58
Ayala, Francisco, 64, 100, 104

Barbour, Ian, 102
Barr, Stephen, 102-4, 108-9, 111
Basil, St., 164-66
Becker, George J., 45, 47-48
Benedict-Joseph Labre, St., 29, 75-76
Bible/Scripture, 49, 68, 80, 82, 89, 92, 95, 120, 137, 154-56; Acts of the Apostles, 91-95; 1 Corinthians, 94; 1 Timothy, 155; Galatians, 90, 94; Genesis, 68-69, 109; Hebrews, 55; Luke, 32, 49, 71, 77, 81, 91-92, 95-96, 117; Mark, 61, 64, 66; Philippians, 93-94, 155; Romans, 90, 137, 155
Bollandists, 145-46
Bossy, John, 162
Brandsma, Titus, Bd., 71, 113

Brooks, Peter, 43, 45-47, 58-59
Brown, Peter, 7, 19, 120, 158, 161
Burrus, Virginia, 22-25, 38, 120
Bynum, Caroline Walker, 157

Catherine of Siena, St., 29, 38, 138-39
Charles de Foucault, Bd., 52
Christopher, St., 29, 72
Collins, Francis, 109-10, 112
Cunningham, Lawrence, 29, 37-38, 40-41, 159-61

Damien of Molokai, St., 71
Daniel the Stylite, St., 39
Darwin, Charles, 107; Darwinian science, 47, 107-8
Davies, Brian, 110
Davies, Paul, 100-101
Dawkins, Richard, 64, 100, 106
Dawson, Christopher, 107
Delehaye, Hippolyte, 12, 145
Donofrio, Beverly, 30-37, 41, 97
Dorothy Day, Servant of God, 13, 15-16, 49-50, 56, 140
Dreiser, Theodore, 47
Drexel, Katharine, St., 80, 142-43, 146-48

Edith Stein/Teresa Benedict of the Cross, St., 56-57, 113, 138

171

Elizabeth Ann Seton, St., 83-84, 118;
    Daughters of Charity, 83
Ellsberg, Robert, 1-3, 52, 56, 113
Eucharist, 35, 90, 94, 99, 120, 128, 141-
    42, 147

Fitzmyer, Joseph, 154-55
Francis of Assisi, St., 39-40, 129
Fullness of Time, 135, 139, 142, 150, 153,
    168

García-Rivera, Alex, 54-55, 61
God the Father, 81, 89-90, 167. *See also*
    Trinity
Greeley, Andrew, 169-70
Gregory of Tours, St.: *Life of the Fathers*,
    141; *History of the Franks*, 143-45
Guibert of Norgent: *On Saints and Their
    Relics*, 159-60

Hagiography, 1, 5, 7, 10, 22-23, 25, 30, 37,
    43-44, 46, 53, 55, 58, 61, 67-68, 70-72,
    76-78, 88, 99, 135, 139-46, 148, 153-66
Hanby, Michael, 107
Hedrick, Charles W., 61-62, 64-66, 68,
    76-77
Hill, William J., 167-68
Historiography, 55, 62, 144-45, 150-51;
    medieval annals and chronicles, 140-
    41, 331
History, 4, 6-7, 9, 12, 18-19, 22-23, 25-26,
    29, 37, 40, 42-44, 55, 61-64, 70-72, 75,
    84-87, 101, 108, 113, 119-21, 123-25, 127-
    30, 134-52; history of sainthood/
    saints, 29, 40, 139, 145, 160-61
Holiness/Sanctity, 7, 37-39, 48-49, 81,
    96, 116, 118-19, 122, 132, 141, 143, 153-
    54, 158, 162
Holy Spirit, 18, 71, 77, 81, 92-93, 95, 99,
    128, 158, 167-68. *See also* Trinity
Hospitality, 71, 94, 96, 126, 128-33
Hume, David, 106-7

Icons/Iconoclasm, 88-89

Illich, Ivan, 124-31
Images, 5, 21, 79-96, 161
Imbelli, Robert, 17-18, 79

Jacobus de Voragine: *The Golden Legend*,
    113, 141-42, 146, 163-65
Jägerstätter, Franz, Bd., 55-56, 137-38
Jesus Christ, 1-3, 7, 16-17, 32, 38, 49, 56,
    61-62, 65-66, 70-73, 75-78, 80-96, 99,
    112-13, 119-20, 123, 125, 129-31, 136-50,
    154-55, 162, 167; crucifixion/cross, 16,
    33, 49, 54, 56, 58, 65, 81, 84-85, 87, 90,
    112, 124, 129-31, 138, 144, 165; incarna-
    tion, 53, 68, 70-73, 78, 86, 90, 99, 106,
    125, 127-29; resurrection, 16, 65, 81,
    92, 95, 99, 143-44, 155, 157, 160
John of Damascus, St., 89-91
Johnson, Elizabeth, 17-22, 24-25, 27, 38,
    157
Johnson, Kelly, 75

Kingdom/Reign of God, 9, 49, 57, 66,
    96, 136, 139, 142
Kitzinger, Ernst, 86
Kolbe, Maximilian, St., 52, 113, 138

Langton, Christopher, 104
Lawrence, St., 76-77
Lombardi, Jack, 118
Lucy, St., 163-66

Mandela, Nelson, 14-15
Martin de Porres, St., 54-55, 80
Martin of Tours, St., 144
Martyrs/Martyrdom, 1-5, 37, 51-52, 56,
    69-71, 82, 113, 130-31, 137-38, 142, 149,
    156-57, 161-64
Mary, Blessed Virgin, 30-38, 41, 45, 57,
    81-85, 89-90, 97, 154, 157
Mary Magdalene, St., 65
Materialism, 35, 44, 56, 64, 72, 99, 101-2,
    104, 108-9
Maurin, Peter, 140
McCarthy, Michael, 22-23

McGrath, Alister, 106, 108

Metaphor, 5, 43, 77, 85-86, 108, 136, 169

Metaphysics/Metaphysical, 2, 4-9, 21, 24-26, 31, 37, 44, 46, 53, 56-58, 60, 67, 73, 97-101, 104, 112, 115, 128, 146, 148-53, 166, 169, buffered self, 16, 24, 33, 35, 37, 42, 57, 128; middle realm, 33, 35, 37, 44, 56, 58; porous self, 16, 30, 33-34, 37, 110, 113, 166, 170; supernatural, 2, 35-36, 61, 64-65, 77, 97, 109, 112, 144, 146

Miller, Kenneth B., 100, 108, 111

Miracles, 3, 6, 9, 92, 97-114; definition of, 109-12; of saints, 112-13, 117, 147-48, 150

Modernism, 12, 40, 44, 63-64, 169

Narrative, 2, 21-22, 30-31, 36, 43, 47, 61, 69, 71, 76, 87-88, 99, 129-30, 135-36, 164-65; narrator/storyteller, 1, 3, 66, 70, 117

Naturalism, 43, 45, 47-48, 72, 100

Nereus and Archilleus, Sts., 69-70

Orsi, Robert, 19

Padre Pio, St., 115-17, 123, 131-33, 170

Paul, St., 73, 79, 90-95, 137, 155-56

Percy, Walker, 58-59

Perpetua and Felicity, Sts., 156-57

Peter, St., 16, 65, 80, 82, 91-93, 95, 140, 142

Pilgrimage, 6, 9, 26, 28, 32-36, 41, 113, 115-33, 147, 156, 158-59

Polycarp, St., 1-5, 37, 51, 113, 138, 156-57, 164

Porpora, Douglas, 26-27, 60, 150, 169

Postmodernism, 11-15, 21-22, 24, 40-41, 44, 64, 166, 169-70

Prayer, 6, 48, 73-74, 81, 88, 112, 117-18, 131-32, 146-47, 155-56, 158, 160, 162

Pro, Miguel, Bd., 52, 71, 80

Progress, 6, 10, 47-48, 50, 58, 75-76, 107, 115, 122-28, 135, 139-40, 144, 151, 170

Rahner, Karl, 153-54

Realism, 5, 12, 36, 42-64, 66-72, 76-78, 84-87, 99, 105, 143, 146, 170; figurative, 5, 59, 61; hagiographic, 5, 43-45, 51, 55-56, 58-59, 66, 69-71, 77-78, 82, 143; literary, 45, 58, 66, 99; nineteenth century, 43-44, 46, 58, 61, 63

Reformation, 161-62

Relics, 88, 118, 120-21, 125, 141, 157-62

Romero, Oscar, Archbishop of San Salvador, 13, 15-17, 40, 56, 148-50

Rose of Lima, St., 20, 38, 72, 80

Sacrament/Sacramental, 35, 45, 57, 78, 82, 86-87, 119, 124, 147-48, 164-66, 169

Saint Anthony Shrine Parish, 5, 82

Saint Patrick's Church, 79, 82

Saints/Sainthood, 29-42; ascetic, 142, 157-58; being in Christ, 2, 7, 16-17, 65, 70-71, 76-78, 91, 99, 120, 128, 136-50, 154-56, 161, 164, 169; canonization, 57, 116, 160-61; communion of saints, 4-5, 7-10, 12, 17-18, 20-21, 24-27, 48, 57, 76, 82, 88, 96, 98-99, 114-15, 120, 123-25, 135-36, 142, 150, 163, 166; cult of the saints, 3, 7, 19, 88, 120-21, 123, 125, 157-59, 161, 164, 166; definition, 7, 10-11, 13, 37-38, 40-41, 53, 57, 72, 116, 124, 128, 147, 161-62, 166; exemplars, 4, 81, 93-94, 167; feast days, 68-69, 145, 161; holy fool, 72-74, 76; virtue, 38, 93-94, 120, 147, 161-62. *See also* Martyrs/Martyrdom; Veneration

Salvation, 2, 7, 49, 80, 90-91, 96, 119, 137-38, 153, 155, 160, 167; salvation history, 44, 80, 85, 87, 137-38, 144, 150

Saward, John, 73

Science, 44, 47-48, 61-62, 64, 99-112, 123, 126, 134, 151, 170

Shrines, 32, 82-83, 87, 113, 115-16, 118, 120-22, 132-33, 148, 156, 159, 162

Social desire, 3-4, 9-28, 30, 37, 72, 80, 152, 169

Statues, 5, 25, 79-80, 82-84, 86-88, 96
Stephen, St., 38, 138

Talbot, Matt, Ven., 52, 73-76
Taylor, Charles, 16, 24, 26, 33, 35, 44, 47,
    56, 58, 60, 63, 122
Teresa of Calcutta, Bd., 16, 78, 118
Thérèse of Lisieux, St., 40-41, 48-52, 74,
    84, 118, 146
Tkacz, Catherine Brown, 136-37
Trent, Council of, 161-62
Trinity/Trinitarian God, 7, 18, 89, 93,
    167, 169
Typology/Typological, 124, 136-39, 142-
    44, 150

Veneration, 3-4, 38, 53, 75, 82, 86, 88-90,
    131-42, 152, 154-55, 160-62, 170

Weil, Simon, 56
Welsford, Enid, 72
White, Hayden, 47, 62-63, 134-36, 143
Wilken, Robert L., 79, 82, 96
Woodward, Kenneth, 12, 97-99
Worship, 3, 38, 79, 86, 88, 89, 156, 160,
    162, 164; liturgy, 68, 142, 161, 164. *See
    also* Saints/Sainthood: feast days
Wyschogrod, Edith, 13-15, 25, 38

Zahn, Gordon, 56, 137
Zola, Émile, 46, 59